W9-ARH-500

AGUILAR MAIOR

LITERARY ROUTES OF SPAIN

All rights reserved.
This publication must
be not reproduced,
stored in a retrieval
system, or transmitted,
in any form or by any means,
electronic, mechanical,
phrotocopying, recording
or otherwise, without the prior
permission of the publisher.

Cover and jacket design
by Abdón Flores

© TURESPAÑA. Madrid, 1990
© de la traducción: James Brander
Título original: *Rutas literarias de España*
© de esta edición:
1991, Aguilar, S. A. de Ediciones
ISBN: 84-03-60199-9
Depósito legal: B-27883-1991

Iniciative and coordinator of Rubén Caba

Literary routes of Spain

Translation by James Brander

Carmen Bravo-Villasante
Rubén Caba
Julio Caro Baroja
Juan Cruz Ruiz
Juan Cueto Alas
Luis Mateo Díez
José Esteban
Joan Fuster
José Antonio Gabriel y Galán
Salvador García Jiménez
Ian Gibson
Ildefonso-Manuel Gil
José María Gironella
José Hierro
José Jiménez Lozano
José María Merino
Baltasar Porcel
Julio M. de la Rosa
Miguel Sánchez-Ostiz
Gonzalo Santonja
Andrés Sorel
Jesús Torbado
Manuel Vázquez Montalbán

AGUILAR

CONTENTS

.

FOREWORD

A great part of Classical literature is itinerant and adventurous. Not only minor poems like the *Argonautica* of Apollonius of Rhodes, but also the two great poems of Antiquity, the *Odyssey* and the *Aeneid,* are based on travel. Equally vagabond has been classical Spanish narrative: *Lazarillo* and the other picaresque novels, several of Cervantes' *Novelas ejemplares* and, of course, *Don Quijote* and *Persiles y Segismunda.* But Spanish literature had been "on the road" long before the discovery of America. The *cantares de gesta,* the *Cantar de Mío Cid,* the works of Gonzalo de Berceo, the *Libro de buen amor* and the romances of chivalry, were all there to incite readers to take to the road in search of adventures. Though many or most passages of these works have an itinerant setting, all of them have a story line or plot, which distinguishes them from the travel book as such.

The pure travel book, however, can also boast a long history in Spain. Nine centuries before Marco Polo dictated his "book of marvellous things" to Rusticiano of Pisa, the abbess of a Galician convent, named Egeria or Eteria, gave an account in late Latin, under the title of *Pilgrimage to the Holy Land,* of her voyage to Palestine about the end of the fourth century. During the later Middle Ages, Spanish contributions to travel literature included such singular books as the *Embassy to Tamerlaine* (Embajada a Tamorlán), wherein Ruy González de Clavijo describes, in the Castilian vernacular rather than Latin, his voyage to Persia in 1403; also the *Wanderings and Voyages of Pero Tafur in Various Parts of the World,* made in 1436-39 through the north of Africa and several parts of Europe. And in the 16th century, amid the abundant crop of travels and chronicles of the Indies that appeared in those times, Andrés Laguna anonymously wrote his excellent *Voyage to Turkey.*

Authors of all periods have left written witness of their passage through Spain: the Greek Strabo in the first century BC; various Arab writers from the 11th to the 15th centuries; Venetian ambassadors in the 16th; and Cardinal De Retz in the 17th. The Pleiade of foreign writers who focussed on Spain in the Enlightenment and the 19th century —from the Duc de Saint-Simon and Stendhal to George Borrow and Richard Ford— had their counterpart in numerous Spanish writers who cultivated the genre of books about travels in Spain: Antonio Ponz, Bosarte, Viera y Clavijo, Iriarte, Jovellanos and Pedro Antonio de Alarcón, to cite a few of the best-known. The tradition of wandering and observing was continued by the Generation of '98; later by Ortega, Plà and, in our own days, by Cela and other more recent writers.

Plutarch tells us that the geographers of Antiquity, when they knew nothing about some part of the map, were in the habit of writing there: "Beyond here there are only waterless sands, or impenetrable swamps, or snows like those of Scythia, or frozen sea". Nowadays, when the whole globe has been more or less explored with the seven-league boots we have snatched from the ogre of technology, there are no more places to which a monstrous or miraculous nature can be ascribed. Such abridgement of the scope of fantastic voyages makes it all the more inviting for us to review the old roads, but with new eyes.

Since all travel is, now more than ever, a pilgrimage to the past, an invocation to history where images are to be refracted in the prism of culture, some time ago I conceived the project of writing a book of travel routes through Spain that would turn upon the life and work of our classic writers. But other occupations, as occupations will, kept me busy; and I kept putting off this project, which dates from 1978, when in the magazine *Viajar* I published such a route on Gonzalo de Berceo. Before this delay gave way to total abandonment of the design, it occurred to me that the time involved in producing such a book would be greatly shortened by farming the task out among different writers; the resulting book would also be enriched with a variety of viewpoints and styles. Twenty two colleagues have accepted my invitation with a readiness which leaves no doubt that the wandering bent of our classic writers is very much alive in the present generation. It only remained for the cartographer Javier Belloso to convert into precise maps the itineraries sketched, with more will than skill, by our wandering writers.

When I set forth my idea to Ignacio Fuejo, president of Turespaña, he showed great interest in it and gave me his full confidence and backing to carry it out. The thanks I here reiterate to him should be extended also to all those at Turespaña with whom I had assiduous contacts: Miguel Ortega Álvarez-Santullano, who backed the project and offered me useful advice and orientation during the work, and Carmen Paulogorrán, who provided efficient and professional cooperation in all phases of the process.

Af a few final comments, toward the better understanding of his book. The very geographical amplitude of the undertaking gave rise to certain requirements. It was established that each one of the seventeen autonomous Communities of Spain was to be represented by at least one literary route; thus, it was necessary to include several authors of the past who, though of undoubted literary quality, have never enjoyed the sort of national or international recognition accorded to the other writers we have chosen.

In the ordering of the texts, an alphabetical sequence has been adopted. The autonomous communities are arranged alphabetically according to their gentilic adjectives and official toponyms; if a single autonomous community contains various routes, these are arranged by surnames of past authors or by titles of anonymous works; and the biographical notes on present-day authors, according to their first surnames.

When the route extends, over two or three autonomous Communities, it appears in the index assigned to the Community where it begins. Thus "Pío Baroja: his land and his people" appears under el País Vasco and not Navarra; "The places of Gonzalo de Berceo" in La Rioja and not Castilla y León; "Places of Lazarillo" in Castilla y León and not Castilla-La Mancha; and "Going to Explore the Sierra with the Archpriest" in Castilla-La Mancha and not in Madrid or Castilla-León.

The Archpriest of Hita, in fact, is very apropos to these final remarks, as I hope his restless and festive outlook may accompany the reader in his travels on the literary pathways of Spain.

RUBÉN CABA

LITERARY ROUTES
OF SPAIN

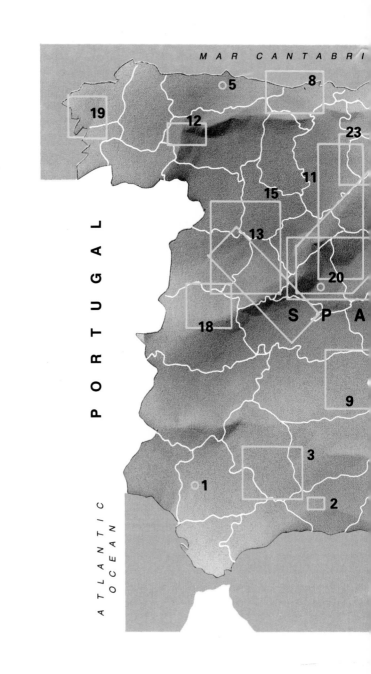

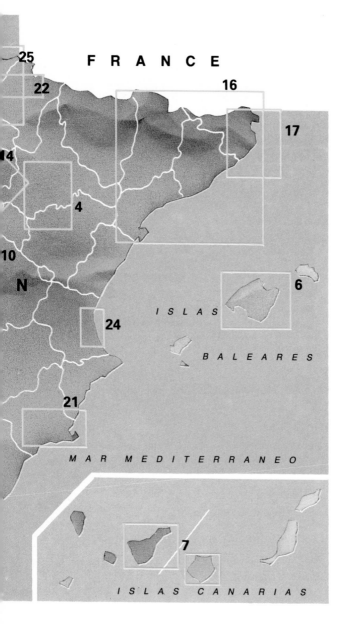

F R A N C E

25

22

16

17

4

4

10

N

6

I S L A S

24

B A L E A R E S

21

M A R   M E D I T E R R A N E O

7

I S L A S   C A N A R I A S

LITERARY ROUTES OF SPAIN

ANDALUCÍA

SEVILLIAN ROUTE OF GUSTAVO ADOLFO BÉCQUER

by

JULIO M. DE LA ROSA

GUSTAVO ADOLFO BÉCQUER
(Sevilla, 1836-Madrid, 1870)

Orphaned of his father at five years old and of his mother at ten, Bécquer spent his childhood and early youth in Sevilla, full of dreams and projects; and left for Madrid in 1854, seeking fame and glory, but found hard disillusionment and years of obscure drudgery and sacrifices. There was persistent illness, and a petty employment in the Dirección de Bienes Nacionales. In 1858 he met Julia Espín; and in 1860, Casta Esteban, daughter of the physician Francisco Esteban, marrying her in 1861. González Brabo appointed him censor of novels, with a salary of 24,000 reales. Excepting his Historia de los templos de España, *written in collaboration with Juan de la Puerta, Bécquer never saw, in his lifetime, his* Rimas *or* Leyendas *published in book form; but much of his work was published in periodicals, notably* El Contemporáneo, La Ilustración *and* El Museo Universal.

After Bécquer's death, his friends financed a first edition of his most representative work in verse and prose, in two volumes (1871), with a prologue by Rodríguez Correa.

An exquisite poet of enormous lyrical talent, Bécquer was also an exceptional writer of prose, a stylist of the first order. "The prose of Bécquer" wrote Luis Cernuda, "like his verse, seeks cadence, not sonority; suggestion, not eloquence."

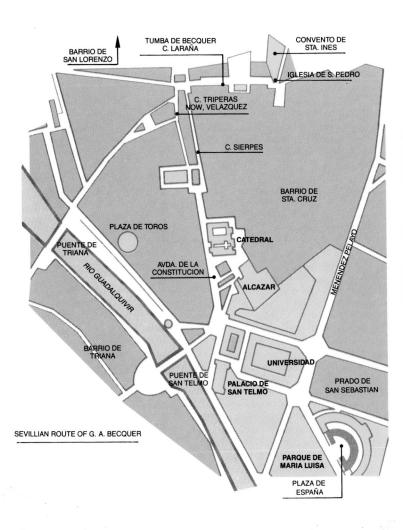

BARRIO DE
SAN LORENZO

TUMBA DE BECQUER
C. LARAÑA

CONVENTO DE
STA. INES

IGLESIA DE S. PEDRO

C. TRIPERAS
NOW, VELAZQUEZ

C. SIERPES

BARRIO DE
STA. CRUZ

PLAZA DE TOROS

CATEDRAL

PUENTE DE
TRIANA

AVDA. DE LA
CONSTITUCION

ALCAZAR

RIO GUADALQUIVIR

MENENDEZ PELAYO

BARRIO DE
TRIANA

UNIVERSIDAD

PRADO DE
SAN SEBASTIAN

PUENTE DE
SAN TELMO

PALACIO DE
SAN TELMO

SEVILLIAN ROUTE OF G. A. BECQUER

PARQUE DE
MARIA LUISA

PLAZA DE
ESPAÑA

SEVILLIAN ROUTE
OF GUSTAVO ADOLFO BÉCQUER

1

INTRODUCTION

The traveller interested in the Sevillian route of Gustavo Adolfo Bécquer ought to arrive in Sevilla, if possible, about the middle of October. The relentless light of summer is now losing its force. The air of Sevilla is transparent in October. The traveller must not be hurried. We must make as slow approach to the landscape of Gustavo Adolfo Bécquer and to this end the newly arrived traveller, before beginning his Becquerian route, should imagine a carriage shaken by the trot of the mules, and the snapping of the coachman's whip. It is unusual to arrive in a city and think that the person we wish to find there is just leaving it. In fact we are to explore the streets of Sevilla in search of the traces of a shadow. Let us imagine it is 1854, and about the end of October. A young man whose large eyes are desolate with sadness is undertaking his great adventure. Gustavo Adolfo Bécquer is about to realize his adolescent dream. After many hours, the capital appears: "Madrid dark, dirty, ugly as a fleshless skeleton, shivering under an immense shroud of snow" appears before his eyes. It is then that Gustavo Adolfo Bécquer, who feels the cold even in his soul, turns his head back the way he came, and understands that he has lost, perhaps for ever, that city to which you, dear reader, are now arriving many years later.

Gustavo Adolfo Bécquer is eighteen years old. His is one of those lives dominated by passion and destined to burn each day in a more intense fire. The young man who has just arrived at Court to conquer Fame with his pen in hand, has already passed the equator of his life. When Bécquer steps off the stagecoach, he is still impregnated with the spirit and knowledge of his native city, whose every corner he had explored. The reader of his work now sets about seeking some of these corners, where Bécquer's roots lie; a difficult, but subtle and suggestive task.

Gustavo Adolfo Domínguez Bastida Insausti Vargas Bécquer was born on Wednesday 17 February 1836, at N.º 9 of the Calle Ancha de San Lorenzo, now N.º 26 of the Calle Conde de Barajas. In the intimate neighborhood of San Lorenzo, presided by the celebrated image of the Cristo del Gran Poder, devotion and myth of Sevilla, we begin then the route of the "eagle of pain". Bécquer always carried within him the inimitable light and sound of this quarter, in whose parish church he was baptised on 25 February; a quarter "where lovers still speak through window grilles, where the neighbors converse in the middle of the street, the women set out pots of flowers on the roof terraces, and the balconies have green jalousies". What Bécquer saw and learned in his childhood, he never forgot.

But the reader and visitor may easily be misled when he is dealing with the kaleidoscopic Bécquer: "It is costing me great effort (writes the poet) to know which things I have dreamed and which have really happened to me".

On 23 February 1852, when the bridge of Triana was opened amid popular festivals, Bécquer saw once more a girl who lived in the Calle de Santa Clara, also in the quarter of San Lorenzo. Seized by love, the young Bécquer passed along the enchanted street numberless time to spy the house of the nameless girl; but the door was always closed though sometimes in the balcony the eternal lover thought he perceived a hope-giving movement of the blinds or a fleeting shadow. It seems already a fulfilment of the *XV rima* of the future poet:

> *Tú, sombra que, cuantas veces*
> *voy a tocarte, te desvaneces*[1].

Bécquer, in the narrow streets of his quarter, was already awaiting a woman who never arrives. The streets of Sevilla, "moorish, tortuous and narrow, in which one seems to hear still the crunch of the footfalls of the executioner King", are already the incipient scene of the lyrical legend which, years later, was to be perhaps Bécquers major literary achievement.

The cliché of Bécquer's miserable childhood is still spoken of. It is not true. Gustavo Adolfo's father, José Domínguez Bécquer, was an outstanding painter, a well-known master of that period, who lived in very easy economic circumstances. His canvases brought good prices even in London. He was (and this is important for the understanding of his poet son's sensibility and bent for observation) an excellent *costumbrista*, i.e. interpreter of folklore and local colour: the Seville of the people, of *romerías* (pilgrimage) and fairs, of the famous processions and the typical street life of the city, were the incessant themes of his painting. The childhood home of Bécquer always enjoyed tranquillity, even luxury: three servants and a carriage.

---

[1] Thou, shadow who, whenever I reach out to touch thee, vanisheth.

The father died young however, in 1841, at 35 years of age. The family then lived at N.º 25 of the Calle del Potro, very near their previous house, in the same quarter and the same ambience. Death was always a faithful companion to this boy who, at the age of ten, received the terrible shock of the death of his mother, Joaquina Bastida y Vargas. A year earlier, Gustavo Adolfo had entered the Nautical School of San Telmo. The family lived in the Calle del Espejo, now Pascual de Gayangos. Gustavo and his brothers were taken in by their aunt María Bastida, who lived at N.º 27 of the Alameda de Hércules, one of the most popular and lovely quarters of Sevilla. Thus Gustavo Adolfo Bécquer was left alone with Sevilla. Alone with his dreams.

2

THE SEVILLIAN ROUTE

School of San Telmo

Gustavo Adolfo Bécquer is now ten years old. The reader-visitor must now seek the banks of the river Guadalquivir, the great river of the poet's finest dreams. Here he will find the splendid palace of the Dukes of Montpensier, formerly occupied by the School of Pilotage and Navigation of Triana. Gustavo Adolfo had all the requisite conditions for entering this school: orphanhood, lack of means, and gentle birth. Bécquer may now be imagined as a schoolboy in the Palace of San Telmo, wearing a uniform, earning good grades, always willing. He meets here a classmate named Narciso Campillo and together they write a disjointed drama, also they plan together the plot of a novel. But the School of San Telmo is suppressed by

royal decree. This is our schoolboy's first serious frustration, as he will now never be a navigator. Gustavo Adolfo
takes refuge in the library of his godmother, doña Manuela
Monnahay y Moreno, daughter of a French perfumer. Gustavo Adolfo discovers the fascinating world of books: Ho-
racio, Zorrilla, Espronceda and, above hall, the Tales of
Hoffmann: supernatural routes and paths of fantasy for a
future inventor of legends. Doña Manuela, a godmother
with her feet on the ground, tries to make Gustavo into a
decent *costumbrista* painter.

The studio of Joaquín Domínguez Bécquer

Gustavo Adolfo Bécquer is now sixteen years old, a
whole life for this youth who knows the dream of love and
the cold of solitude. He lives with his brother Valeriano in
the Calle de Mendoza Ríos, in a humble tenement house,
now disappeared. The Sevillian poet Rafael Laffón, in a
letter to Rafael Montesinos —no doubt the greatest authority on the person and biography of Bécquer— describes
this place:

> "(...) A little door, like that of a shed, gave access to a squalid
> square patio of perhaps three or four metres to a side. Pas-
> sing through the portal, another door painted grey but ob-
> scured with accumulated filth, you stepped into that little
> courtyard of black earth, with puddles of wash-water and
> the odd fractured shard of brick, vestiges of what must once
> have been a pavement. Overhead, roofing tiles slumped and
> leaked water, so low they could almost be touched, over-
> grown with foliage of weeds. On to this patio there opened
> four or five doors, leading to as many dens of squalor.
>
> An ancient landlady prowled around the place; it was she
> who said to my father that the inhabitants of her slum were
> always 'nice folks' and that even, a long time ago, there had
> been 'a young gentleman who wrote verses' in the house."

So Bécquer is poor and cannot continue his studies. He has just written *Oda a la muerte de Alberto Lista.* Gustavo Adolfo now decides to study drawing with Don Antonio Cabral Bejarano and, in 1852, begins work in the studio of his uncle Joaquín Domínguez Bécquer. Every morning, not necessarily having eaten well, Gustavo Adolfo passed by the Cathedral, murmuring curses about girls and phantasms, and went up to a salon in the Alcázar. Here he would draw, sitting in a luminous balcony. For two years, Bécquer worked here, in front of the Giralda, Sevilla's unique tower. Perhaps without knowing it he was storing up images of his beloved city, upon which he would feed in his future exile. Don Joaquín Domínguez Bécquer never believed in the pictorial talent of his nephew; but he did offer him money for his trip to Madrid.

The banks of the Guadalquivir

From his quarter of San Lorenzo, Bécquer would walk toward the Guadalquivir. His gaze is far off, lost in his world of daydreams: "In Sevilla, on the bank of the Guadalquivir that leads to the convent of San Jerónimo, there is a sort of backwater that fertilizes a miniature valley formed by the natural configuration of the riverside, which in this stretch has steep high banks." This spot, so important in the Sevillian youth of Bécquer, no longer exists. The reader-traveller again must exercise his imagination to picture the poplar trees, the bulrushes and yellow lilies of this hidden corner. Now we are on the route of dreams, in the lost Eden. Gustavo Adolfo is fourteen or fifteen years old. He carries on a silent dialogue with the Petrarchist Fernando de Herrera, and the poet of flowers, Francisco de Rioja. Bécquer daydreams here on the banks of the Guadalquivir, and drinks the waters of immortality. He imagines his own

Río Guadalquivir and Torre de Oro.

tomb: a white stone, a cross, a name. Of his whole existence, the most intimate hours were spent at this spot on
the riverbank, which today we are unable to specify the location of.

Calle de Triperas

This was the name in those days of the present Calle
de Velázquez, in the very centre of Sevilla, near the famous Calle de Sierpes. At N.º 8 of the old Calle de Triperas
lived the sweet and resigned Julia Cabrera. This first swee-
theart of Gustavo Adolfo died an old maid at the age of
eighty, taking with her a wealth of secret memories. Always with the hope of an impossible return, Julia saw and
suffered the departure of the poet to Madrid. Waiting always, surely she saw his return, dead, to Sevilla. But the
house in the Calle de Triperas was, for a time, the very
centre of the Becquerian route of love: "I could never explain to myself, in those days, why it was that, when I
wished to go to any part whatever of my native city, it was
necessary first to pass in front of her house."

Convent of Santa Inés

Now we are in the very heart of the route of legend, at
a convent of Clarissine nuns founded in 1374, in the Calle
doña María Coronel. Sevilla is the frame of reference for

---

[2] Sevillian legend of the times of Pedro I of Castile. The husband of
doña María Coronel, don Juan de la Cerda, was killed by order of the
King. Coveted in love by the monarch, doña María took refuge in the convent of Santa Clara. Discovered there and pursued by Pedro I, she splashed
boiling oil on her face to destroy her beauty, and frustrate the desires of
her husband's murderer.

one of the finest legends of Gustavo Adolfo Bécquer: *Maese Pérez, el organista.* The taste and smell of the city impregnate the pages of this story. Bécquer had a deep sympathy and understanding for the world of convents and churches. In his childhood in the quarter of San Lorenzo, surely he had deciphered the feminine language of the bells of San Clemente or Santa Clara.

The reader-traveller must now make his way to the Calle de doña María Coronel through some of the charming narrow alleys of Sevilla: the Calle de Chicarreros, formerly Calle de las Culebras; the Plaza de la Encarnación. He will find, at the convent door, the admirable solemnity of the Mass of El Gallo. An old woman near the convent tells us tales from the old days of Sevilla. All the quarter is wrapped now in a thick, unreal fog. The reader-voyager may now see the Marquis of Moscoso paying court to the widow of Villapineda. Presently in the alley of Las Dueñas there appear the followers of the Duke of Medina Sidonia. Swords and bucklers glint amid the darkness. In the Plaza de San Pedro appear the men of the Duke of Alcalá.

Bécquer, in his exile, evokes and recovers the Sevilla of his dreams. Then there is silence, and we hear the organ of Maese Pérez.

La Venta de los Gatos

We are now, dear reader-traveller, in the quarter of La Macarena, indeed at the very portal of La Macarena, with all the popular flavour that this supposes. Our best choice, probably, will be to take the old road that leads to the convent of San Jerónimo. Not far from the cemetery of San Fernando there was in Bécquer's time a famous inn, "a whitewashed building", frequented by travellers and traders, which is now no more than a collapsed and abandoned ruin, little more than a few walls. Everything seems dead now in the forgotten Venta de los Gatos, which inspired the Becquerian legend of the same name. Nobody sings there now with sidelong glance; the cheerful poor girls with their kerchiefs of a thousand colours exist no more; nor the swing, nor the hidden pairs of lovers, nor the active waiters serving the festive customers with glasses of manzanilla and dishes of olives.

La Feria

By the Calle de San Fernando we now reach the old fairground of the Feria de Sevilla. Here the gentry and the populace paraded in the inimitable sunlight of spring in Sevilla. This fair constituted a spectacle difficult to describe, the feeling of April in Sevilla. The young Gustavo Adolfo, among the trees of the Murillo Gardens, views the incessant counterpoint of colours. Neither the word of the poet nor the brush of the painter can capture "the gauze of gold that seems dust", as Bécquer was to remember in a magazine article, *La Feria de Sevilla,* published in *El Museo Universal* of Madrid, on 25 April 1869.

Where oblivion dwells

On 10 April 1913 the mortal remains of Gustavo Adolfo Bécquer arrived in Sevilla. The city, with her tenacious cultivation of silence, received the poet of the *Rimas* with an overcast sky of rain and storm. One might think Sevilla was crying for Gustavo Adolfo.

Like a beautiful stepmother to her best children, some romantic writer said of the mourning of the city for her great poet, for there occurred an eclipse of the Sun at Se-

Monument to Bécquer in the Parque de María Luisa.

villa half an hour after the death of Bécquer. At the end of Bécquer's route is Death, his faithful companion.

Gustavo Adolfo Bécquer, next to his inseparable brother Valeriano, rests in a tomb hidden in the old chapel of the University in the Calle de Laraña. We shall now finish this brief itinerary before the figure of the funerary angel who, without sword in hand or index finger to his lips, watches over the eternal sleep of the boy from the Quarter of San Lorenzo who died of cold in Madrid one day in December 1870.

The monument to Bécquer, in the Parque de María Luisa, inaugurated on 9 December 1911 and ceded to Sevilla by the brothers Álvarez Quintero, is now closed and solitary. Gustavo Adolfo Bécquer is presently being restored and repaired. An anonymous hand has written on a loose chunk of marble: "Where oblivion dwells".

A VISIT TO THE TOWNS
OF GARCÍA LORCA

by

IAN GIBSON

FEDERICO GARCÍA LORCA
(Fuente Vaqueros, 1898-Granada, 1936)

Born at Fuente Vaqueros, in the heart of the Vega de Granada, Federico García Lorca is today the most widely translated and commented Spanish writer of all time, Cervantes included. It is by now impossible to maintain that such phenomenal popularity is owing only to the circumstance of his death as a victim of fascism in the civil war of 1936-39, as the world readership of his work transcends this biographical accident. It is evident that the mythical, primitive nature of the Lorquian vision, expressed by means of densely metaphorical and earthy language, is the true explanation of the remarkable acceptation his poetry and theatre have enjoyed. Lorca himself said once that, if he had not been born among the peasantry of the Vega de Granada, he would never have been able to write Bodas de sangre. *No doubt he said this in all sincerity. Thus, any admirer of his work who wishes to understand the roots that Lorca grew from, will do well to visit the villages and fields of the Vega de Granada, where the poet spent his childhood, before the family settled in the city of Granada when he was eleven. Turning to the famous death of Lorca, this happened near Fuente Grande, in the municipality of Alfacar, some nine kilometres northeast of Gra-*

nada. The site, now Parque de Federico García Lorca, is dedicated to the memory of all those perished in the fratricidal conflict.

Apart from Bodas de sangre *(1933), Lorca's best-known theatrical works include* El público (1933) and La casa de Bernarda Alba *(1936). Among his lyrical works are two unforgettable books:* Romancero gitano *(1928) and* Poeta en Nueva York (1940).

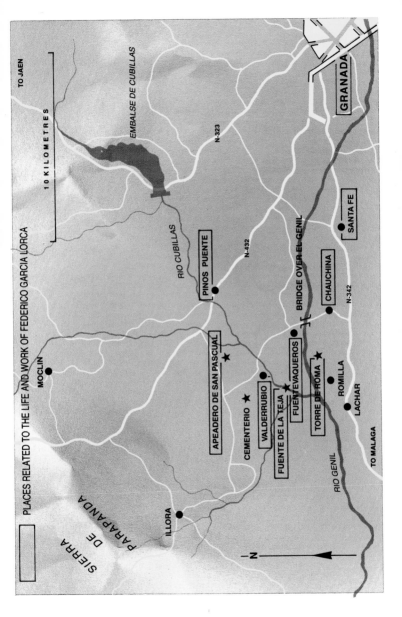

PLACES RELATED TO THE LIFE AND WORK OF FEDERICO GARCÍA LORCA

A VISIT TO THE TOWNS
OF GARCÍA LORCA

The lovely Vega de Granada, with its ring of mountains, is the background and source of all the work of Federico García Lorca and, as the poet never tired of emphasizing, he was a man of the country more than of the city. Thus any admirer of the work of the Granadine genius ought to have some knowledge of the towns where Lorca spent his first eleven years, before his family moved to the provincial capital.

When I first visited Fuente Vaqueros in the spring of 1965 there still existed the picturesque tramway which, penetrating the Vega, covered the eighteen kilometres between Granada and the poet's native village. But this tramway, like the other one to the Sierra, is now a thing of the past. There is practically no alternative but to use a car.

Worth a visit first of all is Santa Fe, a village on the Vega about ten kilometres from the capital on the road to Loja, Málaga and Sevilla (N-342). The Reyes Católicos had their camp here in the last stages of the Granadine campaign; and here, at the end of 1491, Fernando and Isabel signed with Boabdil's emissary the famous capitulations of

Granada, establishing the conditions under which the city was to be surrendered: conditions later shamefully ignored by the Christians. Also at Santa Fe, on 17 April 1492, just after the surrender of Granada, the Reyes Católicos signed their agreement with Cristóbal Colón, which led to the discovery of América. No doubt the young poet was well informed of these historical facts, as his maternal grand-parents were from Santa Fe and, when he went to the capital, he passed through the town in the "old coach" mentioned in a letter to Melchor Fernández Almagro.

Leaving Santa Fe, we again take the N-342. Far off in front of us rises the curved back fo the Sierra de Parapanda, whose fame as the baromether of Granada is reflected in a refrain cited in *Mariana Pineda:*

> *Cuando Parapanda se pone la montera*
> *llueve aunque Dios no quiera*[1].

A few kilometres beyond Santa Fe we turn right to-ward the nearby town of Chauchina.

Here lived the gipsy prototype of Antonio Torres Heredia, "son and grandson of Camborios". His name was Luis Cortés Heredia; he was famous throughout those parts for his grace, his style and his success with women. Aurelia González García, one of Lorca's favourite cousins, in 1956 remembered: "How witty he was, Luisillo el Camborio, as we called him. He could play the guitar like nobody else. A real artist. The emotion he put into a guitar! It realy gripped you. We were all crazy about him. In my house, a party was hardly worth the name if he wasn't at it."

Cortés Heredia, like his father a butcher by trade, met his death on the night of 11 June 1904, at the age of thirty,

---

[1] When Parapanda has its hat on
It will rain in spite of God Himself.

Vega del Genil, near Granada.

when he fell off his horse on the way back to Chauchina. Young Federico might easily have met the gipsy at Aurelia's house, and we may suppose he was impressed by the news of his death.

On leaving Chauchina we suddenly find ourselves in the very midst of the Vega, surrounded by dense rows of poplars, fields of maize, and plantations of tobacco. A few minutes brings us to the bridge over the Genil. This stream has precious little water in the summer, and its dry bed brings to mind the scene of the Lorquian romance, *La casada infiel.* Before we arrive at Fuente Vaqueros, now only a short distance away, we recommend a turn to the left, just before the bridge. This leads us to a Moorish tower where the poet in his childhood used to play with friends.

After a kilometre and a half, the dense poplars on our left disappear and we find the tower we are looking for, known locally as the *Torre de Roma* — a name which perhaps deserves a short commentary, before we proceed to Fuente Vaqueros.

In the centre of the Vega there extended a spacious land-holding known as the Soto de Roma, which had belonged to the Moorish kings, and on whose south edge we are now standing. The origin of the term Roma is controverted. It would seem to have nothing directly to do with the city of Rome. In medieval Arabic, Christians were generally referred to as "Romans", and this may well be the source of the Roma used here.

Such an etymology receives support, if not complete confirmation, in the fact that in the town of Romilla (sometimes called *Roma la Chica* or Little Rome), which is visible from here, there lived, according to an Arab tradition, the unfortunate Florinda, daughter of Count Julián. The inhabitants of Romilla are known as *romerillos* or *romanos,* which seems to pinpoint the origin, in the Granadine world, of the character Pepe el Romano in *La casa de Bernarda Alba.*

Santa Fe.

If our etymology is acceptable, the name of the latifundio Soto de Roma would be roughly translateable as "Domain of the Christian".

Fernando and Isabel distributed the fertile lands of the Vega among their knights. But they were careful to keep the Soto de Roma for the Crown, the holding being later distinguished with the term *Real Sitio* (royal site or residence).

Referring to the Soto de Roma in the first part of his famous *Guerras civiles de Granada* (1595), Ginés Pérez de Hita notes that the land is "thick with trees", and adds that «he who is not very familiar with the paths may easily get lost in it»; also, "in it there is an infinity of game, both beast and fowl". Four hundred years later, anyone who is not very familiar with the paths may still easily get lost in the thick groves of the Soto de Roma, with their present dense growth of poplars: alluded to perhaps in the mysterious dank woods of *Bodas de sangre.*

In 1765 Carlos III gave the Soto de Roma to his ex-Minister of State, Ricardo Wall, son of Irish exiles. In the then tiny village of Fuente Vaqueros, Wall began construction on the parish church of Nuestra Señora de la Anunciación, but died before seeing it finished. The Soto then returned to the Crown, being later given to Manuel Godoy, the so-called *Príncipe de la Paz;* he never visited it, however.

Four years later, in 1813, the history of the Soto de Roma took an unexpected turn; being given in perpetuity to Sir Arthur Wellesley, Duke of Wellington, by the Cortes de Cádiz, in appreciation of his central role in driving Napoleon's armies out of Spain.

The population of Fuente Vaqueros, and of the Soto de Roma in general, grew rapidly in the 19th century, due primarily to the cultivation of linen and hemp. About 1880, it was found that the soil of the Vega was extraordinarily favourable to the growth of sugar beets. The introduction of this plant, for which there was a booming market, soon revolutionized the economy and landscape of the Vega.

Among the new rich of Fuente Vaqueros was Federico García Rodríguez, father of our poet. When Lorca was born at Fuente Vaqueros in 1898, the town was experiencing an economic boom, and the Vega was infused with an optimistic outlook hardly typical of these parts.

The plaza of Fuente Vaqueros today, with its monument to the poet, bears little similarity to that which Federico knew in his childhood, more of a meadow than a plaza, where the village women washed the laundry and spread it out to dry.

The poet's birthplace, now House and Museum of Federico García Lorca, is a stone's throw from the monument, on the left, at N.º 4 of the Calle de la Trinidad. It has been restored by the Diputación Provincial de Granada in excellent good taste and, since opened to the public on 29 July 1986, under the sage direction of the Granadine poet Juan de Loxa, has received many thousands of visitors, including (before he published his *Satanic Verses*) Salman Rushdie.

The village church, of course, deserves a visit. Here our poet was baptized Federico del Sagrado Corazón de Jesús García Lorca on 11 June 1898. The ex-teacher Vicenta Lorca was a sincere Catholic, and the young Federico would frequently accompany her to the church, whose processions, festivals and liturgy were to have a profound influence on his artistic development. The Masses celebrated in this church were studiously imitated by young Federico. His favourite game was to "say Mass" in the patio of his house. Then one day a puppet show visited the pueblo. This soon displaced Federico's religious inclinations, and a puppet theatre replaced the improvised altar in the patio.

Lorca's father was the eldest of nine brothers and sisters. Thus Federico had more than forty cousins in this village which belonged to the Duke of Wellington. His childhood was spent in the unusually wide world of such an extended family: most of them, perhpas, of scant formal schooling, but rich in skills such as music and storytelling, aptitudes which the future poet may be said to have carried in his blood.

After the García Lorca family moved, first to the nearby town of Asquerosa (now Valderrubia) about 1905, and then in 1909 to the city of Granada, Federico never returned to live in Fuente Vaqueros. But the influence of those early years on his sensibility had been decisive. All his life Lorca was to have what he called an "agrarian complex". "I love simplicity", he said in Buenos Aires. "This mode of simplicity I learned in my childhood, in the village. For I was born not in Granada, but in a village called Fuente Vaqueros."

From the plaza of Fuente Vaqueros there extends a long straight avenue, bordered with elms, leading to Valderrubio.

One kilometre out, on the left side, is the so-called Casa Real. Here, in 1831, Richard Ford spent a few days with the bailiff of the Duke of Wellington, leaving to posterity a few delicate pencil drawings of the building.

A little further on we reach the poplars along the stream of Cubillas, which marks the western limit of the Soto de Roma, and the bridge over this stream.

Beyond the dense wall of poplars, we enter a wide cultivated plain. Here the poet's father had some ample fields, planted with sugar beets. Don Federico was one of the principal shareholders of the San Pascual sugar factory, now closed, whose chimney may be seen to right of the highway.

Immediately to the left there begins an earth road bordering the course of the Cubillas. This is not without inter-

est; half a kilometre along it brings us to the spring of
Fuente de la Teja, which wells up on the right bank of the
stream, near a backwater covered with dense vegetation.
Lorca often came to this spot when, in his teens, he spent
the summer with his parents at Valderrubio. It is not a
bad place to sit and re-read some of Lorca's work, such as
the pieces in the *Libro de poemas* specifically ascribed to
the Vega de Zujaira (these fields around us), or the *Suites,*
which have a great deal to do with the Cubillas.

Before entering Valderrubio ("one of the loveliest villages of the Vega", wrote Lorca in a letter, "for its whiteness, and for the serenity of its people") let us devote a few
words to the possible etymology of the foul-sounding
name the village bore in Lorca's time, Asquerosa. This
name in fact has nothing to do with the disagreeable, ho-
monymous adjective (*asquerosa,* disgusting or nauseating).
Asquerosa, to give it its old and, we are tempted to say,
real name, is a village much older than Fuente Vaqueros.
Its name is to be found, in various spellings, in various medieval Arabic texts, and no doubt dates from before the
Muslim conquest in the 8th century. It may proceed from
the Latin *aqua,* water, signifying either "acuerosa", watery,
or «aguarrosa», sweet water. Another derivation commonly
suggested is *Arquerosa,* from *arquero,* archer; to support
which derivation, students of the (admittedly inexact)
science of etymology propose there may have been here a
camp of Roman archers. Roman tombs found recently
near the town perhaps support this hypothesis.

As soon as we enter the town, we see the church, whose
façade contains a plaque commemorating the ceremony on
15 August 1943 when the name of Valderrubio was given
to the place, as if the town had appeared from nothing on
that day. The new designation referred to the plantations
of blond (rubio) tobacco which were then proliferating in
the valley, though now there are not as many of them.

When the García Lorca family arrived here they set up house first, but not for very long, in the Calle Ancha, now Calle Real, to which we arrive in a minute, by going just behind the church. The García Lorca house was the first one after the church itself. In a corner, across the street, is the house that belonged to Frasquita Alba Sierra, proto-type of Lorca's Bernarda Alba.

Frasquita Alba was born in 1858. Of her first marriage she had a son and two daughters; and of the second mar-riage in 1893, three daughters and another son. Thus the exclusively feminime composition of Bernarda Alba's fam-ily is a poetical exaggeration. A woman of strong person-ality though not, it would seem, quite so tyrannical as Ber-narda, Frasquita died on 22 July 1924.

The García Lorcas soon moved to the Calle de la Iglesia, N.º 20. This is the next street parallel to the Calle Real. Here they occupied an ample house purchased by don Federico in 1895, now the local seat of the Spanish Socialist Party (PSOE).

This house is worth a visit. The patio or courtyard in the back is much changed; the neighbours tell me it used to have trees, bushes and flowers. Perhaps I am not in error when I suppose that in the splendid poem *1910 (In-termedio),* from *Poeta en Nueva York,* the "little eyes" of Lorca are seeing this house with its "garden where the cats ate the rats" and at the back of which, in the stable there were always, as I have been told in the village, several bulls that served to pull the plough. This may explain, among the memories of the house contained in the poem, the reference to the "bull's snout". An intensely nostalgic poem in which the poet, from New Work, remembers his childhood paradise in the Vega.

From Valderrubio we take the road to Pinos Puente, which starts from the other end of the village. At one ki-lometre, just after the bridge over the railway, we find on our left the cemetery of Valderrubio, where Frasquita Alba and her second husband are buried, as well as other members of the family. From across the highway we may see the Apeadero de San Pascual, the now abandoned railway station that Lorca used to give as his postal address in Asquerosa.

Now we are in the zone of dry-land cultivation, with olives and wheat fields, descending slowly to the immense green plain of the Vega, with which the dry uplands form a clear-cut contrast of temperament and colour. The poet, as is evident from a fine passage of the *Suites,* was by no means insensitive to this contrast.

A few hundred metres further we take, on our right, the road to Pinos Puente, a very straight road that borders the Vega between huge olive trees until connecting with the N-432. It is said to have been at Pinos, concretely, on the bridge, that the messengers of Fernando and Isabel caught up with Colón, who had left Santa Fe disheartened by the monarchs' initial cold reception of his project.

Leaving Pinos toward Granada, we see two old sugar factories. Of the first, Nueva Rosario on our right, the poet's father was an important shareholder. A few kilometres further, on the left, where the bare Sierra de Elvira practically touches the highway, is La Vega, founded in 1904 as a date on the chimney tells us, and the last to close.

Two roads take off from this stretch of highway, both of which, crossing the railway that runs on our left, enter the fertile plain. These roads offer us an alternative route to Santa Fe and Fuente Vaqueros, in case we wish to go on exploring the marvellous Vega de Granada, birthplace and inspiration of one of the greatest of Spanish poets.

THE CORDOBAN COUNTRYSIDE OF JUAN VALERA

by

CARMEN BRAVO-VILLASANTE

JUAN VALERA
(Cabra, 1824-Madrid, 1905)

The Andalusian Juan Valera is one of the most singular writers of the nineteenth century. Of aristocratic birth, he enjoyed a distinguished political, diplomatic and social career; he never, it seems, took his writing work as seriously as it might have been taken by a less multi-faceted man. Nevertheless he passes for the best stylist of the nineteenth century. His novels include Pepita Jiménez *(1874),* Juanita la Larga *(1895),* Genio y figura *(1897),* Doña Luz *(1879),* Las ilusiones del doctor Faustino *(1875),* El comendador Mendoza *(1877), and* Morsamor *(1899). Valera makes the "costumbrismo" or local colour of his native Córdoba and Andalucía serve the ends of subtle psychological analysis. His fluent style no doubt reflects his wide linguistic horizons; he translated into Castilian* Daphnis and Chloe *and several other works in both classical and modern languages. His production of essays and letters was profuse and letters was profuse and of high quality. Of his extensive travel on diplomatic missions, he has left a similarly extensive body of letters which practically constitute an autobiography. Here, grace and wit alternate with critical and philosophical acumen. His* Cartas americanas *or American letters (1888-1900) make him the first major Spanish writer of the 19th century to take an interest in the political and literary complexity of Spanish-speaking America.*

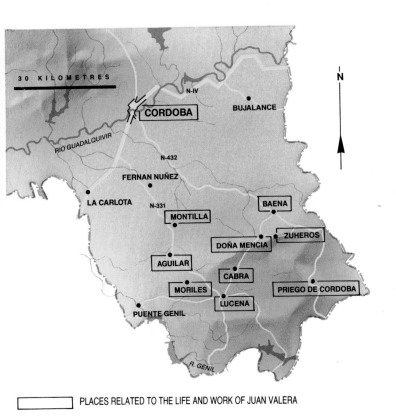

PLACES RELATED TO THE LIFE AND WORK OF JUAN VALERA

THE CORDOBAN COUNTRYSIDE
OF JUAN VALERA

The writer and diplomat Juan Valera was assigned to posts in Naples, Lisbon, Rio de Janeiro; he had been Minister Plenipotentiary in Frankfurt. He had been in Dresden and Russia, at the orders of the Duke de Osuna. He had often been to Paris, and spent long periods there. Upon the Revolution of 1868, he was appointed Subsecretary of State, and in 1872, elected Senator for the province of Córdoba.

In all his diplomatic wanderings Valera never forgot his native land. Born at Cabra, near Córdoba on 18 October 1824, son of the Marquise of La Paniega and of Don José Valera, an officer in the Spanish Navy, Valera, both for reasons of inheritance and of personal taste, all his life retained a close connection to the towns of Cabra and Doña Mencía, which appear often in his novels and his correspondence.

We have cause to be thankful for Valera's ostracism from politics in the year 1873, as it allowed him to devote some years to his writing. Academic sessions, lectures at the Ateneo in Madrid, private meetings and discussions, the salons of society, were not enough to fill up the vast gulf of free time with which Valera suddenly was faced;

and his old desire to write something fine and substantial returned to his mind with new vehemence. We may be sure that his lengthy sojourns at his houses in Cabra and Doña Mencía were not without influence on his decision to embark upon the writing of a novel.

Disillusioned with the Court, his political ambitions left behind, Valera turned to the delights of literary creation, and found that he was now capable of writing the work he had always aspired to write: a novel perfect and apparently simple, though a deeper analysis reveals its complexity; a work which left Valera quite satisfied, and of which he was always proud.

This novel was *Pepita Jiménez,* followed by *Las ilusiones del doctor Faustino, Doña Luz* and *Juanita la Larga,* all of them set in the Andalusian or, more specifically, the Cordoban countryside.

It the traveller wishes to re-create for himself the scenes of these novels, and get to know the fields and hills of the region of Córdoba he can, of course, do no better than to go to Córdoba. Our writer spent several years of his childhood in this city. The Cordoban patios or courtyards will help him understand the love for flowers so often manifested by Pepita Jiménez, who ornamented the rooms of her florid house with pots of aspidistras and odorous climbing plants, hanging among them the gilded cages of her singing birds.

The beauty of Córdoba, its mysterious and labyrinthine streets of whitewashed houses, gives a foretaste of the marvellous towns of the Cordoban region, to which we are about to proceed. From the 1st to the 25th of May the visitor to Córdoba may see the *Festival de los Patios Cordobeses,* when the Cordobans outdo one another in embellishing their courtyards with floral extravagance, each hidden patio being a secret paradise of colour and perfume, with conversation, gastronomy and music prolonged throughout the

Cordoban patio.

Andalusian night. This too is a foretaste of the style of the small towns.

From Córdoba we take a route through the countryside on secondary highways, well paved but with little traffic, to Baena, 61 kilometres from Córdoba, where we make a halt to see the church of Nuestra Señora de Guadalupe ad the Convent of San Francisco. Leaving now the highway, we take a local road, and a few kilometres from Baena takes us to Doña Mencía, a town immortalized by Juan Valera. Here the charm resides in the town itself, whitewashed and sun-drenched; from it we may see the village of Zuheros, high in the mountains, set like an eagle's nest among the crags. Valera made one of his protagonista a native of Zuheros: this was the monk in the novel *Morsamor*.

Ten more kilometres takes us to Cabra, passing through extensive fields of vines and olives on a winding road that takes us up into the hills of the Serranía de Cabra; the views becoming more and more beautiful as we go along. In other days this route would be done on horseback at a more leisurely pace. It leads us all the same, however, to the estate of Alamillo, which belonged to Valera.

In Cabra itself, in the Calle de San Martín is the house where Juan Valera was born, three stories high, with Neoclassical façade, columned portal and central balcony on the first floor. The ground floor balconies are enclosed with grilles, as is usual in Andalucía. This whitewashed house gives a great sensation of simplicity, cleanness and whiteness, characteristic of Andalusian town houses.

In the Parque Alcántara Romero, there is a bust of Valera. The Bibliotecas Públicas (public libraries) of the Municipality and the Institute were promoted by our writer. The old Palace of the Counts of Cabra stands in one of the typical local plazas; and the parish of Nuestra Señora de los Remedios in another plaza, planted with palm tress.

Now, without hurry of touristic worry about seeing

sights, the visitor should settle down in the simple but comfortable pension-hotel and live the sweet life of an Andalusian town of this one and the others he is about to visit. Also he should devote his spare moments (and since he is a tourist, presumably most of his moments will be spare) to a leisurely reading of the novels *Pepita Jiménez* and *Juanita la Larga*. Siesta time is especially suitable for such reading. This will help him understand what he is seeing. The action of the novels takes place in these Andalusian towns of labourers and of well-to-do landowners, as was the famili of Valera himself. Far off in the distance stretch the olive groves and market gardens, where the intelligent and intensive cultivation of Man has made Nature yield exceptional wealth. The town in Valera's novels is called Villaalegre; it is a sort of fusion of elements of both Cabra and Doña Mencía.

Each real image suggests a far-off background of ideas and memories. The Andalusian countryside and the minute description, in the novels, of the labour in the fields and the way of life in the *cortijos*[1], gives glimpses in the background, tinged with an ironic light, of the Bucolics of Virgil. How well done, how pleasurable to read, are the long drawn out descriptions of the popular festivals of these towns: of the procession of Holy Week, which the visitor may see if he comes at that time of year; of the *encolchados*[2]; of the vigil supper prepared for Juana la Larga, with all the rustic viands of Andalucía: the *alboronía* of aubergines, tomatoes and spices; the cod with *sobrehúsa;* the savoury *ajilimójili* sauce of garlic and pepper in which the delicious tortillas are dipped.

In Cabra we must take a walk to the Fuente del Río, just outside the town, now declared a scenic site; it was

---

[1] Farms, farmhouses.
[2] Persons wearing quilts.

Cordoban countryside.

also immortalized by Valera in his novels, when the protagonist, with a water jug under her arm, came to the fountain here. Another walk we recommend, is that made by
Pepita Jiménez in the company of Don Luis, the Canon,
and several other local personalities, where we may discover all the beauty of the Cordoban countryside. "When
the stream runs slowly", says Valera, «there appears lush
growth of reeds and bulrushes, the banks are perfumed
with bergamot, marjoram and sage». Lilies and roses adorn
the paths along which walk Pepita and her jolly company.

Valera took great pleasure in the springtime of Córdoba, and appears to take equal pleasure in describing in
to the reader; but the visitor may here verify the accuracy
of his descriptions. Here are the buttercups, the musk-rose
in rich profusion, the oleander tress. Rosemary and thyme
perfume the air. Hedges of pomegranate and blackberry
divide the fields, orchards and gardens. Robins, goldfin-
ches, sparrows and other birds delight the ear with cheerful song. Swallows swoop and dive in the diaphanous air,
above the houses festooned with the fresh green of fig and
walnut trees. The visitor stops, as did Valera, to marvel at
the wealth of the orchards: cherries, apples, quinces, apri-
cots all promise an abundant harvest.

Valera transmutes all these natural beauties to produce a
poetic Andalucía, no less convincing than the real one; yet
artistically sublimated by a systematic idealization of its
most beautiful features. If the traveller, instead of in Holy
Week, visits Cabra on the 24 th of June, for the festival of
San Juan on Midsummer's Eve, he will see how the magic
night of San Juan is celebrated here; a night of witchery and
love, impregnated with the perfume of verbena, much as
described in the novel *Pepita Jiménez.* The aromatic ambience, the nightingales in the groves are still there to be experienced; and the diaphanous, subtle air in which the brilliant stars and moon seem to be hanging closely overhead.

On the night of San Juan, as in other festivals and celebrations, the streets are full of people. All the population of Cabra, needless to say, is in the streets, plus untold numbers from out of town. Numerous stands serve candies, marzipans, fruits or doughnuts. Guitars are heard wherever one goes.

The *Romería* or pilgrimage of Gipsies to the sanctuary of the Virgen de la Sierra takes place on the third Sunday in June, ascending to an altitude of 1,200 metres, as does the festival of the same Virgin from 4-8 September. Valera mentions these festivals in *Pepita Jiménez;* also the festival of La Cruz in May, the festivals of the grain and grape harvests, and that of the olive. All of these give occasion for fairs, romerías, bullfights and games.

It would be interesting if the visitor were able to see the interiors of a few typical houses, instead of meerely peeping in at the patio from the street entrance; this of course will depend on the acquaintances he may make during his visit. Valera in his novel *Juanita la Larga* describes the lands of Don Paco, a wealthy landowner who courts Juanita, and the house he lives in, thus: "He had two holdings near the town; one, of three *fanegas,* the other of one *fanega* and five *celemines*" (*fanegas* and *celemines* are old measures of land area, now obsolete; but to express them in hectares would detract from the period atmosphere and local colour). "Don Paco also possessed fifteen *aranzadas* of olive groves; the olive trees in them were by no means the scrawny specimens you often see, but were thick with foliage, and almost every year yielded an abundant harvest of olives, the fat ones being especially famous; and Don Paco personally supervised the preparation of them... Lastly, Don Paco possessed the town house he lived in. This dwelling was not without its wine cellar, with ten huge vats of the best Lucena, a small wine-press, and a rack containing some twenty barrels both large and small... This was the finest town house in the village, with a yard full of chickens; a patio, paved and full of flower-pots extravagant with basil, roses, don-pedros and a hundred other plants.

Obviously, for the rustic chores of the wine-press, the oil-press and the vats, there was a back gate through which men and beasts might come and go with their barrels and wagons. All in all, the house was comfortable, even lordly..."

The genre of the regional novel, represented in the 19th century by figures such as Pereda, who sang the praises of the Cantabrian mountains; Emilia Pardo Bazán with her scenes of Galicia; Galdós, the essential Madrilenian; the Valencian, Blasco Ibáñez; finds its most distinguished Andalusian exponent in Juan Valera. There is not a single work of this author that does not have some allusion to the counryside of Córdoba and the folk-ways of Andalucía.

Years later, when Valera was in Washington as Spanish Ambassador, he had the satisfaction of seeing *Pepita Jiménez,* his most famous novel, translated into English. Yet later, in Vienna, he was known as the Universal Andalusian, thanks to his psychological novels rendered in the regional colours of his land.

Times have changed, more than a century having gone by since Valera wrote; it is all the more interesting to read his article on *La cordobesa,* i.e. the housewife of a typical house in a Cordoban village, not unlike the house of Don Paco we have just described. He wrote this article about the same time as the novels set in Cabra and Doña Mencía when, out of politics and recently returned to his land, he seems to take special delight in painting verbal pictures of its scenery and customs and, in this particular case, of Cordoban women. How much love is infused in these descriptive passages, how much mastery of language and wealth of terminology! Valera obviously enjoyed writing and, in his unforced style, makes a fine passage out of a mere enumeration of the products of the land:

"The Cordoban Woman is all vigilance, thriftiness, cleanliness and care. The keys to the pantry, the cupboards, chests and closets are never out of her sight. The pantry shelves are wont to be laden, in provident and rich profusion, with a vast treasure of edibles... There you will find walnuts, chestnuts, almonds, sweet potatoes, plums; cherries steeping in jars of strong liquor, strips of dried peach or apricot, and a thousand other titbits. The peppercorns, chili peppers and garlic are stored beside the codfish, in the less tidy part of the pantry. In the tidier part you will see sugar, coffee, sage, camomile and, often, tea, which not too many years ago was only to be found at the town pharmacy. From the ceiling, there hang a number of egregious giant hams and, alternating with this bucolic manifestation of the animal kingdom, great bunches of grapes, pomegranates and other fruits. In deep glass-covered trays the lady conserves quantities of tenderloin of pork, covered in lard; also chitterlings, kidneys and spleens of the same quadruped; other vessels are found to contain artichokes, mushrooms, asparagus... Nor is there any lack, in due season, of the monstrous cherries of Carcabuey, the pears of Priego, the melons of Montalbán, the peaches of Alcaudete, the figs of Montilla, the oranges of Palma del Río, nor even of those egregious plums that only grow on the slopes below the castle of Cabra: plums sweet as honey, that smell better than roses. As far as grapes are concerned, we need not make any possibly invidious comparisons of one variety with another, for all are excellent: Lairenes, Pedrojiménez, negras, albillas, Dombuenas, Moscateles, Baladíes and a thousand other lineages of grapes."

All the towns mentioned by Valera in this article may be visited by the traveller, as the writer himself visited them from his native town, as they are only a few kilometres distant. If he visits Lucena, he should not neglect to visit the Torre del Moral, a tower in which Boabdil, last

Moorish king of Granada, was held prisoner; and the parish church of San Mateo, with the Baroque chapel of the
Sagrario.

Another day will serve for a visit to Priego de Córdoba,
where he may view the various noble houses of the town,
the castle and the parish church of Santa María de la
Asunción. The Baroque retables of these churches are fine
examples of the work of this period in Andalucía.

Since everything is near and well connected, the traveller may return to Lucena and continue on a good highway
to Montilla, a town famous for the quality of its wines,
where the grape harvest is celebrated in a festival lasting
from the 21st of August to the first Sunday in September.
Before reaching Montilla he will have passed the town of
Moriles, also famous for its wine; and Aguilar de la Frontera, whose name reminds us that this region was long a
frontier with the Moorish kingdom of Granada. It is tempt-
ing to make a stop in any of these towns, as did Valera,
who had friends in practically every corner of the Cordoban region, many of them possessed of ample mansions of
the type described in his novels.

And when the traveller returns home, he may savour a
glass of amontillado and re-read the page of *Pepita Jiménez*
with enlarged comprehension and, we hope, with pleasant
memories and a desire to return some day to the unforgettable land of Córdoba and of Juan Valera.

ARAGÓN

JARNESIAN ROUTE

by

ILDEFONSO-MANUEL GIL

BENJAMÍN JARNÉS
(Codo, 1888-Madrid, 1949)

Born in a family of few economic means, Jarnés studied on a scholarship at the Royal Seminary of San Carlos in Zaragoza. In 1910 he abandoned his ecclesiastical studies; he enlisted then re-enlisted in the army and in this period of military service completed his studies as a teacher. He obtained a minor bureaucratic employment, and while posted in Jaca and Morocco began contributing articles to newspapers and magazines. Settling in Madrid, he became known in literary and artistic circles of the so-called "avant-garde" and contributed mostly to publications of the same tendency. From 1925 until the Civil War he was an assiduous contributor to the Revista de Occidente. *He was soon famous as a narrator and essayist. His novels were well received:* El profesor inútil, *1926;* El convidado de papel, *1928;* Paula y Paulita, *1929;* 1929; Locura y muerte de nadie, *1929;* Teoría del zumbel, *1930;* Viviana y Merlín, *1930;* Escenas junto a la muerte, *1931;* Lo rojo y lo azul, *1932. Also biographies:* Zumalacárregui; Sor Patrocinio, *the stigmatized nun of the Isabeline period;* Castelar; Gustavo Adolfo Bécquer; *and essays collected in book form:* Ejercicios, *1927;* Rúbricas, *1931;* Fauna contemporánea, *1933;* Cita de ensueños, *1936;*

Cartas al Ebro, *1940. Many of the novels have been through various editions. After the Civil War he had to leave Spain, settling in Mexico and continuing his work with more novels:* Venus dinámica, *1943;* La novia del viento, *1940; among various other productions. Having fallen very ill, his relatives managed his return to Spain. He had lost his mental lucidity; and though after his arrival in 1948 he improved slightly, he died in Madrid on 10 August of the following year.*

In better histories of Spanish literature, Jarnés is considered a major figure of the 20th century. Doctoral theses at Spanish and foreign universities, and whole books upon his work, show the growing interest in Jarnés. In recent years several of his books have been reprinted and some, previously in manuscript, published for the first time. Some of his short stories have been reprinted by the cultural service of "Iberia" and are to be translated into German.

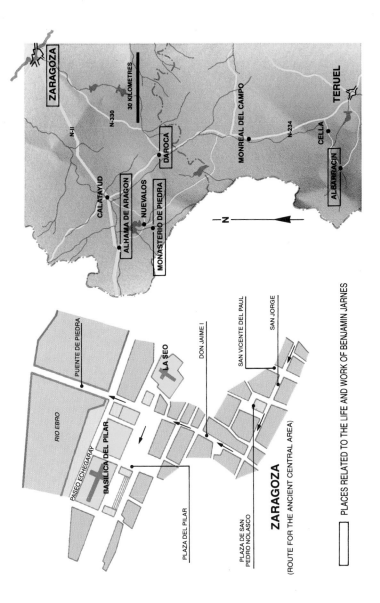

ZARAGOZA

RIO EBRO

PUENTE DE PIEDRA

PASEO ECHEGARAY

BASÍLICA DEL PILAR

PLAZA DEL PILAR

LA SEO

DON JAIME I

SAN VICENTE DEL PAUL

SAN JORGE

PLAZA DE SAN PEDRO NOLASCO

ZARAGOZA
(ROUTE FOR THE ANCIENT CENTRAL AREA)

ZARAGOZA

N-II

N-330

CALATAYUD

ALHAMA DE ARAGÓN

NUÉVALOS

MONASTERIO DE PIEDRA

DAROCA

30 KILOMETRES

—N→

MONREAL DEL CAMPO

N-234

CELLA

ALBARRACÍN

TERUEL

PLACES RELATED TO THE LIFE AND WORK OF BENJAMIN JARNES

JARNESIAN ROUTE

The spacious novels of Benjamín Jarnés are strictly set in a scenery of real geography, though the names are normally altered. Usually the real place-name is rather thinly veiled. Thus Zaragoza —the Caesaraugusta of the Romans— is called Augusta; not just occasionally, but in many of his novels.

Sometimes the fictitious name is further from the real, but only in the geographical aspect. Alhama de Aragón is converted to Aguas Vivas to serve as the setting of the novel *Paula y Paulita,* sharing novelistic space with Abadía de los Fresnos, an arbitrary name for Monasterio de Piedra. In another case, a real city is presented without any name whatever. It has been identified from the closely realistic description, with various faithful details, given of it in the novel, *Escenas junto a la muerte.* The city in question is Albarracín.

Our suggested Jarnesian route is anchored in four main places.

First Day: Alhama de Aragón and Monasterio de Piedra

Alhama de Aragón (Aguas Vivas) is on the banks of the Río Jalón, on the Madrid—Barcelona higway, 208 km from the capital. The town boasts an abundance of thermal waters. Paula, a woman of autumnal beauty, is spending a few days at the spa, accompanied by her daughter Paulita. Paulita is the image of her mother but, of course, more favoured by the splendour of youth. However, what interests us at the moment is not these ladies themselves, but the places they visit; places we may contemplate through the eyes of Julio, the first-person narrator and principal personality in several of Jarnés' novels. Julio, as we might expect, bears a great personal resemblance to Jarnés himself.

Though not, we must suppose, in the plot, certainly in the person of the narrator and the description of the setting, *Paula y Paulita* is, like all Jarnés' novels, faithfully autobiographical: Jarnés often visited the spa of Termas Pallarés at Alhama. This novel is the fruit of his first visits there. For the narrator, the "Termas", with their complex of buildings and gardens, are an enclave set apart, not only from the countryside, but also from the rest of the town. We may affirm that the traveller who sticks to our route with similar faithfulness will see the same scenes as did the alter ego of Jarnés some sixty years ago. The buildings of the Termas Pallares have suffered from the passage of time, of course, and from the changes of fashion. The theatre and the casino are long since closed, and moulder now in neglect and abandon. The lake in the park has lost its aura of social pretension, and is now a crowded public swimming pool.

The novelesque scene in the park, from its prehistory onwards, is thus seen through the ironic eye and limpid prose of Julio: "At first there was the ground; bare, or with a few stones on it. A legendary wand struck the most hostile of the rocks, causing hot water to burst forth, and the first buildings rose not long after. The ravine was walled in, and like all the aseptic marvels of the globe, submitted to a regime of closure and the payment of a tariff; Man is always the lord of Creation, as long as he pays the fee demanded. But the therapeutic marvel attracted few pilgrims; and it was found necessary also to construct an ambience. ... What in the protohistory of the thermal waters was only a classical growth ill copied from Theocritus, is now a fine parterre imitated from Winthuysen. Less roses, but thicker fronds. One day two lovers were seen to have a certain lyrical temperament, and in no time a green lake with ripples appeared from between the reeds and bulrushes. Another traveller was seen to be carrying in his luggage a copy of *Treasure Island;* on the following day a cute little island appeared in the middle of the lake, with three craggy rocks, a couple of palm tress and a hanging of moss. ... In the little park, the same juxtaposition of ambience. Here are Spring, Summer, Autumn and Winter, lined up shoulder to shoulder in a small compass. The same allegories decorate the grand staircase of the hotel. The same nude maiden, the boy with his handful of wheat, the grape-laden harvester caught in mid-song, the old greybeard shivering under his philosopher's cape."

Later, his attention turns to the town in general: "As there is little useable land, the last houses of Aguas Vivas wedge themselves into the spa, and the spa prolongs its hotels into the very midst of the town. ... Now we arrive at what I call the neutral bridge. For the town is split in two to make way for that river, which was already put to shame by the cynical epigrams of Martial."

From Aguas Vivas (Alhama) the novel proceeds to Abadía de los Fresnos (Monasterio de Piedra). When Julio, having failed in his attempt at Paulita, is now the lover of Paula, there appears a strange personality called Mr. Brook, who several years earlier had been a business partner of the then husband of Paula. The two women, Mr. Brook and Julio go to visit the Abadía. Let us say merely that this final chapter, "Petronio", is not recounted by Julio, but by an omniscient narrator, less digressive and more attentive to dialogue. The person who talks most is Mr. Brook, and it comes as no surprise that total silence falls upon the novel when he commits suicide. But before we accompany the four travellers leaving Aguas Vivas, let us mention that this same place is, with somewhat less descriptive precision, also the main setting of the novel *Teoría del zumbel*, published in 1930.

The Monastery of Santa María de Piedra is 17 km from Alhama de Aragón. The highway between them passes through a lovely village, Nuévalos, only about three kilometres from the monastery. The foundation of the monastery is attributed to the initiative of one Abbot Peter, from the Monastery of Poblet, with the support of Alfonso II of Aragón. Construction commenced in 1195, and the original building was finished in 1218, in the reign of Jaime I. The new Cistercian monastery received numerous royal privileges, castles, villages and other possessions in the provinces of Zaragoza and Teruel. With the application of the Law of Mendizábal it became the property of the State, later sold to a private owner, which has been its situation since the middle of the 19th century.

Of its old artistic wealth, the original Romanesque architecture to which the centuries have added Gothic, Renaissance and Baroque elements, there are valuable remnants, though the church is in ruins. The abbot's palace, however was converted to a hotel both splendid and comfortable, and still functions as such.

All in all, the present main interest of the Monastery, which qualifies it as a major tourist attraction, is its mar-

Monasterio de Piedra.

vellous park. The small stream of the río Piedra is interrupted in its course by a cliff a stone's throw from the monastery, producing a fine series of waterfalls. A beautiful spot, whose election by the Cistercians suggested a sharp comment by Benjamín Jarnés: "the location of the ancient Bilbilis (Calatayud) is strategic; that of the Monasterio de Piedra is voluptuous. The roman soldiers and the rotund monk of Cister knew well that it was necessary to defend against the enemy without and the enemy within, respectively. The 'enemy within' of the monk was the spirit, which was kept at bay by the sensual pleasures of the site of Piedra. The Satanic guest could not shriek his rebellion here; one could only sing hallelujahs to the creator of so much beauty, while gourmandizing on the savoury trouts of the river... The monk of Piedra, ultraepicurean, licked his lips at the magnificence of the Lord. What would have happened to St. Jerome if, instead of retiring to the desert, he had retired to this well-watered valley?»

This comment is found a manuscript notebook of Jarnés, dated 1932, a few years after the appearance of *Paula y Paulita,* and maintans the ironic tone already found in the novel: "On entering the Abbey, a traveller loses weight in proportion to the volume of rhetoric he displaces. One who, like Julio, displaces no rhetoric, begins to doubt the fact of his own existence, as if, on getting into the bathtub, the water had not risen even a millimetre." The legends that appear about the waterfalls are soon substituted by other ones invented by the nihilist spirit of Mr. Book. Some of these fantasies conserve, as does the river, their original names, as in the tourist guides, whose duly mentioned prototype is Baedeker. Others are re-christened, thus:

"Legends, like scarlet serpents, keep on sprouting from the mouth of the master of illusion. A rich assortment of different kinds of moss —green velvet of different sorts and prices— come and go, with flowers, mushrooms, all the growths of fancy, legends of lovers pursued by ghosts, troubadors pursued by dwarfs. The conjuring of Brook peoples the Abbey with jocund fantasy. The water suggests the sound of exquisite chamber music. They had only known the torment of slowly dropping water; now they knew its prodigies. Falling water may slowly drill through thoughts', or construct images. Always monotonous, it drills through an argument or sculptures a metaphor... here the water, in all the ruins, produces its finest work."

Apart from such wandering digression and theatrical rhetoric on the theme of its natural beauties, the marvellous garden of the Monasterio de Piedra offers a simple abundance of visual pleasure with which few places in the world can compare.

Concluding this first day, the traveller on our Jarnesian route may spend the night at the hotel in the monastery itself or in one of those in Nuévalos, or proceed 27 km to Calatayud on a good highway. To the traveller who does not know this town, we recommend a visit to any of its fine churches, so beautifully presided by the Colegiata de Santa María.

Second Day: Zaragoza

From Calatayud to Zaragoza (the Augusta of the novels of Jarnés) it is 88 km on the Nacional II highway. Here the traveller will find himself in the principal novelistic space of Jarnés. In Augusta occurs, in whole or in part, the action of *El profesor inútil* (1926), *El convidado de papel* (1928), *Locura y muerte de nadie* (1929), *Teoría del zumbel* (1931), *Lo rojo y lo azul* (1932), and *La novia del viento* (México, 1940).

El convidado de papel is the most autobiographical of all these. Julio, whom we have met as a visitor to the Spa at Alhama and the Monasterio de Piedra, is here seen as a schoolboy, a seminarian at the Semanario de San Carlos. We suggest that, starting from the fine building of the Seminary, in an interesting part of old Zaragoza, the visitor should follow the itinerary of Julio and his classmates toward the groves on the left bank of the Ebro, where they spent their recreation hours. But this walk should not begin without a previous look at the church of San Carlos, a spectacular Baroque work, and the neighboring house of Morlanes, now under a slow process of restoration. Here is the route that appears in *El convidado de papel:*

"On their way to the edge of town the schoolboys may study the past and present of Augusta. The route mostly consists of narrow alleys, but widens out on two occasions, into plazas so singular that they seem not to belong to the same city. In the first of these there is a market, thick with hoarse shouts, acrid smells of garden and stable; hemmed in by cheerful façades, either new or modernized, with access to the heart of the city by way of a wide street recently opened, for which an authentic jewel of the Plateresque palace style was demolished, to be replaced by a sumptuous bank building, repository of the more shameful jewellery of Augusta. A little further on, they come to the second plaza. This is a wider one, without plebeian crowds or slaughterhouse aromas. Here we perceive only the subtle perfume of heroic centuries and municipal acacia trees. Amid the acacias stands a fountain into whose basin a Biblical woman perpetually pours the contents of two jugs. Around the fountain, some petty gardens and, around these, the emblazoned walls of old houses. To one side, the grey façade of a church, and to the other, an ochre-coloured palace."

We may follow the same route: Plaza de San Carlos, Calle de San Jorge. This street, crossing the Calle de San Vicente de Paúl and passing through the Plaza de San Pedro Nolasco (the picturesque market no longer exists) opens onto the Calle de Don Jaime (popularly known as Calle de San Gil). By this street, turning to the right, we arrive at the Plaza de la Seo. No longer here, but in another plaza not far away, stand the fountain of La Samaritana. Now the plaza described by Jarnés is incorporated in the Plaza del Pilar.

The explorer must, in faithfulness to the text, continue to the Ebro. This river and its name are never absent from the novels of Jarnés. And, at the very least, have a good look at the ancient and famous bridge of the Puente de Piedra. The novelistic scenes of Augusta are distributed not only throughout the old Zaragoza, but also in the suburbs. Thus, there is a curious reference to the Cabezo de Buena Vista, presided by the outsize figure of Alfonso I the Battler:

"It is well known that the word "picnic" in this city means an outdoor meal in the shadow of the great sword of King Wamba. This King dominates the city, standing on a pedestal as outsize as his sword and the King himself. 'Larger than life size', say the guides. The city is always presided by giants. Of all mythology, it always prefers the Titan, and ought to be consecrated to Polyphemus or Hercules. The fiestas are presided by giants, and the trials too: the former by giants of papier-maché, the latter by giants of stone, perennial sentinels of the Palace of Justice."

So many are the Zaragozan places written of by Jarnés that an exhaustive tour or even listing of them would be impossible; we have already said that Augusta appears in almost all his novels. Not in *San Alejo, Viviana y Merlín, Eufrosina* or *Su línea de fuego;* but in all the others. Thus we advise the visitor to the city to see, or see again, museums of Zaragoza, most of them installed in the Plaza de San Felipe; the Camón Aznar Museum, in the Calle de Espoz y Mina. Not less interesting is the Palace of the Counts of Sástago, in the Coso near the Plaza de España; the wonderful Patio de la Infanta, installed in the central branch of Ibercaja; and above all, the great castle-palace of the Aljafería.

This second day might, with a certain infidelity to our strict tour planning, last two days, for the city really offers too much to take in in one day. Indeed if the reader is a fervent Jarnesian he may to spend his second afternoon by making a visit to the birthplace of Jarnés, in Codo. But only if he is a really fervent Jarnesian.

Third Day: Daroca and Albarracín

Without too early a rising, but without dawdling, the traveller should take the Nacional 330 highway, which goes from Zaragoza to Valencia. He will cross the Campo de Cariñena and, at 83 km from Zaragoza, reach the ancient walled city of Daroca. Jarnés was in this town on the day the Republic was proclaimed, 14 April 1931, and was an important participant in the doings of that day. He left a record of this in a text published under the title of *Viaje al corazón de un pueblo.*

Daroca is officially described as a "monumental and historic" city. An arch, flanked by crenellated towers, admits us within the city walls. On one side and the other, the wall runs uphill, festooned with towers, some in good condition, others in ruins, others totally disappeared. On the right side is the castle, abandoned and in ruins, occupying a small plateau overlooking most of the city. Here are various churches, the most important being the Colegial de Santa María, ensemble of prodigious works of art and sanctuary of the Santísimos Corporales: its Romanesque apse, its Plateresque side portal, its Gothic naves, Renaissance, Baroque or Neoclassical chapels, the Berniniesque tabernacle of the main altar and the filigrained Gothic work of the chapel of the Corporales, the fine primitive painters and the parish museum all concur in exalting the beauty of the ensemble. There are other old churches in Daroca, some no longer used for services, but used for cultural purposes, like that of San Juan with its Romanesque apse, topped with brick but without altering the purity of its style; and that of San Miguel, Romanesque with rich mural paintings above the main altar. All of this may be cursorily viewed in not too long a time.

Returning to the Calle Mayor, which starts from the entrance arch, we leave the walled circuit through another arch, also flanked by two fine towers. Outside which, we might stop and look back on it. An old fountain with twenty tubes adds a singular beauty to this gate, the Puerta Baja of Daroca. A few metres away on the left, we take a bypass leading us tack to the Nacional 330 highway. It is 99 km from Daroca to Teruel. The road runs closely parallel to the Río Jiloca. Just past the town of Villarquemado, near the old pass of Cella, is the access to Cella, three kilometres away, where we begin to climb the Sierra de Albarracín.

The road leaves Cella and takes us to the foot of the singular city of Albarracín. Nowadays, stuck to the abrupt base of the mountain there are several buildings, "roadside businesses" that did not exist when Jarnés visited the city in the spring of 1931. From the novel *Escenas junto a la muerte* we may excerpt a few passages characteristic of the Jarnesian vision, and typical of his prose style: "the little city comes closer to us, silent, defiant. Extended along a strategic breach in the mountains, it looks down upon us with a stony frown. Hermetically closed, it presents an unwelcoming façade. Covered with a secular patina, as under a mantle of ashes... this city, like other old cities of Aragon and Castile, is in no hurry to present the visitor with pleasant groves or fountains or appeal to his sensitivity. Above

Corner of Albarracín.

all, the city has no fuzzy, indeterminate outlines in the modern manner; its limits are not blurred by the usual aureole of vague parks and detached houses. Here the line between city and country is rigid and well-defined. In general, they are the same limits as in the Middle Ages: the city walls. If the traveller approaches these, it is because he presumes that inside there is a heart, perhaps sleepy, but alive... This city makes no courtesan winks, but martial salutes. Not from windows with geraniums, but from crenellated battlements. ... We climb up interminable, fatiguing ramps, half country, half city, paved with cobbles. On the façades, shields crowned with heraldic emblems, incrustations of ancient pride in faces now humble, ascetic and tired, the eaves worm-eaten and sagging. Houses piled up, constructed in two or three different epochs, of volumes superimposed like boxes in a shop, overhanging, epileptic, threatening collapse; magnificent ironwork, mouldy filigree, in the shape of birds and leaves, climbing up the grilles to the eaves; an abundance of unalterable iron on the crumbling, decaying stone; nerves of the city displaying their black hardness upon the bruised flesh of centuries; iron and stone, black arabesque on ashy grey, on yellow and ochre; a thick crust, sometimes childishly painted over, with no suggestion of cordiality... may we somehow perceive a warm undulation of life under the crust of this town?... The city is here, like a tough woman of these parts, awaiting, not an easy conquistador to break her heart, but a cordial spirit who will recognize her beauty."

Fortunately, Albarracín is about as good an example of respectful restoration as the lover of medievalism has a right to hope for in the late 20th century. Most of the ruins seen by Jarnés have now been restored, in a matter-of-fact style that generally manages to abstain from kitsch.

Our return to highway 330 should be made by means

of the mountain road running beside the río Turia. Before doing so, we may wish to spend the night in Albarracín. If the visitor does not know Teruel and has an extra day on hand, it will be well spent in seeing that city, and in it, one of the purest and loveliest of Mudéjar towers. In any case, highway 330 will take him to Monreal del Campo, only 55 kilometres from Teruel. There he may take highway 211 through Molina de Aragón, coming out onto the Nacional II highway near Alcolea del Pinar, the end of our Jarnesian Route.

PRINCIPADO
DE ASTURIAS

THE PATHS OF VETUSTA,
OR THE PROVINCE AS SPECTACLE

by

JUAN CUETO ALAS

LEOPOLDO ALAS, CLARÍN
(Zamora, 1852-Oviedo, 1901)

Alas was of an old Asturian family, but happened to be born in Zamora, where his father held the post of Civil Governor. After living in León and Guadalajara, the Alas family moved to Oviedo in 1865. Here in the capital of the Principality, Leopoldo finished his secondary schooling and in 1869 entered as a student in the Faculty of Law at the University of Oviedo. During 1871-72 he was at Madrid taking a doctorate in Law and studying Letters at the Universidad Central. He now began to be known as a journalist in Madrid, and on 2 October 1875 first used his famous pseydonym Clarín in El Solfeo. *He obtained his doctorate in 1878 with the thesis* Law and morality *and, although he passed the examinations of that year for the chair of Political Economy and Statistics at the University of Salamanca, the Count of Toreno, minister of Cánovas, vetoed his candidacy. Some years later, the Liberal government of Sagasta granted him a chair at Zaragoza, where he imparted classes in 1882-83. In July 1883 he was posted to Oviedo as professor of Roman Law, and later of Natural Law. From then on, Clarín never left Oviedo.*

He was a disciple of Salmerón, Camús, Canalejas, Castelar,

Amador de los Ríos and Francisco Giner de los Ríos. The liberal revolution of 1868 determined his adhesion to the principles of criticism and reform. A convinced Republican, educated in the ideals of Krausism, he introduced into Spain the mode of literary naturalism and positivism, though corrected by certain metaphysical inclinations and a spiritual and moralizing restlessness that distinguishes him from his more radical European colleagues. He was the most popular and feared critic of current events, both literary and otherwise, of his time. His journalistic work, articles and essays, appears collected in the books Solos de Clarín *(1881),* La literatura en 1881 *(1882),* Sermón perdido *(1885),* Nueva campaña *(1887),* Ensayos y revistas *(1892), and* Palique *(1894). From 1886 to 1891 he published eight* Folletos literarios *composed of essays, commentaries, satires, speeches, etc. Also, and above all, Alas produced short stories, though many of them might well be called short novels; another genre in which he was an undisputed master in his time:* Pipá, El señor y lo demás son cuentos, El gallo de Sócrates, Cuentos morales, Doctor Sutilis, Doña Berta, Cuervo, Superchería, *etc. He began writing* La Regenta *in 1883, and in January and June of 1885, Volumes I and II of the novel came out, published at Barcelona by Daniel Cortezo in the Biblioteca Artes y Letras, with illustrations by Juan Llimons and engravings by Gómez Polo. In 1890 his second novel came out,* Su único hijo, *undeservedly eclipsed by the success, and scandal, of* La Regenta.

PLAN OF VETUSTA

ACCORDING TO LA REGENTA, BY LEOPOLDO ALAS «CLARÍN»
(TOWARDS THE END OF THE 19TH CENTURY)

TO LA FABRICA VIEJA

TO EL CAMPO DEL SOL

CONVENTO DE LAS CLARISAS

SALESAS

CONVENTO DE STO. DOMINGO

CONVENTO DE SAN BENITO

PLAZUELA DE A. ACEBEDO

CONVENTO DE LAS RECOLETAS

CATEDRAL

C. DE LA HERRERIA

C. DE STA. ANA

PLAZUELA DE LA CATEDRAL

PLAZUELA DE LOS TRASCORRALES

C. PLATERIA

CASINO

C. DE LA RUA

C. DE CIMADEVILLA

PLAZA NUEVA

C. DE SAN JUAN

CARCEL

CASERON DE LOS OZORES

PLAZUELA DE PORLIER

C. SAN FRANCISCO

CONVENTO DE SAN VICENTE

THE PATHS OF VETUSTA
OR THE PROVINCE AS SPECTACLE

Let us start off on the right foot, with a useful proposition for this literary route which bites its own tail: *La Regenta* does not present a more or less faithful map of Oviedo, as have insisted, and continue to insist, to the point of boredom, numerous critics and specialists blinded by the theory of social reflex, not to mention local scholars and journalists either angered or flattered by possible resemblances between the real city and the imaginary Vetusta, Hispanists fanaticized by the hard-core school of realism, lecture-hall antifranquists or seminar sociologists. Quite the contrary. Oviedo has ended by resembling Vetusta, from a century of gazing at itself in the pages of the novel.

Let us make this clear. Alas laid out Vetusta on the scale and likeness of Oviedo, the city he knew best, and the provincial model he had most to hand when he was writing *La Regenta.* But to build the novel he used only *some* urban and human materials of that nineteenth-century Oviedo, veiling those he did use in a more or less subtle manner to avoid scrapes with the live forces of local

society, and often crossing them with other provincial references, which in the first instance had nothing at all to do
with the plan of the city. What has happened, and it is not
the first time such a phenomenon has appeared in history,
is that the fiction of Vetusta, after a hundred years of sickly-
intimate relations with Oviedo and the Ovetenses, has had
its influence on reality. This means that the traces left by
the novel are much more visible and visitable in the Oviedo
of today are the references in stone or bone of that Oviedo
of the Restoration that Leopoldo Alas used to construct a
part (a third, perhaps) of his Vetusta.

Our first and only recommendation for the tourist who
explores Oviedo faithfully following the plan of the *Regenta*
and, suddenly, thinks he has found a ruin of Vetusta (an
idle, backstabbing conversation overheard, a casino personality, a ridiculous institution, a rumor from another century, a Magistral, a Mesías, a Catholic lady of adulterous
glance): the visitor who sees these things should consider
his retirement from active service in the wars of literature.
For these, or similar analogies with the novel are not the
same phenomena that moved the pen of Alas to describe
them. Simply, they are influences of *La Regenta.* More or less
happy consequences of the stormy and not very healthy
marriage of a hundred years between city and novel. Knowing this, one may wander at will in the alleys of the capital
of the Principality without danger of seduction by the ab-
ject theory of Social Reflex, and also, enjoy the monuments
with the same pleasure and vertigo that reading gives. All
without knowing whether he is walking though the pages
of the city or treading the pavements of the novel.

The Cathedral of Vetusta exists. This we cannot deny.
The needle of its tower is the first thing we see in Oviedo.
However I do not know if it is still possible to get away
with pronouncing the bit about "romantic poem of stone",
because after a century of intense repetition of this Clari-

Cathedral of Oviedo.

nian description of the Cathedral tower by people who in many cases have never opened the novel, the phrase has a smell of kitsch-cult about it. Similar value erosion has been suffered by the famous siesta of the Heroic City. But it is one thing to recite the Cathedral cliché of *La Regenta,* and another thing to undertake the task of trying to get up into the belltower and enjoy the privileged view of the city possessed in the novel by don Fermín de Pas, the Magistral, with telescope in hand.

It is not so easy to conquer the exalted height from which the Magistral peered down upon his domain of Vetusta. The best way is to get into the graces of the sacristan or of some tonsured person with authority in the place; perhaps slip him a bank-note not in the manner of a tip, but as alms for the work of the parish; put on a poncho like Clint Eastwood used to wear in the Sergio Leone spaghetti Westerns, to keep your better clothes clean of the dandruff-like dust that crumbles from the sick stones of San Salvador, and launch yourself on a respectable climb up a spiral staicase. During the climb you might remember another, less celebrated passage about the Cathedral tower: "It was not one of those towers whose thinness is forced to an extremity of skinniness rather than slimness, and look as affected as certain refined young ladies do who tighten too much their corsets; it was robust without prejudice to its spiritual grandeur, and up to its second stage, with elegant balustrade, it rose like a strong castle; shooting up from thence as an obelisk of gracious angle, inimitable in its measures and proportions. Like a bundle of muscles and nerves, stone rose on stone into the upper air, balancing like an acrobat..."

I assure all readers that the climb is well worth the physical effort. Especially if the climber is a lover of nineteenth-century novelry, i.e. a connoisseur of the techniques of chemically pure literary realism. From the upper balconies of the Cathedral tower he may not only inspect one of the best panoramas of Oviedo (or of Vetusta; why argue the point), but also usurp for a few moments the very same narrative viewpoint the author used to create *La Regenta*. Or to hammer the point home more boringly, the traveller will enjoy the *narrative point of view* that determined the realistic novel and revolutionized the style of the principal genre of fiction. Alas utilizes the height of the Cathedral belltower and the precision of the Magistral's telescope to draw a plan of Vetusta and situate all his creatures correctly in it. Because Clarín accumulates, right from the start, in the first pages, practically all the narrative procedures that altered the course of novel-writing, from Balzac to Flaubert: the invisibility of the author, the omniscient narrator, the efficient and neutral description of scenery and objects that surround and round out the personalities, the protagonism of urban spaces, the discovery of quotidian reality, social determinism, the psychology of current time. And for this, obviously, the author needed to set himself at a certain height and distance, aided by the telescopic vision of a personality who also uses the confessional as a microscope.

But after visiting the narrative viewpoint of the author of *La Regenta,* a viewpoint, let us not forget, that connects the Spanish novel with modern culture, the visitor may also admire some less abstract views from the belltower. Around the Cathedral of San Salvador extends the old quarter of the city. An old, humid Oviedo, no longer as noble as it was still in Clarin's time, which has now become the circuit of post-modernist alcoholizing and drug-taking, with bars called *La Regenta, Tigre Juan* and other landmarks and myths of Oviedo fiction. Six plazas comprise the principal nuclei of the literary core: that of Alfonso II, in front of the observatory of don Fermín de Pas; la Corrada del Obispo, neuralgic centre of the present clergy; that of Las

Corrada del Obispo.

Pelayas or of Feijoo; that of Porlier; that of the Ayuntamiento or Plaza Mayor, with the church of San Isidro, and
the pedlar's plaza of Fontán. Each of these plazas that surround the Cathedral retains today a specific urban function: religious, ecclesiastical, academic, judicial, bureaucratic and mercantile, respectively. All are connected by
narrow, capricious alleys, solitary passageways where you
may still hear murmurs of liturgical latin mixed with the
piano notes of maiden aunts; old churches and chapels of
arcane devotions; crumbling mansions emitting an aroma
of solitude, of rural aristocracy come down in the world;
literary ruins of the lower nineteenth century occupied by
the urban tribes of deafening decibels. A building ensemble
not far different from that of the time of creation of Vetusta, miraculously saved from the real-estate speculator
and the wrecking crane: this is indeed the model for the
Vetustan quarter of the Encimada, which the Magistral
contemplates from atop the tower with a mixture of hatred
and admiration. His prey. And not only because in the garden of one of those palaces walks Ana Ozores, the coveted
wife of the Regente.

"Almost all the streets of the Encimada were narrow,
winding, humid, sunless; grass grew in some of them; the
cleanliness of those streets where the inhabitants were
noble or of pretensions as such, was sad, almost miserable,
like the cleanliness of the kitchen in a hospice for the poor;
it seemed as if the municipal broom and the broom of decent nobility had left in these plazas and alleys the sort of
marks a brush leaves in threadbare cloth."

Clarín, as we have said, used only some references from
the real Oviedo when he drew up the plan of Vetusta. One
of these was the Cathedral. Not only the 70 metres height
of the famous tower, with its great bell Wamba, dated
1219, "which called the most venerable canons to choir,
the Cathedral Chapter of preeminent qualities and privi-

leges", but its interior too. The sacristy, above all, a sinister counterpoint to the formidable watchtower whence the Magistral dreamed of his prospective sin. "The sacristy was a chapel in the form of a Latin cross, large and cold, with four high vaults. Above the drawers hung canvases by unknown painters, most of them antique; and a few not bad copies of good artists. Between picture and picture a few cornucopias flaunted their gilding; and mirrors that hardly reflected anything, on account of the accumulated dust and flyspecks." Also the Choir, the Pantheon of Kings, the chapel of Santa Eulalia or of Santa Clementina; and the Ambulatory, with its splendid collection of confessionals, worthy of inclusion in the best museum of penitential art, in one of which Ana Ozores recounted her mystical-adulterous temptations to don Fermín; Baroque furniture, microscopes of the soul, that were more or less mute witnesses to the real intimate history of the city.

Let us not forget the relics of the Cámara Santa or San Miguel, re-christened in fiction as the Chapel of Las Santas Reliquias; an obligatory tourist visit, though probably more enjoyed by amateurs of fantastic literature than by those of the realistic novel: here resides the Holy Ark that came to Oviedo from Jerusalem, in flight from the persecution of Chosroes of Persia. Nowadays the Ark is empty, due to the revolutionary excesses committed in the rising of 1934 but, when Clarín wrote his novel, the Ark contained the following inventory: "wood from the True Cross; a scrap of the tunic of Jesus Christ; some crumbs of bread from the Last Supper; a piece of the Holy Shroud; some earth from the Holy Land; clothes worn by the Virgin, and a vial with some dried remains of milk from her breasts; relics of St. Peter, St. Thomas, St. Bartholomew; bones of the Prophets and of all the Apostles, and of many other Saints whose names are known only to the infinite wisdom of God". Happily, not all was lost. Today in the cha-

pel of Santas Reliquias, the visitor may admire other, no
less fabulous objects: a sandal of St. Peter; the wallet of
St. Andrew; five Thorns from the Crown; another piece
of the Holy Shroud —a formidable competitor perhaps,
to the better-known Holy Shroud at Turin, especially since
this one has not yet been subjected to carbon-14 tests by
the drearily literal-minded technicians of NASA.

In any case, before leaving the Cathedral, epicentre of
the novel, the traveller would do well to have a look at
some of its artistic treasures, though not all of these are
mentioned in the novel. The tower called Torre Vieja, dating from the 11th century, and the Cámara del Aposto-
lado, one of the most impressive sculptural ensembles of
the Romanesque, are among these; and the main retable,
mentioned in the novel, work of the masters Giralte (Gri-
jalte, says Alas), Alonso de Berruguete and León Picardo:
perhaps the third best in the country, after those of Toledo and Sevilla. And recommendable not only for its
beauty, but also for the sense of humour it breathes: St
Jerome appears with glasses, there are people in the windows with a profoundly ludicrous air about them, the
devil is represented with two comic faces, realistic coun-
tenances are mixed at random with caricatures, and winks,
and even gags. It is a real precursor of the comic-book.
And of course, the Cloister. A marvel of the 14th century,
whose days are numbered as it unfortunately suffers from
"stone disease", the AIDS of the great cathedrals; so that
you had better hurry if you wish to see "live and direct"
the fantastic mythological and caricaturesque sculptures
on its Capitals, some of them X-rated.

Outside the Vetustan epicentre, the tourist game consists in following the route marked by the telescope of the
Magistral. As far as the Palace of Ozores is concerned,
residence of the coveted Ana, local dispute continues. Some
say it is the Palacio Ducal del Parque, now belonging to

the Marquesses of Valdeterrazo; others, no less erudite identify the Ozores palace with an old mansion on the corner of the Calle San Juan and the Rúa; others swear on their ancestors' graves it is another great house between the Calle Jovellanos and the Calle Gascona. Or, between Cimadella and the City Hall. The novel's narrator says only that the conjugal prison of Ana Ozores was *toward the Plaza Nueva*. But there are times when the descriptions of literary realism, however precise they may pretend to be, and perhaps for that very reason, are just as difficult to pinpoint as the toponyms of fantasy literature.

Upon the murmuring Casino, another of the central spaces of Vetusta, there is more unanimity. Everyone agrees it is the so-called Palacio de Valdecarzana, right on the Cathedral plaza; a building now occupied by the slow-grinding bureaucratic dependencies of the Judiciary. The main façade is of the 18th century, and late in the 19th, when Clarín wrote *La Regenta,* it was the seat of the Casino de Oviedo. Chroniclers inform us it was one of Clarín's favourite places; he dropped in here every day to read the Madrid papers, and try a few carambolas at billiards with his friends. He immortalized it thus: "A huge old solitary house, of stone blackened by the outrages of humidity, in a dirty sad plaza near San Pedro, the ancient church next to the Cathedral. The younger members wished to move; but the change of domicile would mean the death of the society, in the view of the more serious and rooted element. Three generations had yawned in those narrow and obscure salons; and this solemnity of boredom must be thrown away for the hazards of a doubtful future in the new part of town, the Colonia. Also, said the elders, if the Casino were no longer to reside in the Encimada, goodbye Casino. It was an aristocrat."

We have again mentioned the Encimada. The quarter of old and ruined palaces which don Fermín, when the height of his belltower went to his head, described as a *huddled mass of old blackened houses,* and which the vain old Vetustan families, its denizens, considered a constellation of palaces... The Encimada also exists, as we have said already. And as in Vetusta, it was the original nucleus of Oviedo: "The centre, before the city extended to the northeast and southeast. The quarter of the nobles and the quarter of the poor. Aristocrats and beggars lived there close together; the latter in cramped tenements, the former in ample palaces. All true Vetustans were residents of the Encimada. Many were those who esteemed highly the value of a house, however mouldy or miserable it might be, as long as it was there, in the high part of the city, in the shadow of the Cathedral. .. The Magistral saw at his feet the ancestral quarter, composed of great houses that called themselves palaces; convents as big as villages; and slum houses, crowded with proles too poor to afford rents in the new working-class quarters on the outskirts of town, in the Campo del Sol, beside the chimneys of the factory."

It is said that Alas was inspired by the then principal street of Cimadevilla when he invented the name Encimada for the urban matrix of his narration This may be. But in this rapid tour of Vetusta, the least important thing is the vain search for coincidences between the toponyms of fiction and reality. Though these exist: Calle de la Rúa, Calle de Quintana, Convento de las Salesas; plus many that offer facile analogies: Fábrica Vieja for Fábrica de la Luz, Santa María and San Pedro for La Corte and San Tirso, el Espolón for the Paseo de los Curas del Campo de San Francisco, the Calle del Rosario for the Calle del Rosal, the villas of the Colonia for those of the Calle Uría, Tarsa for Tarna, etc. The important thing in this tour is atmosphere: to recognize in some streetcorner the lost atmosphere of the favourite quarter of the Magistral, to overhear in an idle conversation the echo of local rumour and boredom, to recognize in a random glance the heirs of those personalities of the Casino, to fantasize about the palace of Ana Ozores, to sit on a bench in the Paseo de los Curas and regain for a moment the vegetable gaze of gardens (or of infancy, as Barthes would say). To lose oneself in the labyrinth of plazas and alleys of the Encimada, as in a Borgian garden of bifurcating paths. To follow the footsteps of the most revolutionary realist narrative in Spanish literature, fabricated with the vision of the blind man of Buenos Aires and the words of the structuralist of Bayonne: *The province as spectacle, History as odour, the Bourgeoisie as discourse.*

ISLAS BALEARES

MALLORCA
IN LLORENÇ VILLALONGA
by
BALTASAR PORCEL

LLORENÇ VILLALONGA
(Palma de Mallorca, 1897-1980)

*Llorenç Villalonga was born at Palma de Mallorca in 1897
into an old rural Mallorcan family. He studied Medicine, specializing in Psychiatry, between which profession and his intense dedication to literature he divided his time.*

Thus, under the pseudonym of Dhey, *in the period before
1936, he published his first novel,* Mort de dama *(1931), and
some plays such as* Fedra *(1932) and* Silvia Ocampo. *But
above all, there was ample journalistic production: he contributed to magazines such as* La Nostra Terra *and* El Día,
and founded the review Brisas *(1934-1936), where he gave
form to his interest in the latest novelties of European thought.
However his independent, exaltedly critical attitude earned him
the enmity of many Mallorcan intellectuals of the period.*

*After a brief attempt at returning to the ancestral existence
of feudal lords (1937-1939), on an estate which his wife, María
Teresa Gelabert, possessed in a rural village of Mallorca, Villalonga returned to Palma and resumed his journalistic activity in*
El Español *and* Baleares. *In 1952 he published* La novela de
Palmira, *favourably received by both critics and public. But it
was in 1961, with the publication of* Bearn, *that he obtained*

his greatest success and definitive acceptance as a writer. In 1966 he began publication of his Complete Works, *and in 1974 received the Josep Plà Prize for his work* Andrea Victrix. *In 1975 he published his last book,* Un verano en Mallorca. *Shortly afterward, in 1977, he fell ill and wrote no more. He died in 1980.*

Villalonga's personality was that of a sceptical aristocrat, observing the profound moral and social transformations that accompany the end of a traditional society. The very act of writing critically about his social class put him in conflict with the old closed traditional aristocracy of Mallorca, so much portrayed in his novels. But he was no classical aristocrat: his thought, though profoundly conservative, was also sceptical and open to ideological freedom.

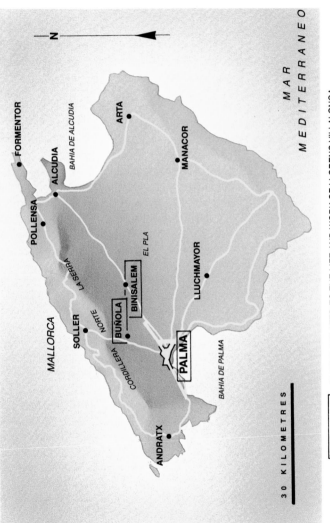

N

MAR MEDITERRANEO

MALLORCA

FORMENTOR

POLLENSA

ALCUDIA

BAHIA DE ALCUDIA

ARTA

SOLLER

LA SERRA

NORTE

BUÑOLA

CORDILLERA

MANACOR

EL PLA

BINISALEM

PALMA

LLUCHMAYOR

BAHIA DE PALMA

ANDRATX

30 KILOMETRES

PLACES RELATED TO THE LIFE AND WORK OF LLORENÇ VILLALONGA

MALLORCA IN LLORENÇ VILLALONGA

Two Mallorcan spaces appear, par excellence, in the novels of Llorenç Villalonga: Palm, the city; and the countryside near the mountains, with its enormous pines through which the wind murmurs majestically. And in Palma, above all he speaks of the old Cathedral quarter, in which Villalonga situates the action of his first novel, *La muerte de una dama*, published in 1931, when our writer was 34 years old. In this book, the Baroque doña Obdulia Montcada dies in a lordly mansion, amid a grotesque and ironical human comedy:

"The quarter is venerable, noble and silent, with narrow streets and ample houses that seem uninhabited. Between the eaves of the houses, the blue of the sky vibrates like a lance. Grass grows in the cracks between the big slabs of stone. The silence is broken, from time to time, by the sound of bells.

Nobody seems to move through the quarter. The true inhabitants of these streets are the cats, as Santiago Rusiñol has said. Mallorca is a privileged world for feline creatures. The cat demands silence, order and cleanliness, like a scholastic philosopher: the noise of the world would not

Cathedral of Palma.

allow him to meditate. There are many analogies between cats and clergy. Thus, they have chosen the same quarter to live in (...) Gentlemen, canons and cats live in a perpetual siesta. The Cathedral bells, slow and clamorous, regulate their existences."

Nowadays, of course, the quarter is more animated, especially in summer, when the guides lead troops of tourists through the narrow labyrinthine alleys. But most of the year, the scene described by Villalonga remains more or less unaltered. The houses date from the 16th to 18th centuries: courtyards with a central well, surrounded by Italianate galleries. They belonged to the island aristocracy, though now, also, to the bourgeoisie. Villalonga himself lived in one in the 1940s, in the Calle Estudio General, number 25; it had belonged to relatives of his wife. Small salons hung with bright patterned cloth, darkened paintings, Isabeline furniture... Villalonga also had the indispensable cat. A black one. "And when it dies, they bring me another black one; so as far as I am concerned, it is always the same cat..."

Another Palma also appeared in that first novel, and is not only still there, but has grown monstrously: touristic Palma, which began to flourish in El Terreno, at the feet of the Castle of Bellver, along the shore. Villalonga described in thus:

"At the other end of the city, in the suburbs, in El Terreno, in Génova, there moves a colonial world, composed of painters, tourists and ladies who smoke. They are weird people, who go swimming in winter and turn their backs on religion. They can, however, make decent cocktails. They give dances and teas. The Old Quarter pretends to ignore them. Lacking either guts or desire to declare war on them, it has opted to declare them non-existent."

In other Villalonguian novels, such as *Desenlace in Montlleó,* neurotic and schizophrenic persons appear. Villalonga had studied Medicine in Murcia, Barcelona, Madrid, Zaragoza; finally specializing in Psychiatry, with practice in Paris. Too many centres, perhaps, for a good student... In any case, he was soon employed as psychiatrist in the lunatic asylum of Jesús, then in the suburbs of Palma, on a road then quiet but now crowded with new buildings, on the northwest of the city. He alludes to it in *Las tentaciones:*

"It was really a strange and terrible crisis. The mother superior of the Clinic of Jesús, where she had spent several years, told us she had never heard so blasphemous a tongue or seen a patient more bedevilled than the sweet, angelical poetess."

On one occasion in my youth, I accompanied Villalonga to the asylum. It was a more or less perfunctory visit, indifferent amid the hallucinatory spectacle of the demented lunatics around us. With his smile between ironical and saintly, with his simulatedly innocent voice, Villalonga mantled himself in lordly distance from any inkling of tragedy. He detested it: in the name of good manners, perhaps, or because of some profound, abysmal sensation? In his mind at least, he wished to live installed in a Neoclassical salon. He confessed that Psychiatry had served him in writing novels, but not at all in understanding human beings.

Llorenç Villalonga also wrote a guide to Mallorca which, it must be admitted, is neither very entertaining nor very useful, as one of a series popular in the 50s, put out by the publishers Noguer. All the itineraries and excursions start, as he notes, "in the little garden of the Glorieta, at the start of the Paseo del Generalísimo (now Borne) a small cheerful garden adorned with a fine monument to the poet Juan Alcover", near the port of Palma. The garden is still there; and the fountain and statue dedicated to the best poet the islands have produced. What has disappeared is Villalonga's real motive for always beginning his excursions at this point. This was the café Riskal.

Across from the Glorieta was an old theatre, the Lí-
rico, and a bar that had been conceived on the canons of
1930s rationalist architecture, the Riskal, with its great
windows. Villalonga dropped in here every morning, late,
after a short walk with his wife, Teresa Gelabert. After
lunch he returned to the Riskal, not far from his house;
and there joined a circle of medical friends which, with
time, became more and more a circle of literary friends.
They would have their coffee, and stay a couple of hours.
My own dedication to writing was determined by my par-
ticipation in this circle. Villalonga presided at it, ironical
and hard to please. From the café windows he contem-
plated the city; here he mentally situated himself to describe Mallorca.

Of the island, there were two areas he knew especially
well: that of Buñola, on the road to Sóller, at the foot of
the formidable mountain chain that runs from Andratx to
Formentor, which drops steeply into the sea, shutting off
the island's central plain from the sea on the north; and
the area of Binisalem, a wine village in the central plain, or
Pla. Also for some years he had a house near Palma, at
Son Quint, a pine-wood now also "urbanized", near the
present luxury hotel Son Vida. Binisalem is some twenty
kilometres from Palma; Son Quint only seven or eight. As
the trip to Binisalem, in his prim little black car, was too
lengthy an expedition for a stay of only two or three days,
the nearby house of Son Quint was more suitable. This
slow rhythm, so typically Mallorcan, enchanted both Villalonga and his wife.

Villalonga had been born in Palma. His father was an
Army officer, Mallorcan; his mother was from Menorca.
Of this other Balearic island there is little evidence in his
novels, though he lived there a while as a child, his father
being posted to the barracks there. They had also lived in
La Coruña, of which he conserved a vague memory. On

Panoramic view of Binisalem.

the other hand, Paris is omnipresent in his books, the ideal city, the ideal country. Villalonga was indeed an *afrance-sado,* a person of Frenchified outlook; and liked to think of himself as an heir to the Enlightenment, though it would be more accurate to call him an heir to the literature and society of the 1920s. He so mythified France, that his best novel bears the name of a French region and family: Bearn.

In *Bearn* we find a symbiosis of the two Mallorcas Villalonga had known, apart from Palma. His family, which he liked to think of as proceeding from an illiterate rural landlord stock rooted in the local earth, came from Buñola, from the lower middle class. Once when as a child Llorenç had been ill, he had spent some time in this town, with its stone houses, staying at his aunt's house. His brother Miguel, also a writer, died there in the 1940s. The town of "Bearn" owes much to Buñola, though the author does not describe it very closely.

But another ingredient comes from his long stays at Binisalem, a plain little village where stood, in the then Calle del General Franco, the house his wife had inherited, belonging to a family that had arrived on the island in the 13th century, in the company of James I of Aragón. The house described in "Bearn" as that of the local lords, Tonet and María Antonia, is based on the house at Binisalem: something between a farmhouse and a mansion. However in the novel, the house has been considerably magnified by poetic license, converted to one of the real stately houses of the great rural landholdings of old Mallorca:

"You enter through a large courtyard oriented to the south, which in Mallorca is called the *clastra* (from Latin *claustrum*), surrounded by the stables, and the quarters of the foreman and the labourers. At the back, an arch of no great architectural pretensions, though the erudite pronounce it Gothic work of the 13th century, leads to a smaller courtyard, where an ample entrance hall contains a staircase lead-ding to the upper floors (...) Upstairs are the quarters of the family, ample and cheerful. The stairway opens on a gallery running along one wall (...) The central door opens on an oval room, almost unfurnished, decorated with Pompeian motifs and illuminated by a skylight. This leads to the main salon, perfectly furnished and symmetrical, with two balconies (between which there is a marble fireplace) giving on the garden. On the left of the salon is the main bedroom; on the right a door leads to two other rooms where the master had installed his bedroom and work room: these rooms have direct access to the garden by way of a spiral staircase..."

The house dominates the book: the house and the landscape, this last much more sparingly described, but it is always there, defining an ambience both remote and poetic: "...the woods and mountains, the fields and rocky escarpments, covered with scrubby bush and aromatic plants: people them with thrushes in autumn and nightingales in spring; do not forget the atmospheric phenomena, the sun, clouds and rain, nor the moonlit nights, nor the magnificent storms in which, as the poet says, the Creator's grandeur is manifested", says the narrator, a priest who is known to be the natural son of the lord of Bearn, an *afrancesado* in whom Villalonga partly portrays his wife's uncle, and partly weaves an ideal image of himself.

Other observations on the landscape and the towns appear in other books. However they are usually brief, often with invented nomenclature, and feeble connections to reality. Real toponyms may appear, such as that of Montlleó, but with no relation to the eastern cove of that name. However, Villalonga's work is totally impregnated with the spirit and being of Mallorca. Thus, our bilingual writer, when he uses the Mallorcan variety of Catalan, achieves effects of freshness and vivacity, as in his brief theatrical sketches called *Disbarats* (freaks or absurdities), fond but sharp caricatures of the local upper classes.

His was a Mallorca which he thought eternal; which, ethnocentrical, provincial and leisured, dated in the form he knew it from the late nineteenth century, and began to change radically from about 1950, with the invasion of tourism and its economy in the island, and rise of consumerism in the world generally. Villalonga, who died in 1980, in his last books attacked this invasion with barely contained frenzy: *Flo la Vigne, La lulú, La gran batida.* In another book, *Andrea Víctrix,* influenced by Aldous Huxley's *Brave new world,* Villalonga paints a depressing picture of a future apparently limpid and brilliant, but in reality sexless and cruel, in which the Guild of Waiters, i.e. the waiters of Mallorca, constitute a ruling Supreme Order in the island. The narrator, alter ego of the author, is resuscitated in a Utopian Palma:

"Having anesthetized me, they had put me in a plastic box and taken me to a cellar of the clinic, kept at forty degrees below zero; along with half a dozen other patients, including Sir Winston Churchill, Madame Vorey and Marlene Dietrich. Most of them had died in the process. The only survivors were a diabetic stuffed with sugar, and myself, stuffed with anxiety and unwillingness to participate in this Frankenstein charade. I had been revived and out of my box, like a butterfly out of its chrysalis, for only a few hours; I wandered aimlessly through the streets of the City of Mallorca, which was, however, known by a new name: Club Turista Mediterránea —or in ordinary speech, Turclub, which the snobs pronounced Turclüf— and I did not like what I saw."

But this Mallorca does not, perhaps, yet exist. And still, beyond the intense environmental degradation of the touristically developed zones, there remain parts of the island where like remnants of a lost paradise, the world of Villalonga's pages may be found.

CANARIAS

JOSÉ DE VIERA Y CLAVIJO: ADVENTURE OF A MAN FROM THE INTERIOR

by

JUAN CRUZ RUIZ

JOSÉ DE VIERA Y CLAVIJO
(Los Realejos, 1731-Las Palmas, 1813)

José de Viera y Clavijo, Canarian thinker, historian and cleric, was born in Los Realejos, Tenerife on 23 December 1731. Throughout his life he felt profoundly attracted by the renovating ideas produced in the 18th century in Europe, especially in France; and translated them into his work and attitude. He early travelled to Madrid and Paris and in both capitals, in spite of his "modorra" or heaviness (the modorra of the guanches, he said, as is mentioned by one of the best students of his work, the researcher Alejandro Cioranescu) he absorbed the Encyclopedic spirit then in the air, and became one of the inaugurators of this intellectual movement in Spain. Though travel was essential to his evolution, another determinant was his contact with the circle of Nava, in La Laguna, and with the city itself, which left its permanent mark on him. His attitude, liberal and open to foreign influences, attracted the attention of the Inquisition, but did not finally prevent him from continuing his literary work of investigation and creation. His History of the Canaries (1776), published in two volumes, is a work essential not only to establish the historical identity of the Archipielago, but to understand the methods of historical investigation of José de Viera y Clavijo. He was at once poet and naturalist, novelist and translator and his culture was, indeed, encyclopedic; one example being his last work, a Dictionary of the Natural History of the Canary Islands, which appeared in 1799. He died in Las Palmas de Gran Canaria, where he was Archdean for Fuerteventura in the Cathedral of the Grancanarian capital, on 21 February 1813. His life was full of travel and ideas; but at the end of it, the disappointing reception of his History of the Canaries, *as Cioranescu says, sank him in a slough of disillusionment, as Canarian as his origin and sentimental geography, which joins Los Realejos, La Laguna, and the Grancanarian quarter of Vegueta in a sort of triangle of insular melancholy.*

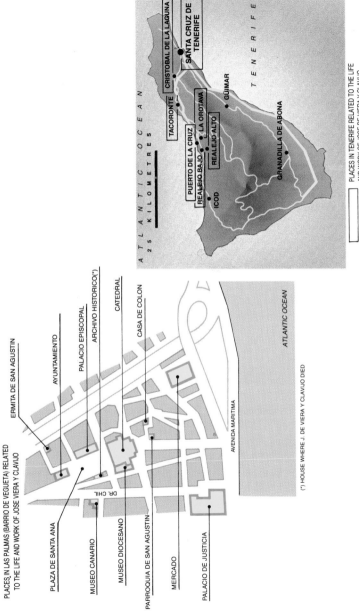

PLACES IN LAS PALMAS (BARRIO DE VEGUETA) RELATED TO THE LIFE AND WORK OF JOSE VIERA Y CLAVIJO

PLAZA DE SANTA ANA
MUSEO CANARIO
MUSEO DIOCESANO
PARROQUIA DE SAN AGUSTIN
MERCADO
PALACIO DE JUSTICIA
ERMITA DE SAN AGUSTIN
AYUNTAMIENTO
PALACIO EPISCOPAL
ARCHIVO HISTORICO(*)
CATEDRAL
CASA DE COLON
DR. CHIL
AVENIDA MARITIMA
ATLANTIC OCEAN

(*) HOUSE WHERE J. DE VIERA Y CLAVIJO DIED

PLACES IN TENERIFE RELATED TO THE LIFE AND WORK OF JOSE DE VIERA Y CLAVIJO

ATLANTIC OCEAN
25 KILOMETRES
SANTA CRUZ DE TENERIFE
CRISTOBAL DE LA LAGUNA
TACORONTE
PUERTO DE LA CRUZ
REALEJO BAJO
LA OROTAVA
REALEJO ALTO
ICOD
GUIMAR
GRANADILLA DE ABONA
T E N E R I F E

PLACES IN TENERIFE RELATED TO THE LIFE AND WORK OF JOSE DE VIERA Y CLAVIJO

JOSÉ DE VIERA Y CLAVIJO: ADVENTURE OF A MAN FROM THE INTERIOR

José de Viera y Clavijo was a man from the interior. He was born in a house that now appears fit for demolition, standing just across from the football field of Los Realejos, in the Realejo Alto. It is a luminous and airy zone, crossed by deep mysterious ravines, in which green is the predominant colour. The house he was born in, which is of "upper and lower", as used to be said in the Canaries of houses before more than two floors were common, has been unusable for many years, although plans for restoration have been announced for just as many years. Probably the autorities have obeyed the subliminal desires of the great encyclopedist, who early in his childhood left that obscure dwelling in the north of Tenerife, to go and live with his parents in a place more appropriate for what was to be his intellectual adventure: El Puerto de la Cruz.

Los Realejos, the place where José de Viera y Clavijo was born, has an upper part and a lower part; and, as corresponds to the inherent logic of place denominations in small urban centres, these are called Realejo Bajo (lower

Realejo) and Realejo Alto (upper Realejo) respectively. Presently the latter which, like the former, forms part of the municipality of Los Realejos, in the Valley of La Orotava, is a place with its own life, full of shops and services, inhabited by a flourishing population mostly employed in the tourist industry, which since the 1960s has been booming more or less continuously in the whole valley, not only in Puerto de la Cruz, which however is the tourist city proper.

This prosperity is intimate and not always visible in the street. Throughout the years, the Realejo Alto has changed remarkably little in appearance. Being a landscape of ravines, its street plan is difficult and thus more or less invariable; and as in all places inhabited by families who have renovated their own properties at the same slow rhythym as their surnames, the houses have the same popular air as they did when José de Viera y Clavijo cried over his baby teeth.

In such towns, the persistence of appearances is always as something to take pride in. And the Realejo Alto is not lacking in such pride as being the birthplace of one of the most illustrious men of the Canaries and of the 18th century in Spain. That the heirs of this motive for pride have ignored the need to repair and maintain the birthplace of José de Viera y Clavijo, does not diminish the value of the motive itself. Los Realejos is not alone in its abandon: apart from solemnities like names of prizes or prestigious nomenclatures (various institutes in the region go by the name of Viera y Clavijo), the great encyclopedist lives in the memory of the people with the prestige merely of an illustrious visitor. He is, of course, not alone in this limbo: others, like Benito Pérez Galdós for example, have long remained in the region of benign neglect which homelands reserve for their most egregious sons.

Viera y Clavijo would not have mourned much over

La Orotava. Street in the old town.

this. The Realejo Alto was, in his biography, an important but more or less accidental link. Just as Leopoldo Alas "Clarín" was accidentally born in Zamora, Clavijo was born in this hill-town in the north of Tenerife. He soon left it, without his own wishes being involved any more than they were with his birthplace; since it was his father, a well-known lawyer, who took him, along with the rest of the family, to a more obviously maritime residence, that of Puerto de la Cruz.

Puerto de la Cruz is a natural prolongation of Los Realejos, and there is one point, now called La Romántica, in the municipality of Las Dehesas, where they join like one sea with another. In that area, indeed, the limits of one and the other municipality coincide in such a natural manner that they make ridiculous any dividing line. Nowadays the division seems ridiculous; but there was a time, that of Viera y Clavijo, when a move from one town to the other was a major displacement, the truncation of a life experience. The family of Viera y Clavijo made this move, and perhaps in so doing changed the course and dimension of their son's life. Puerto de la Cruz is today a prosperous but tranquil touristic town; but even then, in the 18th century, it was a gateway for entry and departure of travellers, as said Domingo Pérez Minik, a great admirer of Viera y Clavijo, speaking of the whole island. Puerto de la Cruz combined this function as gateway with that of fishing port, as it still does today.

Puerto de la Cruz, then, was both cosmopolitan and closed. It treasured carefully its traditions while tolerating the necessary and beneficial flow of tourism. Its maritime processions are legendary, which made of the Virgin a complacent dancer on the aromatic waves (for this, they say, is where the sea smells best in all the island), and which make of fishermen's songs improvised lullabys that are handed down from grandparents to grandchildren with the savour of ancestral feeling: "Mayitas, Virgen del Carmen!". While these traditions have been conserved, the Puerto has maintained what it had already in the adolescence of José de Viera y Clavijo, a disposition to receive and adopt the foreigner, any kind of foreigner. The town's cosmopolitan capacity has taken in everything, and the native of Puerto de la Cruz has never objected to the amalgam because it was all the same to him.

Though the term had not yet been invented, there was even then in Puerto de la Cruz a certain atmosphere of encyclopedism, created by the continuous presence of foreigners, bringing with them their knowledge and ideas, which perhaps arrived here in a very attenuated form but were bound to have an influence sooner or later.

In this open city Viera y Clavijo had his first contact with books and underwent his earliest influences. In his main work, History of the Canaries, there are some allusions to this fact; but it is principally in the spirit of his biography that we note the salutary influence the cosmopolitan atmosphere of the port city must have had on the encyclopedist's personality. Even today we may notice there this influence: in spite of being a closed city upon the sea, well connected with other municipalities on the island, but separate from them because it conserves a well-defined personality, Puerto de la Cruz has a perceptible air of urban heart, with its systole and diastole, its open and closed valves. A heart that beats for those who remain, but also stops punctually: feeding those who inhabit it but also stopping the supply opportunely, perhaps to oblige them to leave. To leave and return. This happened to Viera y Clavijo: he was fed by Puerto de la Cruz, but eventually had to leave it in order to progress in an intellectual adventure that was to take him to the horizons of Madrid and Paris.

Viera y Clavijo had a personality misty and introverted

like the deep autum of the town where he was born. Man is the product of his geography; and in past centuries, at least down to the 18th, geography is an even stronger determinant than it is today. The island of Tenerife has often been described as a continent in itself. England is an island, because the climate is more or less the same in every part of it. Tenerife, much smaller in area, has the feel of a continent, because the climate, and the character of the inhabitants, changes markedly from part to part of it. Nowadays, with communications much more lubricated, everything has become homogenized, including character. But differences persist, and exist even between parts of the same municipality: the people of Realejo Bajo are garrulous and given to street life; those of Realejo Alto, more reserved and silent. Those of Puerto de la Cruz are, like those of Realejo Bajo, given to street conversation, but at bottom have a very private behaviour, almost Anglo-Saxon. Those of Tacoronte, the town Viera y Clavijo had to pass through to get to his favourite retreat of La Laguna, have always lived like birds of passage, a sort of philosophers of the road that have seen history go by, knowing that even what seems most solid is always ephemeral. And those of Santa Cruz, the capital of the island, are talkative but tranquil, conversational but less philosophical than the Realejo people; as being bureaucrats or businessmen, they are more practical-minded.

It is the people of Santa Cruz who refer to all the other people of the island as "inhabitants of the interior". Viera y Clavijo was a man of the interior; this made him adventurous and imaginative: his *History of the Canarias,* principal work of his whole oeuvre, is a reflection of his character, because not all the things he tells of in it really happened as historical facts. One of the best scholars of his work, the Rumanian professor Alejandro Cioranescu, told us in his house at Santa Cruz that the tint of legend in his History was of no great importance, as the identity that Viera y Clavijo was seeking had more to do with the need for making literature than with the precision called for by history. This was a consequence not only of his intellectual vocation and cosmopolitan personality, but of his own island life: people of the interior are much more concerned with essences, and for that reason more prone to distrust bald facts. This attitude to reality excites their imagination.

Viera y Clavijo was thus an interiorizing man to whom, as to a Proustian, the search for the past caressed the idea of immortality like a form of melancholy. His personal voyage thus brought him to an interior courtyard of La Laguna, the cultured city of the Canaries, centre of the University and of intellectual discussion, from which his will for knowledge was to radiate, as Spanish forerunner of encyclopedism. In the Palace of Viana, where the intellectual circle met which his presence made so famous, he lived the best part of his life. Not surprisingly: for these people who live from the imagination and the harvesting of truth, need a circle of listeners, a conversation, to manifest the fact their idea exists, that it is reaching some destination. La Laguna is, perhaps, the best place in the Canaries for thinking of others. Unamuno found it so, and many doubters of history, Spanish and foreign, have found there the calm necessary for comparing with others the nature of their ideas.

La Laguna is an essential intellectual theatre of the islands: it is in the centre, near the legendary Camino Largo: the old Institute that was, in its time, the only institute in the islands, where all the geniuses and all the time-servers that Tenerife ever produced have studied; nearby the Cathedral, with its bordering plaza, looks down on an institution which offers no other feature more notable than its liberal history: the Ateneo de La Laguna. At its side, like a river washing up against the beautiful church of La Con-

cepción, is the Calle de la Carrera, which seems made for
Viera y Clavijo to walk upon; from the Calle Consistorio,
where the finely-proportioned City Hall looks across towards the mysterious convent of Las Clarisas and to one
of the most fascinating markets on the island.

We have said that it is not surprising Viera y Clavijo
should have found in La Laguna the ideal atmosphere of
his life, because the city is an idea, inside and out: warm
though humid, it has the structure of an ideal city. Its
dimensions are suited to the pedestrian; its houses have
the comfort demanded for the formation of a conversational circle. Viera, who was a man of relaxed conversation
and wide knowledge, found in La Laguna his real ecological niche. Those who visit the city today cross the Calle de
La Carrera "which was more like a river than a street",
and enjoy the delight of an air that comes tempered by the
nearby presence of the woods of La Esperanza and La Mesa
Mota. They will understand why José de Viera y Clavijo
felt so melancholy and alienated in his Madrilenian exile,
where he spent years of disappointment and frustration,
even though his intellectual and professional position had
indeed risen to an enviable height. The build-up of his nostalgia, which became more heavy with time, had much
to do with his deep roots in the Canaries. The circles he
moved in at Madrid were more alien, less open to his man-
ipulation. For this reason, and for other reasons of his
complicated life at Court, Viera felt the urge to return, and
did so, though it was to Las Palmas, the other island which,
in those days, was not as now in conflict with La Laguna
for the possession of a University.

Las Palmas was a very important stage in the biographical and geographical itinerary of Vieras; it is a city with
many hidden corners, little understood by those who see
it only as a place to visit during a stopover on a cruise, for
example. It is also a city for conversation, dominated by

a beautiful and legendary old quarter, which has lately seen revived its former splendour with the inauguration of a modern art museum which would no doubt cause great satisfaction for the encyclopedist Viera. This is the quarter of Vegueta, where the Cathedral of Las Palmas, with its history of picturesque priests, learned bishops and other clerics with whom Viera shared the robe, is the centre of a lifestyle more leisurely than is usual amid such a bustling city. It has a certain air of La Laguna, which must have appealed to Viera, a kind of shade in its stone-paved streets, an atmosphere that seems presided and bound by a silence, broken only, and with clerical prudence, by the Cathedral bells whose peal seems an emblem of the city. In the geography of Viera that may be visited today, there are routes to satisfy visitors of the most diverse kinds of cultural curiosity. In the geography of Viera that may be visited today, there are routes to satisfy visitors of the most diverse kinds of cultural curiosity. In the same area there is the Museo Canario, recently renovated, full of ceramics, inscriptions, cloths, offering an overview of the history of the islands; the great unfinished Cathedral; the episcopal palace across from Viera's own house, gutted and reconstructed and now housing the provincial historical archive; the Diocesan Museum, with its patio of orange trees and its vast and only partly researched collections; the parish of San Agustín; the old City Hall, a noble building now only used for Council meetings; the old seminary; the house of Columbus, in which a fine example of museological and conservational work has recently been completed; the shrine of San Agustín, where it is said Columbus prayed; and the plaza of Santa Ana which is, of course, a symbol of this privileged zone of the island.

In that colonial house of Las Palmas, guarded by a pack of stone dogs, Viera y Clavijo died. It is curious: this restless personality, thinker, historian, occasional novelist,

Plaza de Santa Ana and Bishopric of Las Palmas.

traveller, conversationalist, enthusiastic raconteur, cleric convinced that the 18th century was the beginning of great things, he also became the symbol of a geographical doctrine which unfortunately has not prospered in the islands in this final stretch of the 20th century: the islands are part of a territory of water. Vieras lived on both principal islands and is remembered as a citizen of both, their rivalries being set aside. Being the interior adventurer he was, Viera was a discoverer of paths; and wise as he was, discovered good ones. His personal route leads from high in the Valley of Orotava, whose beauty so astounded Humboldt, to the Madrid of the 18th century, passing through La Laguna, the city of the vanguard, where he laid the first stone in building the finest literary circle the islands have known, and Las Palmas and its quarter of Vegueta, where he closed the circle of his adventurer's life. He was a Canarian and also a citizen of the world, universal and inimitable.

CANTABRIA

MOUNTAIN AND SEA
IN JOSÉ MARÍA DE PEREDA

by

JOSÉ HIERRO

JOSÉ MARÍA DE PEREDA
(Polanco, 1833-Santander, 1906)

José María de Pereda is one of the major Spanish novelists of the late nineteenth century. His best works are those set in his native region. He began as a costumbrista (observer of local customs) with his Escenas montañesas *(1864), a compilation of texts published in periodicals. Pérez Galdós, on the appearance of* Tipos y paisajes *(1871) warmly praised the work of Pereda (from whom he himself was far distant in such matters as politics and religion). It was again Galdós who in 1897, when Pereda was received as a member of the Real Academia Española, corresponded to the entrance speech of his friend with a perspicuous critical study of Pereda's novelistic work.*

Among the abundant literary production of José María de Pereda, which includes theatrical work, costumbrista "scenes", seven long and four short novels, we may single out for special notice Sotileza *(1885), received with great enthusiasm by the critics, and* Peñas arriba *(1895). Both are high points of Pereda's work, and occupy a privileged place among the great exponents of the realistic novel in the nineteenth century.*

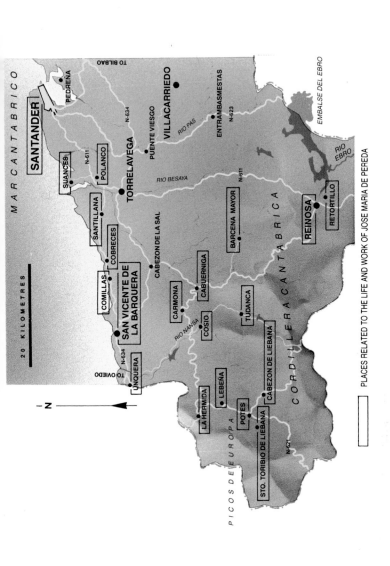

PLACES RELATED TO THE LIFE AND WORK OF JOSE MARIA DE PEREDA

MOUNTAIN AND SEA
IN JOSÉ MARÍA DE PEREDA

This gentleman of reduced stature, dressed with old-fashioned correctness, is don José María de Pereda, our guide. We are in the city of Santander, marked by two catastrophes: the explosion of the ship *Cabo Machichaco* in 1893, noted by Pereda in *Pachín González,* and the fire of 1941, which razed the most Peredian part of the city, the stage where the personalities of *Sotileza* acted out their lives.

We are on a high point of the city, facing the bay, which has not changed too much since the novelist described it:

"He told me the names, pointing them out, of each peak in each mountain of the grandiose range that begins on the East with Cabo Quintres and Galizano (the tail of the huge reptile), and ends on the West with the Picos de Europa (the head) stuck among the clouds. Then, tracing in the air with the same finger the course of each river that rises there and flows downward through the dark ravines of the foothills, he ended facing West; and marking three almost vertical lines, named the Saja, the Nansa, and the Deva... as a special treat he introduced me to the rosary of stepped mountains that on the South side, from East to West, serve as a majestic frame for the admirable bay..."

Now let us go along the Oviedo highway, following a route backward in time: from the city where Pereda died in 1906 to Polanco, the town where he had bee born in 1813. We follow the old route, ignoring the new motor-way hues of green. At Puente Arce we say goodbye to Pas. The river has a salt smell of the Cantabrian sea, into which it empties a few miles away, by the salt dunes of Liencres. Now we leave the main highway onto the road that takes us to Polanco, birthplace of the novelist, which so often appears in his writings under the name of *Cumbrales.*

We make our first stop at the house which Pereda built here in 1872. Much of his best work was critten here. The ambience has been lovingly conserved by his descendants. Perhaps the most moving exhibit on view is a manuscript volume, open at a page where, in red ink, "there is a cross, and a date, between two words in a notebook... God and I know that in the petty space they fill, there is an abyss that separates my present from my past..." The motive for these red marks was the suicide of one of his sons, which happened in the house of the family, while Pereda was writing *Peñas arriba.* Possibly it was in the same house that Galdós showed his friend the drawing, made at the request of Pereda, for the mausoleum he was to build in the cemetery of Polanco, where he wished to be buried himself.

Our route begins here. It reproduces a trip hat Pereda and Galdós made in 1876, and which the Canarian novelist described in *Cuarenta leguas por Cantabria.* We return to the main highway and, following the edge of the estuary formed by the Saya and the Besaya down to the sea, we see, through the magnifying lens of the novelist, "the sea water detained an instant there at the entrance to the valley, to form a sort of gulf, running off towards the left, and lapping there against the base of the mountain". And below, the town of Suances, with its beaches of yellow sand.

Now our route runs parallel to the coast, with the sea to our right. Let us for a moment abandon the contemplation of this wonderful landscape, and descend to Santillana del Mar. Galdós wrote in 1876: "looking all around us, we noticed a weird phenomenon, not seen even on a visit to the deadest of little towns. You don't see any people. There is nobody. Nobody watching us, nobody following... all is solitude, a silence like the grave..."

Can this be the same Santillana that Pereda and Galdós visited a century and a quarter ago? Because the one before our eyes now, is full of every kind of visitor. The doors of the houses stand open; the entrance halls house shops selling souvenirs. The silence has disappeared, displaced by the sound of multitudinous feet shuffling over the old stones, by exclamatory comments in various tongues, by the click of cameras.

From the Romanesque Colegiata —there is a cloister with carved capitals, a Romanesque tympanum, a Pantocrator, a fine retable, a processional cross— by way of the Torre del Merino (14th century) and the Torre de doña Leonor de la Vega (15th century) to the 18th-century palace of the Marquis of Benemejís, with pictures by Mengs and Vicente López, a walk through Santillana is a walk through the ages. But more than the singular art works it contains, the essence of Santillana is the ensemble of buildings both lordly and humble that compose it. As in choral music, it is not the individual voice that counts, but the harmonious unison, radiating a mysterious spell. Try to see it at night, or about sunrise, to experience it sunk in silence, as Pereda did.

We must now continue, returning again to the coastal

Santillana del Mar.

highway. We might have gone up to see *The Sistine Chapel* of Altamira. But these cave paintings, which remained intact for some fourteen thousand years, began to deteriorate under the impact of visiting crowds, and are now closed to the public. We may console ourselves remembering that Pereda in his trip with Galdós did not see them either, as they were only discovered three years later.

Now we come to Comillas, less than twenty kilometres from Santillana del Mar. A seacoast village, which belonged in the 15th century to the Marquis of Santillana. From past centuries not much remains; but from the immediate past, a curious little jewel: *El Capricho,* by Gaudí. But Pereda could not see this either in 1876, as it was constructed seven years later.

We continue along the coast towards San Vicente de la Barquera. On our right, the valley of Valdáliga. Ahead, far off, the mass of Peña Sagra and the Picos de Europa. As we descend towards the village, we are dazzled by the vision of a great gulf of quiet water if we arrive at high tide, or of a vast flat of sand and seaweed creased by shining threads of water, if at low tide. A bridge, begun in the 16th century, takes us to the foot of the village. Above us, on a promontory jutting out into the sea, is the imposing mass of the Castle, venerable carcass of a fortress built in the 13th century. Climbing to it we continue among remains of the wall and of noble houses, till we arrive at the church of Santa María (13th-16th centuries) one of the noblest buildings of the religious architecture of Cantabria. Inside, the chief artistic work is the recumbent statue of the Inquisitor Corro, considered one of the finest Renaissance sculptures existing in Spain. We have a look too at the Baroque retable and the sepulchres of the Inquisitor's parents, and continue on our way.

It is now time, if we have not already done so, to have lunch. Puebla Nueva is a good place for this. The main

Port of San Vicente de la Barquera.

problem is in choosing among the wealth and variety of Cantabrian gastronomy: *cocido montañés*[1], fish, seafood, beef, local cheese... whatever you choose, it is hard to go wrong.

Now we leave the coast. The majestic inlet of Tina Mayor, where the Deva and te Cares merge before emptying into the sea, indicates our direction inland. The definitive goodbye to the sea is at Unquera (to gourmets we recommend the delicious *corbatas*[2] typical of the place). And we enter the canyon of La Hermida, a narrow gorge carved out through the ages by the river Deva. Tight curves here succeed one another, overhung by intimidating walls of rock. But suddenly the dark walls separate into an open valley, bathed in sunlight. On our left, the village of Lebeña, built on a hillside. At its feet, the Mozarabic church of Santa María de Lebeña, built in the 10th century. Of three naves, with barrel vaults and delicate capitals, it is a small but lovely example of the pre-Romanesque architecture of Cantabria. There is a notable 15th-century polychromed image of the Virgin, considered one of the most interesting Marian statues in Cantabria.

Next comes Potes, end of the first stage of our itinerary. Capital of Liébana, surrounded by mountains —Picos de Europa, mountains of León and Palencia, Sierras de Peña Labra and Peña Sagra— the landscape cannot help but astound and enchant the traveller. The old quarter, separated by the río Bullón, and consisting of old traditional style houses, has been declared a National Historical Monument. The single most important historical vestige is a tower, the Torre del Infantado (the Marquess of las *Serranillas* was, from 1445, lord of the town), built in the 15th century.

---

[1] Stew of white beans, meat and potatoes.
[2] Sweets in the shape of a necktie.

We walk the streets of the town a while, then continue on our way toward Santo Toribio de Liébana, a monastery whose construction seems to date back to the 8th century. Of the structures of past centuries there now remain only the Gothic church, begun about the middle of the 13th century; the cloister, built in 1669; and the 18th-century chapel in which is kept, within a cross of gilt silver, a *Lignum Crucis* or fragment of the True Cross: a relic for whose custody the monastery of Santo Toribio was built. Nearby is the Cueva Santa or holy cave, where tradition says the Saint lived: half a cave-dwelling, half a building of Romanesque period. Two other small chapels, that of San Miguel and the shrine of Santa Catalina, complete our visit to the monastery and indicate it is time to return to the village of Potes, where we spend the night. Tomorrow will be another day, when, behind the majestic Picos de Europa, we climb to *Peñas arriba.*

Pereda passed this way in 1871. He came not to take notes for his novel, but, more prosaically, on an electoral campaign in his capacity as deputy for Cabuérniga. Later, with politics forgotten, he returned to clarify his diffuse memories and take notes on the scenery, as we might expect of a realist writer. It seems that rain and snow hindered his observations. Fog blurred the outlines of the mountains, so he had to paint the majestic scene from memory.

Potes now lies behind us, and we begin to climb the pass of Piedras Luengas, overlooking the impressive valleys of Valdeprado and Cabezón de Liébana, almost to the border of the province of Palencia. This is a pure landscape, bare and green geology dressed in blackberry bushes ferns, oaks, pines. But near the Cabezón de Liébana, before beginning the real climb, we turn off to the right and soon arrive at Santa María de Piasca, a monastery whose existence is documented as far back as the 10th century.

There remains the church: three naves, three apses, and crossing. The main portal is a fine example of late Romanesque. Above it, two images, also Romanesque, of St. Peter and St. Paul. The so-called *Puerta del Cuerno* is surmounted by an elegant representation of a boar hunt. But we need not describe in too much detail what you will see in due time on the outside and inside of this church. It is hard to say whether Pereda, who preferred landscape to architecture, visited this place. However, though fans of Pereda, we are not complete slaves to his tastes; so who cares?

Now we climb the pass, with curve after curve. Any point along the road offers vast views over the valleys. Or upward toward the heights of Peña Labra, rising like a rocky castle. Before turning off the highway which would lead us to Cervera de Pisuerga, we make a halt at the Venta de Pepín, for a snack perhaps, but more likely just to contemplate the view. Then we turn left and begin the descent into the basin of Nansa. Pereda saw this impressive landscape through the eyes of the protagonist of *Peñas arriba:* "In the foreground, two high cones united at their base, from North to South, like two twins of a breed of giants; facing them, on my right, the summits of Palorpera, overlooked by the Horn of Peña Sagra extending its colossal ridge toward the West; and in the far distance, closing the gap between Peña Sagra and the two cones, the enormous Peñas de Europa, already crowned with snow, rising from the shore of the Cantabrian..." If don José María, or his novelistic persona, had climbed the Horn, he might have enjoyed an even vaster view of towns and mountains and of the Cantabrian coast from Asturias to Vizcaya.

But we now continue our descent, down the Hoz del Nansa, through a thrilling, lunar landscape. The road hanging on the cliff wall above the abyss, takes us to the valley of Tudanca. In the words of one of the characters in *Peñas arriba:* "...in all this valley there is no flat place, except the salon of don Celso's house...". It is to the house of don Celso, that is, to the *Casona* of Tudanca (called Tablanca in Pereda's novel) that we now proceed.

This village, built on a hillside by the river, was not long ago declared in its entirety an historical-artistic ensemble. But though the town is indeed a place where nature and architecture unite to make a unique impression, it is the *Casona,* a building that belonged to José María de Cossío, that offers the most interest for us. Built in the reign of Philip II by an indiano who had made a fortune in Peru, it has sheltered personalities such as Unamuno, Marañón, Alberti (who wrote here a part of his book *Sobre los Ángeles*), Gerardo Diego and a great number of poets, writers and intellectuals, of whom numerous autographs are conserved in the library. The library also contains some 25,000 volumes; paintings and drawings by Zuloaga, Solana and Vázquez Díaz among others; antique furniture, engravings, etc. These are a few of the sights of the Casona, where a great part of the action of *Peñas arriba* takes place.

Now we keep on going down the valley, through more Peredian places, which the author often veiled with invented names, towards Puente Nansa: here is Cosío, with its stone houses, "the rustic ones predominating over the genteel" (José María de Cossío), and the tower called Torre de los Cosío standing out among them. Then Carmona, the parish church (16th century), and the mansion of Rubín de Celis, now a parador or hotel. We go on, up the Collado de Carmona, towards Cabuérniga. If the traveller passes through here about the end of September, he may see the spectacle of the cattle of Tudanca being brought back down to the valley, after spending the summer in the high pastures. In these towns, the landscape has been tamed. The architecture, whether popular or noble, is like a modest version of Santillana, and seldom without interest.

Leaving the valleys, we go on to the pass of Palombera, following the course of the Saja towards Reinosa, the point where the protagonist of *Peñas arriba* began his trip. The land is again splendid with beech, oak, hazel, and chestnut. The traveller will understand why, amid this formidable natural setting, the Romans had to undertake long, tiring campaigns against the Cantabrian tribes and, it seems, never really succeeded in pacifying the region. A detour of nine kilometres to the left will take us to Barcena Mayor, among all the architectural ensembles of the region one of the finest and best conserved. We need not look for exceptional individual buildings here; rather, the harmonious huddle of traditional buildings, the stone-paved streets, the sloping roofs, the storage lofts hung with maize and peppers, form a dream ambience of great charm. Sunday however, is not recommended for a visit, as the village then is full of tourists.

With every metre we rise, the landscape becomes more naked and severe. Finally we begin the descent to Reinosa, where Marcelo, the protagonist and narrator of *Peñas arriba,* got off the train. Marcelo mentions Juliobriga, though he did not visit it for very long. It is a few kilometres from here, in the village of Retortillo. When Pereda's Marcelo got off the train, on his way to Tablanca (Tudanca), excavations had barely begun on what is now considered the most important Roman town of Cantabria, and nucleus of the region. Very little remains standing. We see foundations of houses, remains of street paving, of some public buildings, of popular tenement blocks. Excavation, a hundred years later, continues, and occasionally some interesting object comes to light: columns, ceramics, mosaics. Juliobriga is a venerable ruin that still poses enigmas to the archaeologists; a motive for melancholy meditations —"Estos Fabio, ay dolor, que ves ahora / campos de soledad, mustio collado"[3]—. Here, where the last Cantabrians were beaten, life continued when Rome had already fallen. One of the vestiges and proofs of continuity is the Romanesque church, built on the ruins of the Roman town. If we return to Reinosa and take the higway to Palencia, we may see one of the finest examples of Romanesque in the region: the Colegiata de Cervatos. The round-arches portal, with its archivolts springing from six columns whose capitals are rich with animal carvings; the lintel with floral themes and other ingenious carvings, are well worth this short detour from the Peredian route.

But our tour ends in Reinosa, the place where the protagonist of *Peñas arriba* began, here getting off the train that had brought him from Madrid. As he did "We cross an old bridge over the headwaters of the Ebro, and go upstream with the river on our left, its fresh green banks arched over with reeds and blackberry bushes". In the distance, the mountain called Pico Tres Mares, watershed of three rivers that drain into the Cantabrian, the Atlantic and the Mediterranean.

Some day, to remind us of our trip, we will re-read some part of *Peñas arriba,* which guided us from Potes to Reinosa, in the opposite direction to the protagonist's movement. We may mention, to be sure, that the geography of the novel does not exactly correspond to the real one, because the trip from Reinosa to Tudanca, according to José María de Cossío, was never made by Pereda: "the topographic references have been changed, often widely, and not one of the mountains named is in its right place. But the novelist's intuition was such that with

---

[3] "These Fabios, how painful to see them now: solitary fields and mouldy holes...".

these shuffled elements and confused data, he could truly capture the essential character of the countryside...".

What image will float on the surface of our memory? The reality of our tour, or the reality of Pereda's convincing fiction?

CASTILLA-LA MANCHA

LA MANCHA
OF DON QUIJOTE
by
JESÚS TORBADO

MIGUEL DE CERVANTES
(Alcalá de Henares, 1547-Madrid, 1616)

In all his luckless, chequered lifetime, Miguel de Cervantes never managed to make the title of don, *in those days borne by all persons of quality, really stick to his name; nowadays he is one of the writers most universally thought deserving of honorific treatment. For he is justly considered the first and greatest of novelists, and not only in the Spanish language.*

He was born at Alcalá de Henares, near Madrid, son of an unsuccessful surgeon probably of Jewish descent, in 1547. He never attended any university. He moved from city to city, thought of emigrating to America, went to Italy and enlisted in the Spanish army there commanded by don John of Austria. At the battle of Lepanto, an arquebus shot permanently paralyzed his left hand. On his way back to Spain, his ship was captured by Barbary pirates, and he spent five years as prisoner in Algiers. In Spain he was employed as a tax-gatherer, which brought him troubles such as excommunication and imprisonment. All his life he was dogged by poverty, problems with women, legal persecution and insult, until his death in 1616.

Cervantes tried his hand at poetry and plays, but is above all known as a writer of prose narrative. The first part of El ingenioso hidalgo don Quijote de la Mancha *appeared in 1605; the second part ten years later, just before the author's death. By this time the book was already popular both in Spain and abroad. It is the story of a man both mad and sane, who seeks to redeem the world with his fantasies and the aid of a faithful, earth-bound peasant. This extensive work achieves its announced purpose: "that the melancholic be moved to laughter and the smiler smile yet more, the fool be not moved to anger, that the witty may admire its ingenuity, and the serious man not disdain nor the judicious fail to speak in praise of it". But it is also much more than that, for the* Quijote, *amid its laughter, is an inexhaustible source of fantasy, of humanism, of literary beauty, of wisdom. The commentaries, theses, adaptations and derivatives it has inspired can be counted in the thousands.*

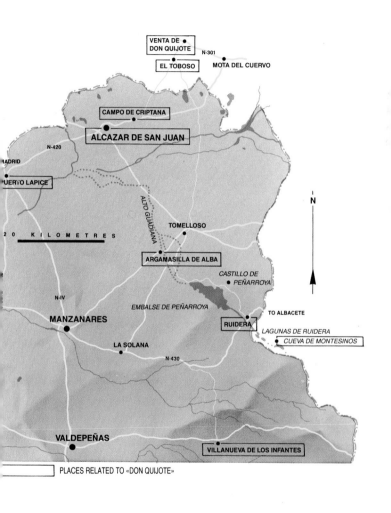

VENTA DE
DON QUIJOTE ●
N-301
EL TOBOSO ●
MOTA DEL CUERVO

CAMPO DE CRIPTANA ●

ALCAZAR DE SAN JUAN ●

N-420

MADRID

PUERTO LAPICE ●

ALTO GUADIANA

TOMELLOSO ●

20 KILOMETRES

ARGAMASILLA DE ALBA ●

CASTILLO DE
● PEÑARROYA

N

EMBALSE DE PEÑARROYA

N-IV

TO ALBACETE

MANZANARES ●

RUIDERA ●

LAGUNAS DE RUIDERA
● CUEVA DE MONTESINOS

LA SOLANA ●

N-430

VALDEPEÑAS ●

VILLANUEVA DE LOS INFANTES ●

PLACES RELATED TO «DON QUIJOTE»

LA MANCHA OF DON QUIJOTE

The visitor to La Mancha is apt to inquire with surprise and bewilderment as to the whereabouts of the "forest" out of which don Quijote and Sancho sallied one day with the intention of enchanting the peerless Dulcinea. The Knight remained "hidden in the foliage" not far from "the great Toboso", according to Cervantes. But the woods have disappeared almost completely since those days; the undulating plain spreads infinite and treeless toward the wild sierras that mark the frontier of Andalucía. La Mancha is the most extensive plain in Spain; no doubt its landscape has been much modified in the last four hundred years. Cervantes surely knew this plateau, to which the Arabs gave its name because it was inhospitable, empty, scattered with woods and sloughs. A land of settlers and of passage, under an unpropitious sky. It is different now.

Near the Caminos Reales or royal highways, some of them now changed to motorways, there appeared the white-washed walls and red-tiled roofs of roadside inns that gave shelter to the traveller. There one might meet mule-drivers, hidalgos, groups of friars, mountebanks and knaves. Miguel de Cervantes, who never stayed very long in one place, must have known them well; and in or around such inns set many adventures of the sanest madman in world literature. But the author of *Quijote* avoided precise description of the geography of these places that were soon to become mythical, for the novel manipulates an invented reality. Thus La Mancha is the first Macondo, the first Yoknapatawpha of literary fiction.

So that today, all of La Mancha is the homeland of Don Quijote, though many students of the novel consider that the bizarre, profound and entertaining adventures of the Knight Errant all took place —excepting the strange journey to Barcelona— within a circle of some 50 kilometres' radius. "En un lugar de la Mancha...", begins the great book. Which place is that? New surprises for the modern traveller: because in all parts of La Mancha, from about 50 km. south of Madrid where the río Tajo basin begins, all the way to the Sierra Morena, don Quijote, Sancho, Dulcinea and other names from the story crop up everywhere. No fantasm of fiction is so ubiquitous. Hundreds of hotels, restaurants, bars, plazas, streets, and vineyards bear Cervantine names. Quixotic nomenclature also extends to brands of wine, cheese and biscuits, barber shops, neighbourhood groups, clubs, choral groups, agricultural cooperatives. Cervantes' characters are represented in hundreds of statues, plaques and other memorials through the length and breadth of twenty thousand square kilometres. But in all this area extending into four provinces —Ciudad Real, Toledo, Albacete and Cuenca— there is only one real museum devoted to those two dreamers or the man who dreamed them. This is in El Toboso, the village of the peasant princess Dulcinea, whose face and word remain veiled throughout all 126 chapters of the two parts of the book. But Cervantes says she was named Aldonza, and this name was then very vulgar and pejorative...

Cervantists have kept up a long smoldering war of polemic, which sometimes flames up into insults and even blows, about the reality that underlies the fiction. In every Manchegan town, somebody maintains a theory that some adventure happened there or that some personality inhabited some house in the town. Cervante's shade must be greatly amused at the insoluble jigsaw puzzle he has left in the fingers of his acolytes; as amused as millions of readers over four centuries have been, at the sovereign invention of this writer whose reputation was so mediocre in this life, and so immense beyond the grave.

However, there do exist real facts and probable conjectures. For example, Cervantes lived some years in Esquivias, with his young wife Catalina de Salazar. A fine old house near the church is considered to have been the temporary abode of the vagabond novelist. This house is still used, with its wine-cellars, stables, courtyard and numerous rooms. The present proprietor intends to convert it into a "typical inn", fulfilling the suspicious prophecy of the novelist, who was afraid his legacy might be profaned in some such way. And in the parish archive, there is the record of the marriage, which must have caused adverse comment. Cervantes was thirty-seven years old and very poor; Catalina was nineteen and brought a substantial dowry. The marriage did not last long.

But the vital centre of the Quijote world is further south. The most widely received tradition considers the hidalgo lived in Argamasilla de Alba. A quarter century of research has led Ángel Ligero to believe that his birthplace must have been at Alcázar de San Juan, the geographic centre of La Mancha, very near El Toboso and the hills still dotted with windmills. Thirty-eight kilometres separate the towns which dispute the honour of the Knight's birthplace. In reality, the Alcazareños also pro-

pose that their town, and not Alcalá, was the birthplace of
Cervantes.

The pilgrim who wanders the highways of today has
no time to peer into the documental or magical ramifica-
tions of these arguments. The advocates of these theories
must settle for the satisfaction of convincing themselves,
and of preaching to the converted.

The first thing this pilgrim will encounter is a modest,
solitary building in whose courtyard, about sundown, a
number of dogs may usually be heard furiously barking. It
is called Ventas de Don Quijote, at 130 kilometres from
Madrid on the Nacional 301 highway to Albacete, just
one league from El Toboso. Of the numerous mishaps
and adventures that Cervantes sets in roadside inns like
this one, did any perhaps befall the knight in this place?
Perhaps here he received his knightly armour, or dis-
puted with priests, or tried to take to bed the good-willed
wench Maritornes, or confronted the mighty Knight of
Mirrors, the giant Caraculiambro or the proud Alifanfa-
rón. Perhaps here the Knight was hung up, or Sancho
thrown in a blanket...

Several inns dating from the 16th and 17th century
still function in the region. There is one at Puerto Lápice, very well set up and decorated, where they serve
many local dishes, including duelos and quebrantos, an
egg dish don Quijote often ate on Saturdays. Since it contains pork, this may have been, as it was for many in that
age, an advertisement of the eater's condition as an "Old
Christian", i.e. not of Jewish descent, as was Cervantes
himself in all probability. "Some say the first aventure to
befall him was that of Puerto Lápice; others say, that
of the windmills; but as much as I have been able to as-
certain of this case, and have found written in the annals of La Mancha, is that he journeyed all that day and

that at night, his nag and he were tired and near dead of hunger..."

Don Quijote well knew that those inns were really castles, and that in them dwelt all sort of princes and villains, as in the world itself. In the open fields or in the yards of these hotels of the period, he faces the great enemies, like a useless redeemer of the poor people and the disinherited of the country. He always loses, but nobody can rob him of the honour of his struggle. Just as nobody can deny to any of these inns of whitewashed walls, from Alcázar to Ruidera, the honour of having sheltered don Quijote. Even those that were built half a century ago, like that of Puerto Lápice. Piles of fleas and rust, perhaps, farmhouses with more ruin that work, amid the dried twigs of the vineyards that surround them they ferment the memory of the deeds of that hero. Such and such a deed happened here, or there, or further down the road? Cervantes wrote a novel, not a book of geography; we should remember this.

Inns and windmills... There remain only three concertrations of windmills in Quijote's La Mancha, unemployed humble giants, all of them reconstructed; at Consuegra, Mota del Cuervo and Campo de Criptana. These flour factories were invented about the 11th century, but not introduced to La Mancha until 1575, thirty years before the publication of *Don Quijote*. Built on windy hills, between growths of scrub and holm-oak now largely disappeared, they must have been an impressive spectacle in their day. The impression of power they projected led Cervante's knight to confuse them with fabulous giants; but some specialists have seen in this struggle a confrontation on the symbolic plane with the great powers of the epoch: King, Church, nobles.

At Campo de Criptana, ten hapless windmills survive on the Cerro de la Paz, on the heights of what some have

Windmills at Campo de Criptana.

considered "the most beautiful town of La Mancha". The houses wear their whiteness with that ancient air that gives the towns of La Mancha so much charm. Other nearby hills must also have had windmills, before obsolescence gradually condemned them to ruin.

A bit further on, we come to El Toboso, amid wide vineyards and occasional flights of crows. This perhaps is in reality the most beautiful town of La Mancha and, of course, that which best conserves the spirit of the seventeenth century. In those days it had 900 households (some 4,000 inhabitants); now it has half that. In the two convents here they sell sweets called Dulcineas, also pelusas. Still firmly in place are the walls of the church that Sancho and Don Quijote "bumped into", though the roofs look in need of repair. Across from the church two wrought-iron statues, not very inspired, represent Quijote's declaration of love to his "very good-looking" peasant princess. And the house in which she is supposed to have lived, a rustic mansion, proclaims one of the most poignant loves of world literature. It belonged to one Aña Zarco (Dulce Ana, Dulcinea), perhaps an impossible love of Cervantes himself; and is now a worthy museum of his imagination.

To the silent charm of El Toboso, the inhabitants add a real devotion to Cervantine relics. In another handsome house, there is a collection of some 350 versions of *Quijote,* in some thirty languages, many of them autographed by famous or remarkable persons.

In Alcázar, however, not much interest in shown in the possibility that it was the birthplace of Cervantes or of the hidalgo Quesada (or Quijada, or Quijano, or...). They pulled down the house in which the writer might have been born; nor do any of the 25 windmills once there survive; of the town's defensive towers only one of seven remains, and the walls and moats have disappeared (this might,

indeed, have been the island Barataria). The town was Cel-
tiberian, Roman and later seat of the Order of St. John. Its
newer quarters still see the opening of new bars and churches (though the latter are no longer built of the handsome
red stone of Santa María la Mayor), for it is a large town of
some 26,000 inhabitants, five times as many as in Cervantes' days; prosperous and devout: the Virgen del Rosario is
its Mayoress in perpetuity, and the inhabitants were consecrated en masse to the Corazón Sacratísimo de Jesús in
1943, as we may read in a plaque on the façade of the City
Hall. On another façade, someone has written: "death to
the unfaithful woman". But the plaza dedicated to Cervantes is shapeless, shabby and poor.

Whether don Quijote proceeded from this town or
from Argamasilla, it is clear that he sought adventures in
the Campo de Montiel, to the south of the city. The pilgrim may try, for example, to find in the environs of the
town the house in which the Marriage of Camacho was
held; but in any case the exegetists tell us that this was
only an irony of Cervantes, mocking the court banquets
that took place at the marriage of Felipe II and Isabel de
Valois (1559). The fact is that no establishment in the town
offers such banquets; not even the famous *galianos* of the
region, a sort of scrambled mix of meat of fowl and other
game, appears in the menus of hotels or restaurants. There
is, however, good ham, partridge, wild rabbit, and magnificent cheese.

It so happens that Argamasilla de Alba, which in 1575,
when it had 600 houses and called itself a "wayside village", grown up around a crossroads and thus open to
news and novelties, set amid its infinite vineyards and irrigated fields, with its distilling and textile industries and
healthy agricultural development, displays also a healthy
interest in things Quijotic. For it is believed here that the

Hidalgo is a caricature of a local gentleman named Rodrigo de Pacheco, who witnessed an apparition of Our Lady "when he was gravely ill, and given for lost by the physicians, on St. Matthew's Eve, 1601", as we may read under his portrait, displayed in the ample and almost bare church. The cold that entered the brain of this gentleman, or better said, an unconquerable fire, may have been the model for the "sane madness" of don Quijote. However, Cervantes had begun writing his book long before the Virgin's apparition to Pacheco.

The successors to the academics of Argamasilla, many of whose verses Cervantes "notes" and adds a few mockeries, affirm that the book was begun in the Cave of Medrano, and not in a Sevillian prison. This "cave" is in fact the cellar of a two-storey house, burnt in 1880; but they now propose to rebuild it for a museum. Some people here will tell you, with abundant detail, the story of how Cervantes was shut up in this hole for an impertinent compliment made to the mayor's daughter, Magdalena Pacheco; or with more plausibility, for trying to collect a debt from the mayor or some other influential person. However, the woman who possesses the key to the ruin, and is no descendant of the wealthy Medrano, knows nothing of this story. When the writer Azorín visited the place some decades ago, they told him of an Englishman who had entered the cellar, knelt and kissed the ground amid shouts of enthusiasm.

The house of Sansón Carrasco, the great blackguard and traitor of the story, belongs now to sixteen owners who cannot agree on anything. In the parks of the town and in the interior of the Cave, there are statues on Cervantine themes, but they do not bear much looking at. Argamasilla however is an agreeable town, handsome and clean. It now has 6,700 inhabitants, twice that of Cervantes-Pacheco-Quijano days. The underground river of the Guadiana sends some of its waters to the surface in the form of the splendid wine that fills the vats of nearby Valdepeñas.

Argamasilla, like El Toboso, Alcázar and Puerto Lápice, like all the Manchegan towns that were first farmhouses and then villages, has resuscitated in the last half-century, after long stagnation. When Azorín visited these places in 1905, he saw little else but desolation, poverty, memories and ruins. Now there are factories, discotheques, renovated houses, lots of new buildings, abundance of automobiles and other symptoms, not all of them agreedable, of the approaching dawn of the 21st century.

Perhaps Villanueva de los Infantes is a bit set in its dauntless past. It is said that here lived the discreet and cultured Caballero del Verde Gabán, with whom don Quijote has a contented conversation on his third journey and in whose house he stays. The handsome stone mension attributed to him stands very near the plaza, among dozens of other sumptuous houses, churches and convents. In the Dominican convent, Quevedo died in 1645 and was interred in the church of San Andrés, under an iron plate which now covers an empty hole. This other star of Spanish letters had been lord of small village nearby, called Torre de Juan Abad.

Infantes is the great monumental city of La Mancha, and exudes almost an aroma of Andalucía. The stone walls of the Late Gothic, Renaissance and Neoclassical mansions were built when don Quijote was already a name popular throughout the world. Knightly monks, communities of friars, tax-gatherers, communities of scholars, and even the inquisitors of the Holy Office have left their dwellings to the curiosity of posterity.

But the world of don Alonso el Bueno was in the inns and the fields. In his journeys through the Campo de Mon-

House of Villanueva de los Infantes.

tiel, he must have skirted the banks of some of the sixteen lagoons of Ruidera, which drain into one another in
a noisy cascade (hence the name Ruidera) of 120 metres,
in a sweet, quiet, rural landscape. This area is now a Natural Park.

After the last of these lagoons, a reservoir created forty
years ago backs up the confused waters of the río Guadiana, whose vague headwaters now drain into this lake
of Peñarroya. Nearby there exists a handsome Moorish
castle not noticed by the Knight of the Woeful Counten-
ance, because it had no sails perhaps, or because he could
not see it amid the oak woods. Nor did he notice here a
strange, whitewashed building called a *bombo* or *tombo* in
which the peasants keep tools and cattle. He did, however, notice the threshing floors where wool was washed,
and of which only a few remains may now be seen. Another thing Cervantes neglected to mention was the castle
of Rochafrida, sung in ancient ballads, now reduced to a
few ruined walls.

The countryside of Montiel is flat and fertile land near
Infantes, but wooded and rocky near the lagoons. From
the town of Ruidera we must cover just two leagues of
road, as the book says and does not lie, to arrive at the
Cave of Montesinos, where don Quijote invented the sport,
or science, of speleology. He arrived there, after having attended the marriage of Camacho, under the guidance of
Primo, a character even crazier than himself. He descended
with a rope, and in the dark humid depths —it is some
forty metres deep— saw a sumptuous crystal palace and
pleasant meadows. No one can doubt that these things are
still down there, with Durandarte, Lanzarote and Queen
Ginebra dwelling in them, as Cervantes frequently repeats
that his book is a *true story*. The cave seems a simple hole
atop a ridge, amid oak woods and bare red earth. Far below

gurgles the underground current of the río Guadiana, also invisible and magic.

This hole which by itself would never have merited mention in history is the last *real* trace of the wanderings of don Quijote and his servant, confidant and friend Sancho in La Mancha. Here begins and ends the fantastic tale of the "most chaste of lovers, and most valiant of knights ever seen in these parts for many a year".

GOING WITH
THE ARCHPRIEST
TO EXPLORE THE SIERRA

by

RUBÉN CABA

JUAN RUIZ, ARCHPRIEST OF HITA
(Last decade of 13th cent-1353?)

Until a few years ago, the only information we had about the author of the Libro de buen amor *proceeded from the text itself. He tells us his name and ecclesiastical post in strophes 19 and 575. We know he was born at Alcalá (Alcalá de Henares? Alcalá la Real?) by strophe 1510. And strophes 1485-89 give a parodic description of his facial features. In the colophon of the Salamanca manuscript, work of the copyist Alonso de Pardiñas, we find the comment that the Archpriest composed his book "while imprisoned by order of Cardinal don Gil, archbishop of Toledo". In 1972, the mediaevalist Emilio Sáez published his conclusions: Juan Ruiz (or Rodríguez, in the uncontracted form) de Cisneros, future author of the* Libro de buen amor, *was born at Alcalá la Real (then, Alcalá de Benzayde) about 1295 or 96, and must have died late in the summer of 1353, in Christian lands. When his parents recovered their liberty, having met one another while captives of the Muslims, Juan Ruiz went to Castilla to be educated by his uncle Simón de Cisneros, bishop of Sigüenza. Though it is not known in what years Juan Ruiz de Cisneros was Archpriest of Hita, Emilio Sáez conjectures that the cardinal don Gil de Albornoz must have relieved him of that post after seeing the second version of his book. Whether these speculations are well founded or not, the Islamic influences in the Archpriest are undeniable.*

Américo Castro sees in the "active, restless, cheerful and sensual" poetry of the Libro de buen amor a *"distant antecedent of the modern literature of moving, seeing and tasting as much as possible of the world". And Claudio Sánchez-Albornoz observes that "his erotism is not less than his irony. He makes mock of clerical prayers, fasts and vigils; ridicules penitences and pilgrimages; parodies the retinues, challenges and combats of the nobility; caricatures the mourning wails in honour of deceased dignitaries; scoffs at the judiciary and the clergy; laughs at himself and takes pleasure in his book".*

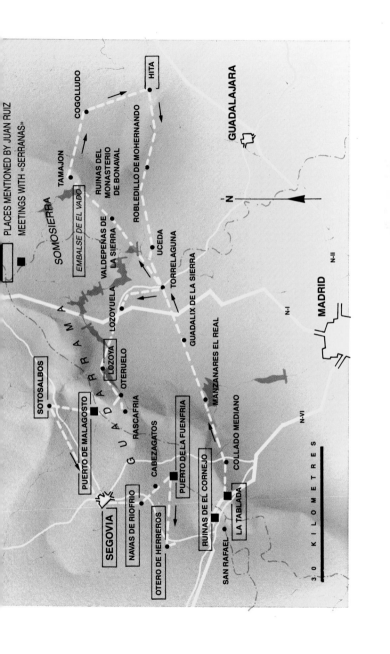

PLACES MENTIONED BY JUAN RUIZ
MEETINGS WITH «SERRANAS»

SOMOSIERRA

COGOLLUDO

HITA

TAMAJON

RUINAS DEL MONASTERIO DE BONAVAL

ROBLEDILLO DE MOHERNANDO

GUADALAJARA

EMBALSE DE EL VADO

VALDEPEÑAS DE LA SIERRA

UCEDA

TORRELAGUNA

LOZOYUELA

—N—

SOTOSALBOS

LOZOYA

OTERUELO

GUADALIX DE LA SIERRA

N-I

PUERTO DE MALAGOSTO

S   I   E   R   R   A

RASCAFRIA

CABEZAGATOS

MANZANARES EL REAL

MADRID

SEGOVIA

G   U   A   D   A   R   R   A   M   A

NAVAS DE RIOFRIO

OTERO DE HERREROS

PUERTO DE LA FUENFRIA

PUERTO DE EL CORNEJO

RUINAS DE EL CORNEJO

LA TABLADA

COLLADO MEDIANO

N-VI

N-II

SAN RAFAEL

3 0   K I L O M E T R E S

GOING WITH THE ARCHPRIEST
TO EXPLORE THE SIERRA

I shall not repeat here the arguments I used in a book to establish details of the Archpriest's route over the Sierra. These derive from the epigraph "Of how the Archpriest went to explore the Sierra, and of what befell him with the Serrana". The signs that have led certain commentators of the *Libro de buen amor* to cast doubt on whether Juan Ruiz was describing a real journey, disappear when we read the in their context; or lose their significance in the face of topographic reality. Be it known to the literary pilgrim that Juan Ruiz situates his erotic skirmishes, though these are no doubt embroidered with fancy, in a setting that is by no means invented. Furthermore, the adventures (strophes 950-1048) happen in the course of a circle journey, with unity of plan and direction. The inconstant, stop-and-go progress of the narration is no less obvious than it is deliberate. If the Archpriest was to tell of his carnal adventures with cowgirls in the first person, then he was obliged to centre his story in the mountain passes and their environs, and well advised not to even mention territories subject to the Crown (el Real de Manzanares) or to the primate See of Toledo (the domain of Uceda).

Let us consider the route the Archpriest took over the Sierra. Although he started from Hita and had to cross the domain of Uceda, the first place name he mentions is the town of **Lozoya.** On the third of March (St. Emeterius' day), he went over the pass of **Malagosto,** where he met the stocky snub-nosed girl; continued to **Sotosalbos** and, from there, to **Segovia,** leaving the city after three days. But, instead of returning the way he had come, he headed for the pass of **Fuenfría,** so as not to meet the snub-nose girl again. Not far from the village of **Riofrío** he got lost, and another mountain girl, Gadea, put him on the path to **Ferreros.** One Monday, before dawn, he left **Ferreros** and at less than two leagues, at the inn of **Cornejo,** stopped to talk with a third cowgirl, Mengua Llorente, escaping from her under pretext of going to find some wedding gifts. From **Cornejo** the Archpriest walked another league, climbed the pass of **Tablada** and here, lashed by the wind, took refuge in the hut of the dreadful Alda. Here the author interrupts his story. He must have travelled through the valley of Real de Manzanares and the lands subject to the domain of Uceda to arrive at **Santa María del Vado,** before returning to Hita.

The literary pilgrim, to be not unworthy of the footloose spirit of the Archpriest, in undertaking to follow in his footsteps ought to do so literally, i.e. arrive at Hita with a light heart, and with his walking boots on. However, those of lesser spirit who prefer to make the journey sitting behind the wheel of a car will find that, with a few exceptions such as certain rocky paths and mountain passes, they can follow his route quite closely in an automobile.

Time has lopped the towers of Hita, a proud walled town in the days of Juan Ruiz, and has seen it creep down the south side of the ridge that protects it from the North wind. Of the "castle mighty and strong" sung by Gonzalo de Berceo, there is nothing left but bits of the foundations, overgrown with grass. With the castle, all the high quarter

Town of Hita.

and most of the town wall have also disappeared. On the esplanade where Juan Ruiz's Romanesque church one stood, a stone slab records the fact: "Here was the church of the Archpriest". Halfway downhill, a handful of houses hem in a rectangular plaza where doña Endrina (of strophe 653) could not nowadays stroll to display her gazelle-like figure, without having to dodge the cars that buzz through it.

The traveller who wishes to follow Juan Ruiz in all stages of his journey, including the areas he does not mention, will pass through Taragudo, Humanes and Robledillo de Mohernando, on the way to Uceda and Torrelaguna; this being the route the Archpriest must have taken to arrive at Lozoya. Before turning to the left, he may view, to the North, the peak of Ocejón, over two thousand metres in height, among the southern spurs of the range known in the old days as Montes Claros; over which rode the Infantes de Carrión on their way to the oak-wood of Corpes, where they abused the daughters of El Cid.

Having left El Cubillo de Uceda behind us, we soon see Uceda itself. According to the Count of Mora's reading of a certain passage in Livy, the Vescelia mentioned there is the modern Uceda. When Juan Ruiz visited Uceda, it was a prosperous, fortified town, and capital of an extensive domain, in the possession of the primate See of Toledo. Juan Ruiz, no doubt to avoid complications with his ecclesiastical superiors, evoided all mention of Uceda or its domains in his ribald poem. To descend to Torrelaguna from Uceda there are two ways: a short cut through Torremocha and a longer route on the highway from Patones.

The poet Juan de Mena met his end by falling off a mule on the outskirts of Torrelaguna. An accident not surprising in a man as absent-minded as Mena who, as his friend the Marquess of Santillana remarks, often became so absorbed in his writing that he forgot to eat for days. The parish church of Torrelaguna, built in the 13th century, was renovated at the end of the 15th on the initiative of Cisneros who, on this occasion, had the western façade adorned with his own figure, sculpted in a kneeling posture before the King. The Torrelaguna that Juan Ruiz saw was still subject to the domain of Uceda, and thus bound in vassalage to the See of Toledo. For a writer of satire who was also a cleric, it was advisable to pass quietly through Uceda and Torrelaguna, and not mention their names. And that is what the Archpriest did.

Having passed the town of El Berrueco, which conserves the medieval pillory where severed heads were exhibited, including that of Sieteiglesias, we enter Lozoyuela, a village inhabited by the descendants of a group who, centuries ago, left the town of Lozoya because of a dispute over taxes, and founded here their "little Lozoya".

Having covered a section of the national Madrid-Irún highway, we turn off to Lozoya. From the first ridge on this detour, the traveller may survey the country that stretches off to Robledillo de la Jara and Berzosa del Lozoya. This land was once frequented by hill girls so pretty they did not appear to be peasants, according to some of the rhymed verses of the Marquess of Santillana, a turbulent gentleman who, in the intervals of war, wrote erudite verse and gallant lyrics. The grotesque cowgirls of the Archpriest were transfigured by the Marquess's pen into fair ladies of cottage and meadow, no less unreal than the others.

Lozoya and Lozoyuela have few features in common, despite the close kinship that unites them. The daughter, who has no reservoir do reflect in, has not the mature charm of the mother, nor her agreeable appeal. And to her own beauty Lozoya adds that of the countryside, and of the reservoir which, appropriating the images reflected in it, makes the swallows part of its aquatic fauna, and the mountain peaks part of its bed.

After losing his mule, the Archpriest passed the town

of Lozoya, on the third of March, heading for the pass of Malagosto. In those days, El Paular was wooded country; the Charterhouse had not yet been built. Here on the outskirts of the village of Rascafría, Alfonso XI was wont to hunt boar and deer.

The route that the republican troops opened along the medieval road in the Civil War is overgrown with bushes now; and whoever wishes to hike over the Malagosto, will do well to obtain of some villager of Oteruelo or Alameda his services as guide. The pass is reached by a long climb, with the scrub-covered slopes of Arrecías on one's right, and the deep hollow of Entretérminos on the left. Towards the top of this stretch there is a waterfall called, logically, La Chorrera (from *chorro,* gush). After skirting the ridge of Peñas Crecientes on its west side, we turn right toward the giant ribbed mass of Poyatas (lower, middle and upper parts) and then, after some three hours march, arrive at the pass of Malagosto and the border of Old Castile. The walker nowadays will not find any muscular mountain girls to throw stones at him, nor invite him to a rustic meal and a "struggle" in the hay. The pass of Malagosto, which could boast a hostel in the days of Alfonso X the Learned, is now an inhospitable place with no shelter but a rough herdsmen's hut which more or less keeps out the wind and water. On a high rock in the pass a cross has been put up, around which is celebrated, on the first Sunday of August, a pilgrimage in memory of the Archpriest of Hita, which starts from Segovia and Sotosalbos.

To descend toward Sotosalbos from the spring of Merendero, we must trust the stream of las Corzas and keep following it downhill, avoiding the ravine of Cambrones and the peak of Valmesado, moving along the ridge of Mataburros. After crossing the río Pirón, we arrive at the houses of La Pellejera; and behind these find a path that penetrates into the oak wood. Leaving behind us the place called

Mata de Pirón, we perceive the belltower of the church of Sotosalbos, the same church, with few alterations, that Juan Ruiz saw rise above the oaks. Those who do not wish to risk getting lost, may take the path that starts from the spring of Merendero, and stay on it for the distance of about two leagues, until it encounters the highway between Torrecaballeros and Sotosalbos, in the stretch between the rivers Pirón and Pironcillo.

The town of Sotosalbos has conserved its Romanesque church, visited by Juan Ruiz. Sotosalbos and its parish priest, don Pablo Sainz, are enthusiastic about the town's connection with the Archpriest, and have organized recitals, concerts and lectures on the subject.

After Torrecaballeros, the towers of Segovia come into the traveller's view. This millenarian city is the work of rival doctrines and of rival hands, moved by a common desire to resist the assault of enemies and time in their fortified town built on a high limestone butte. The cyclopean structure of the Aqueduct connects this butte with the high ground to the south, toward the Sierra. Throughout its history, various names have been bestowed upon this structure. In past ages, the Segovians called it the Puente (bridge); nowadays they call it Los Arcos (the Arches); Zahonero invented the term "harp of stone"; Ramón Gómez de la Serna called it a megatherian reptile; the expression employed by Juan Ruiz was *serpiente groya,* which etymologists consider to mean a stone or granite serpent. The exact date of its construction is not known, but I personally favour the idea that it was built by one of the Flavian emperors or by the first of the Antonines, Nerva. When Juan Ruiz saw the aqueduct, it remained standing by a combination of luck and inherent solidity, for the centuries of abandon it had suffered would have brought down a work of lesser quality. Only later, under the Catholic Kings, was it repaired and restored to service.

After his initial admiration of the aqueduct it is to be

Romanesque church of Sotosalbos.

supposed that the reader, if a sufficiently devoted fan of
the Archpriest, will spend a day or so in Segovia visiting
the places and buildings that Juan Ruiz saw, many of them
little changed since his time. These include the Tower of
Hercules, the Alcázar (though much changed), the churches
of Vera Cruz, San Esteban, Santísima Trinidad, San Juan
de los Caballeros, San Millán, San Martín, and of course,
the plaza of Azoguejo. If the Archpriest found in this plaza
a congregation of mountebanks, an assembly of jugglers, a
faculty of fiddlers, a council of vagabonds, masters in the
art of hunger and of living hand to mouth, the modern observer will find the place is mainly populated with busloads
of tourists, and groups of solid local citizens for whom a
stroll to the Azoguejo is part of their daily routine.

After three days in Segovia, Juan Ruiz decided to return
home: "Desque vi la mi bolsa que se parava mal, / dixe: «Mi
casilla e mi fogar çient sueldos val»"[1]. On the outskirts of
the now vanished village of Riofrío, Juan Ruiz places his
meeting with Gadea, another of the muscular-cowgirl breed
who, after giving him a beating with a stick, takes him back
to her cottage. We must now pass Navas de Riofrío on the
way to Revenga, and from there continue to the meadow of
Cabezagatos, if we are to follow the steps of the Archpriest
as he lost his way when climbing to the pass of Fuel ría.

At Cabezagatos, we must leave the forest path on the
left (this path, following the Roman road, skirts the heights
of Camorca and the Montón de Trigo, and follows the
ridge of Minguete up to the pass of Fuenfría), and hike off
to our right, i.e. to the west, through the pine woods. Then
we skirt the bottom of the mountain they call La Mujer
Muerta, and cross the stream of Río Peces. Now the going
is mostly downhill, but the walter will have to trust his in-

---

[1] "When I saw my purse was in a bad way, / I said: 'My house and
hearth are worth a hundred coins'."

stinct and sense of direction in climbing fences and avoiding swamps and pools, until he comes out on the Madrid-Segovia highway across from the roadhouse of Santa Lucía; here he turns to the left toward Otero de Herreros. Two kilometres southeast from Otero de Herreros stood the village of Ferreros, where Juan Ruiz arrived early in the morning. There is nothing left of it but the ruined walls of the Romanesque church of San Pedro, on whose stones swifts perch and lizards sun themselves.

On the highway that leads to San Rafael, the traveller will arrive at a gate, in the neighbourhood of a depressing, though angelically named, residential development, where he will easily find the drovers' trail or *cañada* of Quebrantaherraduras, which comes in an almost straight line from the site of Ferreros and continues, after passing the inn of Cornejo, to the border of Castilla la Nueva at Tablada. When Juan Ruiz walked the 14 or 15 kilometres that separate Ferreros from the pass of La Tablada, it is very probable he went along the cañada.

From the station of El Espinar, we proceed up the río Moros and soon find the ruins of the house of El Cornejo, in the vicinity of which the Archpriest met a half-witted mountain girl named Mengua Llorente, chopping at a pine. Like the other ugly, sex-starved *serranas* in the Archpriest's story, she took an immediate liking to him and insisted on marrying him; but by outwitting her (which was not too difficult) he escaped her clutches.

Still following the Archpriest's footsteps, we continue up the gorge of the río Moros and take the first canyon branching off toward the southeast. Passing the peak of Mostajo and skirting the ridge of Matalafuente, we climb to the pass by which the Archpriest passed from Old into New Castile.

Nearby, in the valley that descends toward La Tablada, there are a number of great rocks, locally known as Piedrahíta since, by iniciative of the Royal Spanish Academy, some inscriptions in memory of Juan Ruiz were carved on them. On one of the most prominent of these rocks we may read strophe 1022: "Cerca la Tablada, / la sierra pasada, / falléme con Aldara / a la madrugada"[2], and below, as a signature: "a walker in this pass, one morning in March 1329". Another rock, yet higher, is inscribed: "1330-1930. / Al arcipreste de Hita, / cantor de esta sierra, / do gustó las aguas / del río de Buen Amor"[3]. I do not know on what grounds it was decided that Juan Ruiz passed this way exactly in 1329, since he does not mention the year of his journey; but it cannot be far wrong, as the first version of the book was finished in 1330.

In returning to his homeland, there could be no shorter or more natural route for the Archpriest than the valley of Real del Manzanares. Juan Ruiz does not, however, set any of his *serrana* adventures in this region, nor even mention its name or that of any of the villages in it. Which is not surprising in that the Manzanares valley was a royal domain in the reign of Alfonso XI. We may assume Ruiz avoids mention of it for the same reason he avoids mention of the domain of Uceda.

To reach El Vado from Torrelaguna, the terrain makes a route through Valdepeñas de la Sierra and Tortuero advisable. Near the reservoir of El Vado, from the ravine of Palancar, we see on the banks of the río Jarama the stone structure of the monastery of Bonaval, a Cistercian foundation with the rank of Abbey which, we may assume, offered its hospitality to Juan Ruiz in his wanderings. It is interesting that the Archpriest mentions in his book, along with the Orders of Santiago, Hospital, Calatrava and Alcántara, that of Buenaval.

---

[2] "Near La Tablada, / having passed the Sierra / I found myself with Aldara / early in the morning."

[3] "To the Archpriest of Hita, poet of these mountains, where he the waters of the river of Buen Amor."

By the reservoir of El Vado, near the dam, there is a monolith inscribed: "El Vado 1351-1951 / Cerca d'aquesta ssierra / ay un lugar onrrado / muy santo y muy devoto: / Santa María del Vado. / Del ditado qu'el Arcipreste de Hita offreció a Santa María del Vado"[4].

The year 1951 here mentioned marks the six hundredth anniversary of the death of Juan Ruiz, which happened in 1351 or thereabouts. The inscription reproduces strophe 1044. A highway hugs the shore of the reservoir, leading to Tamajón. About four kilometres along it we reach a point where we can see, across the water, the remains of the town of El Vado: a few ruined houses, the roofless church and, on a knoll, the walls of a shrine. Here, either in the church or the shrine, Juan Ruiz went to give thanks for having escaped safe and sound from "all that noise".

In Juan Ruiz's time the rival town to Hita was not Tamajón but Cogolludo. Perhaps the Archpriest was involved in conflicts of jurisdiction with the clergy of Cogolludo; in strophes 1144-1160 he refers to "simple clerics" who "stick their noses in others' business". It is known that, from about the end of the 13th century, there were frequent differences between the towns regarding use of land for grazing and woodcutting. All this must have influenced the fact that the Archpriest makes no mention of Cogolludo, if indeed he passed through it at all; for, having passed Santa María del Vado, he might have gone down the río Sorbe valley through Beleña.

From the height of Portillejo, the literary pilgrim may descry the brown, truncated cone on which is built the town of Hita, beginning and end of the Archpriest's journey to explore the Sierra.

---

[4] "Near those mountains / there is an honoured spot / most saintly and devout: / Santa María del Vado. / From the poem the Archpriest offered to Santa María del Vado."

CASTILLA Y LEÓN

ROUTE OF THE EXILE: THE CID LEAVES CASTILLA

by

GONZALO SANTONJA

THE "CANTAR DE MÍO CID"

The Cantar de Mío Cid, *the "first monument of Spanish literature" in the accurate words of Menéndez Pidal, is conserved in a single copy made in 1307 by Per Abbat, working from an older text, in all probability a copy of the original, which was perhaps written about 1140. The older text lacks the first leaf and another two in the interior, these lacunae being bridged with the prose version of the* Crónica de los Veinte Reyes, *following a copy identical to that used by Per Abbat. The* Cantar *clearly had enjoyed a popularity in its own day, but had been forgotten for centuries when the scholar Tomás Antonio Sánchez discovered the text and published it in 1779. It comprises 3,731 verses, in irregular metre and assonant rhyme.*

Regarding its authorship, Menéndez Pidal's conclusions, though controverted, are widely accepted. He distinguishes the hands of two separate poets: one writing at San Esteban de Gormaz not long after the Cid's lifetime, in living memory of his career; and a later writer at Medinaceli, further removed from the events and less faithful to them. The first wrote about 1110, the Cantar del destierro *and the general plan of the work being his; while the recasting done by the other writer would date from about 1140, producing the definitive* Cantar *as we know it. The modifications introduced by the later writer, noticeable in the* Cantar de las bodas, *are even more apparent in the* Afrenta de Corpes, *characterized by a novelesque tone and even by certain anachronisms, entirely absent in the fragments he did not bother to alter. The variety of the versification, rich and changing in the first Cantar, contrasts with a relative monotony in the other two: a further argument for the hypothesis of double authorship.*

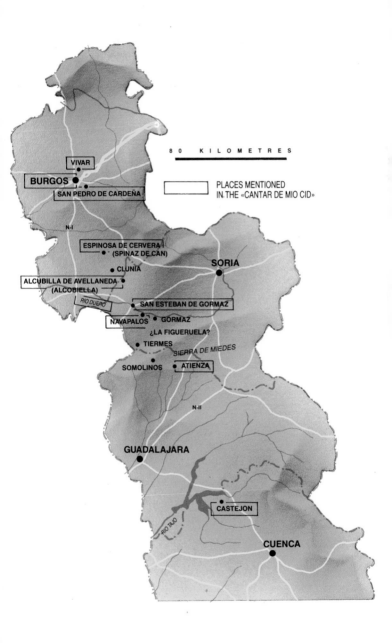

80 KILOMETRES

PLACES MENTIONED
IN THE «CANTAR DE MIO CID»

VIVAR

BURGOS

SAN PEDRO DE CARDEÑA

N-I

ESPINOSA DE CERVERA
(SPINAZ DE CAN)

SORIA

CLUNIA

ALCUBILLA DE AVELLANEDA
(ALCOBIELLA)

RIO DUERO

SAN ESTEBAN DE GORMAZ

NAVAPALOS

GORMAZ

¿LA FIGUERUELA?

TIERMES

SIERRA DE MIEDES

SOMOLINOS

ATIENZA

N-II

GUADALAJARA

CASTEJON

RIO TAJO

CUENCA

ROUTE OF THE EXILE:
THE CID LEAVES CASTILLA

The *Cantar de Mío Cid* begins with Rodrigo Díaz, known to the Muslims as Cid (from Arabic *sidi,* lord or leader), leaving his home at Vivar, on the way to his *destierro* or exile. "De los ojos tan fuertemente llorando"[1], Rodrigo and his followers direct their horses on to the road that leads to Burgos, two leagues away, the first stage on their journey. Here, at Rodrigo's domain of Vivar, by the convent of Santa Clara and facing the *Molino del Cid,* his mill (which attracted the sneers of the Infantes de Carrión, proud idle nobles who considered work a stigma of dishonour) is the starting point of our route. A route which sticks closely to that followed by the Cid, during the strict term of nine days given him by the King to abandon the realm, victimizing thus his brave vassal for the slanders of envious courtiers, who accused the Cid of skimming off a part of the tributes received from Moorish kings in Andalucía, which the King had sent him to collect.

In the Cid's village we may still find two interesting objects connected with the hero.

---

[1] "His eyes weeping copiously."

One is the image of the Virgen del Espino, a delicate carving about one *jeme* in length (the *jeme*, a measure used in the Cid's days, the distance between the tips of thumb and index finger of an extended hand). Another is the old trunk, in which the nuns long kept the manuscript of Per Abbat. The manuscript is now in the National Library at Madrid.

But before leaving Vivar the pilgrim ought to meditate a moment, so as to start off on the right foot. Let his imagination take him to a day in the past, when a shepherd boy ran up to a clergyman and reported a miraculous apparition of the Virgin. The priest laughed at the story. But his scepticism cost him dear, for he was instantly struck down with paralysis. Though sceptical, he was not stupid; he realized he had been crippled as penance for his lack of faith. He repented of his mistake, and had himself carried to the spot of the apparition. Here he bade the labourers delve in the ground, and soon there came to light three images: one of St. Andrew, one of St. Hildefonsus, and one of the Virgin with the Child, carved out of a hawthorn branch. At the sight of this image, the stricken priest was instantly cured of his illnesses both physical and mental, i.e. of his paralysis and lack of faith. From that moment on, he remained a devout believer for the rest of his days. The image that effected this miracle was none other than the famous Virgen del Espino (Hawthorn Virgin), still to be seen here at Vivar. The traveller who visits Vivar and views the Virgin will do well to keep in mind this story and the warning implicit in it.

Now we take the Nacional 623 highway and pass the ridges of Castillo and Grajo, also leaving behind us on our right the ruins of Fredesval, inexplicably forgotten on the maps, unmarked and hidden and only accessible by an earth path. We enter Burgos by the Avenida del Cid, passing under the arch of the Puerta de San Esteban and through a series of narrow streets, to come up against the impressive mass of the Gothic cathedral of Santa María, under whose giant crossing the remains of the Cid and his wife have reposed since 1921. These remains have more than once been disturbed and transported, from their original resting place in the tomb he chose for himself, at his favoured monastery of San Pedro de Cardeña. We shall have more to say about this later.

Also kept in the Cathedral of Santa María is one of the coffers, covered with leather and adorned with arabesques, which our hero filled with sand and stones and offered as collateral for a cash loan from the rich Jews Raquel and Vidas, giving them to understand the coffers were filled with the non-existent treasure he had been wrongly accused of embezzling from the King. The Jews, ready to believe this slander against the Cid's honesty, accepted the locked coffers without inspection. The coffer on display in the Cathedral, according to expert opinion, is a work of the 15th century, while the Cid's adventures happened in the 11th; but remembering the story we have just told of the incredulous priest, and how far his scepticism got him, perhaps we had better agree to consider the coffer authentic.

There are a thousand reasons to prolong our soujorn in Burgos but, determined to continue on our route, we now leave the city through the Arco de Santa María, not before having visited the church of Santa Gadea, where the Cid obliged Alfonso VI to swear an oath that he had no part in the murder of his brother Sancho.

The marvel of San Pedro de Cardeña is not far away. The austere beauty of the countryside is such, especially in autum, that we really ought to do ourselves the favour of covering the distance on foot. The drovers' trail or *cañada* of Palazuelos, strewn with golden leaves in autumn from the trees around it, leads directly here.

The tenth-century tower the Cid knew, jutting up from a horizon that without its presence would seem incomplete, slowly comes into view, a work of great charm. The tower is

Monastery of San Pedro de Cardeña.

square and four stages high, the last stage having been added in the 15th century, to bring its height up to that of the newer Gothic church beside it. There are small loophole windows in the bottom stage, simple round ones in the second and twinned ones in the third; all featuring capitals with imaginative carving of intense elementality, at once delicate and barbaric. When the sun is shining, the tower is splendid and appears gigantic; on a misty day, it insinuates its presence, seems to come closer and bid us approach. Let us do so.

The monastery of San Pedro de Cardeña grew up around the spring of Dina, later called Caradigna or Cardeña, and now officially known as the spring of the Martyrs. Here died the prince Theodoric, son of Theodoric Amalus, king of Italy, and of Queen Sancha who, it is supposed, built the original establishment in his memory. It is not really certain when the monastery was founded, but it undoubtedly dates back at least to Visigothic times. Robust and serene, solid yet elegant, the monastery in autumn rests wrapped in thecold air at the end of its little valley, proud and silent, casting its evening shadows on the low hills that surround it.

Its long history is not lacking in dramatic and sometimes bloody episodes. On 6th August 832, the abbot Sancho, and his monks to the number of some two hundred, were massacred by the Moors, who then burnt the establishment. On the anniversary of this event, a miraculous seepage of blood from the stone pavement of the Cloister of Martyrs was an annual occurrence at Cardeña, at least as late as 1473.

But not all has been miracles and mourning. In 1602, after years of patient lobbying in Rome, the victims of the Moors were canonized. The friars of the monastery in that year, heirs to these Saints, celebrated the occasion with a banquet that gave new meaning to the classic Spanish expression, "to eat like a priest". The menu included, among a long list of other viands, "over a thousand fowl, hens, capons, ducks, geese, nine calves and sixty muttons, all dead; and further provision of the same alive, in case of need...". Of drink there is no mention, but one supposes there must have been abundant flow of savoury wine, and perhaps of excellent strong liquor too. The community today makes and sells both of these commodities, under the brand names of Valdevegón and Tizona del Cid.

But let us return to history. Repopulated in 899 by Gonzalo Téllez, lord of Lantarón, the monastery's domains spread to the banks of the Ebro, Duero and Pisuerga rivers, giving it primacy among all the monasteries of Castilla. Its flourishing scriptorium employed scribes like Florencio, the favourite copyist of Fernán González, founding Count of Castilla. The figure of Fernán González, indeed, is very closely linked with Cardeña, which received one of his sons, Munio, as a monk, and enjoyed special protection from the other son, García Fernández. The father of the Cid, Diego Laínez, in turn son of the judge and leader Laín Calvo, also maintained close relations with this House; relations not only maintained but intensified by the Cid himself, to whom tradition attributes the construction of some dormitory buildings, demolished in 1711 on the completion of the second courtyard and construction of the north wing.

Perhaps the finest moment of the institution's long career was that of the abbot Sisebuto, the abbot Sancho of the *Cantar* (Lat. *abbas Sanctus* or *Sancius,* giving Romance *Sancho*), protagonist of one of the handsomest pages in the universal annals of independence and honour, when he offered protection and hospitality to the Cid, to his wife doña Jimena and their daughters, thus defying the cruelty of a royal command:

"que a mio Cid Roy Díaz que nadi nol diessen posada,
e aquel que gela diesse sopiesse vera palabra

que perdiere los averes e más los ojos de la cara,
e aún demás los cuerpos e las almas"[2].

The Cid and Sisebuto never met again. Sisebuto had been
dead for several years when Jimena, in compliance with her
husband's express desire, transported his body from Valencia on the back of Babieca, the Cid's faithful and long-lived
horse. If there was not in reality more than one war-horse
named Babieca, this noble beast must have lived some forty
years, before his final burial in front of the main entrance to
the monastery, where two elms were planted over his grave.
His master's body, suitably embalmed, reposed in a sitting
position in a sort of marble throne next to the high altar.

It is said that in 1106, not long after the Cid's death and
while his body was still being exhibited in this manner, a
rancorous Jew made a stealthy attempt to pull his beard. The
Cid's right hand was seen to move with sudden violence, in
a gesture as to draw his great sword Tizona from her scab-
bard. This gave the Jew such a start that he fainted on the
spot; and when he revived renounced his faith and professed
Christianity, being baptized with the name of Diego Gil.
It may be supposed that, like the Jews Raquel and Vidas
swindled by the Cid in the poem, Gil had been a moneylen-
der; but he renounced his lucre, and spent the rest of his
days in service, prayer and solitary contemplation, as any of
us might do after such a traumatic experience.

But not all has been miracle and wonder in the later
history of Cardeña, nor has the dead hero's presence always
been enough to ward off ill. Since the Moorish horde in the
Dark Ages, perhaps the worst thing to hit the monastery was
the *francesada*, the invasion of a Napoleonic army fresh from

---

[2] "to the Cid Roy Díaz no one shall give lodging,
and he who gives such lodging, know by this present decree,
shall forfeit all his goods, and also the eyes from his face,
and his soul be severed from his body".

the French revolution, boiling with anticlerical spirit and, more particularly, with greed. Napoleon entered Burgos on 11 November 1808; and the monastery, though in a somewhat secluded spot, was by no means forgotten. Officers and soldiers made the day-trip out to Cardeña and, among other spoliations, sacked the tomb of El Cid, and broke off the forearm of his equestrian statue so as to carry off the sword Tizona.

Further damage was done by the anticlerical movement of the early nineteenth century. The Mendizábal government in 1836 suppressed the monasteries, and declared a *desamortización,* i.e. the sale of all the ecclesiastical lands. A century later, after many intervening vicissitudes, few of them positive, the monastery buildings were used during the civil war of 1936 as a concentration camp. The Chapter Hall was used as a kitchen; the monk's cells, logically, as cells. Finally and, we may hope, permanently, the bad weather cleared in 1942, when the present Cistercian community took possession of the monastery. Though largely wrecked in the hundred years of abandon and abuse we have mentioned, Cardeña raised its head again. Again inhabited, it has lost the depressing air of abandon it must have had before 1942. The visitor undoubtedly will wish to prolong his visit, and stay on as a discreet guest amid these stone walls. It would seem the Cid experienced a similar desire.

For, of the limited term of nine days given him to leave the kingdom, six had gone by when he finally left Cardeña. He had only three days left to reach the frontier. So he lost no time in heading for the río Duero, beyond whose valley lay the mountainous and sparsely inhabited borderlands, and beyond these, the Moorish kingdoms to the south.

By rocky and winding roads, now half forgotten, he proceeded on the first day to Spinaz de Can, now Espinosa de Cervera, quickly crossing the region of Cuevas Rubias (Covarrubias), and no doubt passing by the marvel of Silos, because, contrary to the opinion of don Ramón Menéndez Pidal, it seems improbable that the Cid and his followers would attempt the pass of Yecla, which the modern traveller may view with ease, but which would be in those days most impracticable for a small army on a hurried march. The little-known Romanesque church of Spinaz de Can deserves a visit.

On the morning of the eighth day, the Cid headed for the ford of Navapalos, following sometimes the ancient roadway of Quinea, sometimes the worn stones of the Camino del Santo or of Brujas, a route which would lead him past the ruins of Clunia, the Roman capital of the upper Ebro valley. Under the Empire this town could boast a theatre, a basilica and a forum; its perimeter of some 8 km. suggests it must have had a population of perhaps sixty thousand souls. From here the Cid might see in the distance the Pico de Grado and the Cerro Bordega, in whose foothills rest the no less impressive ruins of Tiermes. Ruins underfoot and more ruins on the horizon, a suitable landscape for the sad journey into exile.

It would be evening when they reached the bank of the Ebro across from Navapalos, a village until recently uninhabited and now in a tentative process of revival. At a short distance is San Esteban, with ruins of a castle, and two Romanesque churches declared national monuments (San Miguel, built by the monks of Arlanza, and El Rivero); and a multitude of emblazoned houses. The town had been the scene, not long before the Cid's time, of a great battle against the Moors, which took place at the ford of Cascajar, so violent that the river ran red with blood. The scales of victory were tipped to the Christian side by the prodigious intervention of an angel arriving to take the place of a knight who, ignorant of the Moors' approach, had stopped to hear a Mass in San Miguel.

And, across from Navapalos, almost a stone's throw away, is the mighty caliphal fortress of Gormaz, set on a strategic

Fortress of Gormaz.

hill, at the foot of which runs the Duero. The author of the *Cantar* seems to have known this region well, and wrote not long after the events of his story. The curious reader may find many proofs of the writer's fidelity to fact. The ford of Navapalos is one occasion for an experiment of this sort.

For the río Duero at this point, just as the poem says, is easily waded across, at any time of year, high water or low. There are numerous places where you can wade across in a couple of minutes, with the water never above your knees. Anyone who wishes to verify this, or simply wishes to wade in the river, has only to go upstream some 200 metres from the bridge, put on a pair of sneakers for the sharp stones in the riverbed, and cross. The great Duero river, which drains such a large area of Spain, is found, at least here in its upper course, to be quite a manageable little stream.

At the now forgotten place of Figueruela, the Cid installed his camp on the eighth night. On the next day, his time was up; but by now he only needed to cross the Sierra de Miedes to be out of Alfonso's domains. The land beyond it was ruled by the Moorish kingdom of Toledo. The Cid and his band crossed these mountains at night. From the top of the pass they might see, stretching off under the stars, the lands of the south, in those days divided in a patchwork of petty kingdoms ruled by warlords feuding, where many a fight awaited the employment of their mercenary swords.

The modern traveller really ought to get out of his car, for reasons not only of exercise and enjoyment of the land, but of simple respect for history, and cross the blustering, inhospitable heights of the Sierra de Miedes on foot. The route begins at Peralejo de los Escuderos, a semi-abandoned village reached by an earth road turning off from the highway to Retortillo. The road in fact is nigh impassible for normal cars after the first snowfall, but we suppose that few of our readers are so enthusiastic as to make this hike in winter. The turnoff may well be overlooked; it also leads to Castro,

Valvenedizo and Losana, villages in a similar state of semi-abandonment. Peralejos is not indicated on the road signs; nor does it appear on most maps. It is there, however.

The hike ends at Somolinos on the other side of the pass, a metropolis of some fifty inhabitants. Just before reaching it we pass the so-called *Laguna sin Fondo* or Bottomless Lagoon, a body of water flanked by the walls of a ravine, and closed by an impressive dam about twenty metres high, eighty long and ten thick; with a building of noble appearance rising on its left bank, which once housed works pertaining to the neighboring silver mine of Hiendelaencina. Later it was used as a paper factory; it seems the paper of the first banknotes emitted in Spain was manufactured here.

The hike is not especially difficult; but it is not, perhaps, advisable to emulate the Cid's passage by night, as the path, little used nowadays, is easy to lose. Nor do we wish to miss the vast panorama to be seen from the top: behind us, the last valleys of Castilla la Vieja; before us, the first lands of the moorish kingdom of Toledo, whose outpost in the Cid's days was the castle of Atienza down the valley.

"Ya crieban los albores e vinie la mañana"[3].

The Cid and his followers were hurried shades, resting by day and hurrying by night. As morning approached, the Cid and his men descended on Castejón, tearing with their shouts the tranquil murmur of the río *Fenares*. Minaya set off toward *Guadalfajara;* "fasta Alcalá llegó...". The present was full of risks, and they were at a crossroads between past and future. They had no rearguard to support them; enemies were everywhere. So the handful of men took the road to Zaragoza, over the sunburned, dusty earth to La Alcarria and Campo de Taraz, their first days of exile already past and soon to be forgotten.

---

[3] "Now spread the dawn light, and the morning came."

THE BIERZO
OF ENRIQUE GIL Y CARRASCO

by

LUIS MATEO DÍEZ

ENRIQUE GIL Y CARRASCO
(Villafranca del Bierzo, 1815-Berlín, 1846)

Enrique Gil y Carrasco, one of the most significant rep-resentatives of the Romantic movement in our country, was born at Villafranca del Bierzo, León, on 15 July 1815. His early schooling was in Ponferrada; later he studied Law at Valladolid.

In 1836 he moved to Madrid, where he was soon acquainted with writers and artists, and especially with Espronceda, who helped and encouraged his incipient literary career. He worked for newspapers and magazines in the capital and developed into a professional journalist.

He was also soon known as one of the great poets of what is considered the second Romantic generation.

In autumn of 1839 the disease appeared which was to destroy him: a tuberculosis which from that time on progressively under-mined his health, though with intermittent ups and downs. Seeking repose, he returned to Bierzo and travelled in the region.

Returning to Madrid, he was appointed second assistant to the Director of the National Library. In December 1843, one of his best friends, González Brabo, was called to the Presidency of Government and, at the end of the following year, named Gil y Carrasco Secretary of Legation. His first mission was to jour-

ney through the lands of the germanic confederation and report on their political, economic and cultural situation.

After a long journey through Europe, he arrived at Berlin with his condition very much the worse. In July 1845, after more fluctuations, his cough worsened and he spent the season at a spa in Silesia, whence he returned to Berlin is very bad condition. At the end of the year he received from Madrid the first copies printed of El señor de Bembibre. He died on 22 February 1946.

Poetry, criticism and narrative are the main facets of his work. A poetry which, in critics' view, is an important link in the chain of Spanish nineteenth-century lyrics. But it is as a narrator, especially in his great historical novel, that he is mainly recognized. El señor de Bembibre *is still considered the best historical novel in the Spanish language. We must also mention:* El lago de Carucedo, Bosquejo de un viaje a una provincia del interior, El anochecer en San Antonio de la Florida, *and numerous articles on manners and travel.*

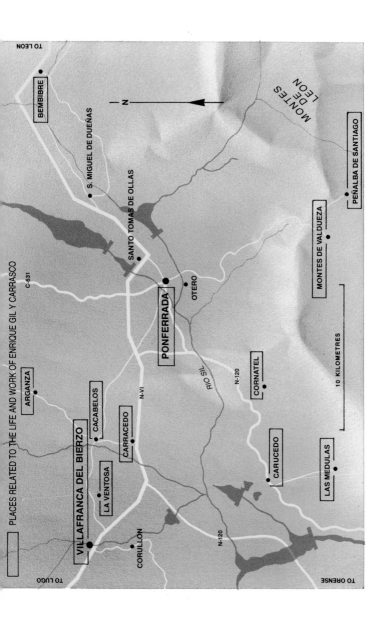

PLACES RELATED TO THE LIFE AND WORK OF ENRIQUE GIL Y CARRASCO

TO LEON

BEMBIBRE

S. MIGUEL DE DUENAS

SANTO TOMAS DE OLLAS

N

MONTES DE LEON

PEÑALBA DE SANTIAGO

MONTES DE VALDUEZA

OTERO

PONFERRADA

C-631

ARGANZA

CACABELOS

CARRACEDO

N-VI

RIO SIL

N-120

CORNATEL

10 KILOMETRES

VILLAFRANCA DEL BIERZO

LA VENTOSA

CARUCEDO

LAS MEDULAS

CORULLON

N-120

TO LUGO

TO ORENSE

THE BIERZO
OF ENRIQUE GIL Y CARRASCO

The town of the writer

At the present number 15 of the Calle del Agua, in Villafranca del Bierzo, Enrique Gil y Carrasco was born on 15 July 1815. A walk along this street of emblazoned houses which maintains, amid the splendour and decrepitude of its walls, the intact atmosphere of a bygone age, may be the most suitable prologue to our exploration of this land, which the Romantic author loved, and recreated in his books with an almost obssesive insistency, as if the landscapes of the Bierzo contained all the esthetic vitamins that were to nourish his creations.

Life and death possessed for our writer, as for so many other Romantics, a biographical proximity to his own situation, urged on by the spectre of tuberculosis, the disease which killed him at the age of thirty-three. Enrique Gil died in the far-off oblivion of Berlin, where he was performing modest diplomatic functions, on 22 February 1846. And he was buried there, in the cemetery of St. Eduvigis, where his remains reposed amid some uncertainty, until his tomb was located. In 1987 they were brought back to Villafranca; and in a short walk from the Calle del Agua where he was born, it is easy to reach the church of San Francisco, where he now lies. Life and death thus meet again, in his native town, at a short distance in space and memory.

Infelicísima (most unhappy) was the adjective Gil applied to the location of Villafranca, an unavoidable point of confluence in the old Way of St. James, bordering on the rivers Burbia and Valcarce; and it is difficult to understand this negative reference to what to most of us seems a very congenial spoot. It is indeed true that, within its walls, the town keeps its undeniable beauty much to itself, and the geographical site could be changed for another without perceptible loss. Villafranca is one of those unusual urban redoubts, preserved from the effects of time, which give a certain sensation of being in a living museum, a reasonable equilibrium between the monumental and the day-to-day, between the heraldic emblem and the neighbour's laundry, so to speak.

A seigneurial town grown up in proximity to the Bierzo, Villafranca has been enhanced with important monuments in the styles of different centuries, from the Romanesque of the church of Santiago to the Gothic of San Francisco with its surprising Mudéjar coffered ceiling, the Collegiate church of Santa María, instituted in 1533 upon what had been a Cluniac abbey, or the Baroque of San Nicolás and the Anunciada.

Landscapes of memory

The roads that are to take us through the Bierzo of Gil de Carrasco are oriented, under the suggestive influence of his work, at least in three directions, in which there come together references of a mythical, historical or cultural character, which always controlled his imagination. Roads, in any case, garlanded on either side with the perennial splendour of the landscapes of Bierzo which, so frequently, hide the ruins of abandon, of which our author often complained.

The Romantic view of Nature, the stylized, sensorial, idealizing or exalting vision, assumes for Gil y Carrasco, as we have noted, the form of a return to his homeland; and it is not difficult to recognize in the captivating spirit of the Bierzo's landscapes, wrapped in so many legendary aureoles, an attraction deeper than that of mere nostalgia. They possess a peculiar tone of melancholy beauty, in whose contemplation the writer no doubt found a deep response in his own ambit of esthetic interests. The literary sensibility of Gil y Carrasco, so moulded by the Romantic movement, had a confessed apprenticeship in the natural spaces of land so propitious as a source of inspiratorion in his memory.

In the direction of these roads we shall find the mythic legacy of ancient Bierzo, the Asturian *Bergidum*. This is an old watchtower of pre-Roman days, though with Roman and Visigothic additions. The traces of Roman rule, which later we shall visit in the stripped landscape of Las Médulas, where the myth of precious metal still lies buried, of the gold that also had a presence in the mysterious waters of the Sil. And we shall find the lands of the señor de Bembibre, the scenery of the great novel of Gil y Carrasco which relates, beyond a pathetic love story, the decline of the Templarians, who had several bastions of power in the castles of Ponferrada and Cornatel. And under the advocation of some Visigothic saint, we may approach the Valle del Silencio, the Tebaida, the hidden places where the world's solitude may still be found.

A symbolic watchtower

But before starting on this route, we should first have a look at the panorama seen from El Bierzo, from one of its ends, and go to Corullón, some six kilometres to the south of Villafranca. From its castle, a fortress of the 15th century overgrown with ivy, we get a view of the ample flatland stretching off into the foliage of fruit trees, spread like a green shadow on the land, which the green seems to be invading, and crawling up the lower slopes of the hills. In Corullón there are three splendid Romanesque churches: San Fiz, San Miguel and San Esteban. Sometimes, as in the case of San Fiz, we have to push our way through undergrowth to find them.

The sort of watchtower which for El Bierzo is a symbol of the remote antiquity of civilisation in the region, and of the town called "Bergidum" by the Asturians and Romans, stands beside the road from Villafranca to Cacabelos, about opposite the village of Pieros. It is called the Castro de Ventosa. A truncated hill which seems to survive on its own mysterious memory, like a strange symbol of what is buried there. The stubby crest, grown up upon the refuse of the myth and of history, is now used, more than anything else as comfortable nest for grapevines.

Gil y Carrasco mentions an excursion with two friends, one afternoon in July "the cool western breeze moving the vines upon the ruins of the temple of Bacchus", and describes the panorama seen from the top of La Ventosa: Cacabelos, el Cúa, the white mass of Carracedo, Ponferrada, Los Castros de Columbrianos and San Andrés, the range of the Aguiana, El Sil "glittering like a golden-scaled serpent", El Oza, the plain of Toral de Merayo, Priarzana, Cornatel, Las Médulas...

The scenes of the novel

Continuing toward Cacabelos we enter the scenery of *El señor de Bembibre:* Arganza, Carracedo, Ponferrada, La Villa del Señor (Bembibre). Gil y Carrasco's great novel, considered the best historical novel in Spanish, came out in 1844. It fits, with some liberty, within the canons of the historical novel defined by Walter Scott and, as we have mentioned, narrates a pathetic love story —that of don Álvaro Yáñez and doña Beatriz Osorio— in the historic framework of the suppression of the Order of Knights Templar, and the nobiliary struggles in the time of Ferdinand IV of Castile.

The novel begins on the roads of Cacabelos and Arganza, on an afternoon in May, in the 14th century. And to enter Cacabelos, there is no better way than to take the Calle de Santa María, which traces, from the hilly border where the Way of St. James passes, a straight course through the town, leading to the Romanesque apse of the church of Santiago. This, then, is a street of pilgrims, flanked by handsome emblazoned houses, on which time, inclemency and neglect have left their dark patina.

Toward Arganza, where the sleeping palace at the entrance to the town recalls the house of don Alonso Ossorio, father of the unfortunate doña Beatriz, all the roads are bathed in sunlight if not covered with vines, which spread everywhere like a green invasion.

The vineyards are of similar splendour in the vicinity of Carracedo, whose monastery, in the words of Gil y Carrasco, is surrounded by "meadows and gardens all exceedingly fertile, luxuriant groves, fields of wheat and maize and flax, furrowed by pure crystalline rivulets that keep them perpetually green". In the Bierzo landscape, such fertility is the norm, gardens alternating with vineyards.

In the year 990 Bermudo II founded the monastery of

Ruins of the monastery of Carracedo.

Carracedo, later restored by doña Sancha and Alfonso VII, under the Cistercian reform. The 12th-century Chapter hall, the 13th-century Royal Palace, a handsome work of the Romanesque-Gothic transitional period, and the marvellous Mirador de la Reina, are some of the most notable monuments in this ancient monastery, which has suffered from neglect and from the sale of ecclesiastical lands in the last century. Our author regretted the spoliage of Carracedo, the vandalistic destruction committed by men in top hats.

The Templarian fortress

Ponferrada, to whose Templarian castle don Álvaro so often rides to visit his uncle don Rodrigo, master of the Order, is situated on the Roman road, beside the Way of St. James.

It was, precisely, Ferdinand II who in the 12th century established the knights of the Temple in this spot for the protection of the pilgrims. The town has grown and continues growing, under the industrial and commercial impetus of its condition as provincial capital; and the castle, one of the most perfect monuments of medieval military architecture, maintains itself erect, a proud ruin situated —in the words of Gil y Carrasco— "on a beautiful height, from which may be seen all the Lower Bierzo, with its infinite variety of features; and the river Sil, running by its feet on its way to join the Boeza, seems to pay it homage".

The writer lived at N.º 6 of the Plaza del Ayuntamiento, in an old house, porticoed and emblazoned, seat of the Administración de Rentas Reales, in which his father worked.

There are two small jewels in the vicinity of Ponferrada

which the traveller ought not to miss: the church of Santa María de Vizbayo, in Otero; and that of Santo Tomás de las Ollas. The former is one of the oldest Romanesque structures in the Bierzo, from the late 11th century. From its discreet height the city, with the emblem of its Templarian fortress, appears as an undiscovered panorama, tranquil in the pervasive silence that wraps this humble shrine and its no less humble adjoining cemetery. Santo Tomás de las Ollas is a Mozarabic church of the 10th century, which hides in its interior an unusual chapel of oval plan, with nine blind horseshoe arches.

We reach the Burgh of the Lord of Bembibre at one end of our tour of the scenes from the novel, but first we ought to visit the convent of Bernardine nuns of San Miguel de Dueñas, "on the fertile banks of Bembibre, below the hill of Arenas". A foundation of the 10th century which has undergone many vicissitudes, but remains perfectly conserved and alive today; most of the buildings dating from the 17th century.

The estate of don Álvaro is in Bembibre, this active town of the Bierzo with its industry, commerce and mines. Of his castle it is hard to find any remains today, though Gil y Carrasco in the last century saw "something of its walls". And of course, there is the viewpoint on the hill, which was "a place chosen for rest from his warlike fatigue".

The solitude of the world

The peace and rest and that solitude of the world, which we have already mentioned, may be sought in the Valle del Silencio, a hidden corner of the Valle del Oza, to which we ascend from San Esteban de Valdueza, hardly six kilometres to the south of Ponferrada, by way of the villages of Toral, Villanueva, Valdefrancos, San Clemente, Manzanedo, Montes and Peñalba. Twenty and some kilometres of winding road toward the heart of the Leonese Tebaida, in the Sierra Aquiliana, where San Genadio restored the monastic life about 895 AD.

It was Salomón, a disciple of San Genadio, and like him Bishop of Astorga, who in 937 constructed the church of Peñalba, dedicated to St. James, one of the purest jewels of the Mozarabic style. Not far away, where the Río Silencio runs, the founder's hermit cave may still be seen.

At Montes, in the Sierra de la Aguiana, the Visigothic foundations of San Fructuoso survive. Fructuoso was a noble who elected a life of retirement and prayer, as his friend and disciple San Valerio narrates, "in the terrible, narrow and isolated solitudes of the Cordillera, where he constructed the Rupianensis monastery, secluding himself in a tiny narrow cell, near the sacred place". This is the monastery of San Pedro, in whose present 12th-century church there are conserved a few sculptural remains and a long inscription from those remote times.

Gil y Carrasco dwells on the emotion and secret beauty of these sacred spots. "The choice of site", he says, "could not be more appropriate for the severe thoughts of those anchorites. The view of those rocky heights, that sad, dark solitude where, as the clouds are torn in winter, perhaps Heaven was revealed to the contemplative monks in all its splendour and majesty; and also the superfluousness of human vanities and the fragile hopes of earthly life."

The green shadows of the chestnut trees continue growing over the fallen remains of the monastery, so deeply hidden by undergrowth that walls involved in deeper mystery than these of the Tebaida would be hard to find. Here Time, coloured with the penitential spirituality conferred by remote memory, seems definitively preserved in the silence of the valley.

The gold of the mountains

Ponferrada is again our point of departure, now to vary our journey with an exploration of the Roman past, taking the highway to Orense, which leads us to the spectacular ruins left us by the greed and gold fever of antiquity. "One of the richest stores of gold", our writer says, "that Nature opened to the Romans in this lands, witness of her grandeur and her crimes".

But before arriving at Las Médulas we cannot help but inspect the castle of Cornatel, the other great Templarian bastion of the Bierzo, overlooking "rough and sombre crags" like a proud nest of eagles, from which we may view one of the most profound landscapes of this countryside with its "views of the far distance".

From the viewpoint of Orellán, the enclave of Las Médulas may be seen in panoramic view. These weird badlands are the remains of a Roman gold-mining operation, carried out in Imperial times by the procedure called *ruina montium.*

"The broken mountain collapses in upon itself with a thunder such as the human mind can hardly conceive", writes Pliny, who speaks of over twenty thousand pounds of gold per year extracted from these mines, significantly lowering the price of that metal in the Empire; and mentions that some sixty thousand slaves worked here.

The system depended on vast amounts of slave labour. The mountain was undermined with shafts and galleries, then water was directed through the tunnels to provoke its complete collapse or *ruina montium,* these hills being composed of loose sedimentary material. Water and earth then flowed to a system of basins in the valley, where the sand was washed and gold extracted. The water was brought in by a system of canals, some of them forty kilometres in length.

Las Médulas.

This ruined landscape, this fleshless skeleton of mountains, peopled with capricious, fantastic peaks and solitary needles, weird minarets, rising from amid the green luxuriance of the chestnut forest, is like a dream country, a rare monument to the forgotten devastation of another age.

From the village of Médulas we can enter and explore some of the remaining tunnels, and walk round the strange buttes and towers, mute witnesses to the past amid the exuberant green foliage of the present.

The crystal of legend

A place highly emblematic of the work of Gil y Carrasco is the Lake of Carucedo (lago de Carucedo), whose name forms the title of his first novel and reappears often in his other writings. It is, no doubt, a suitable culmination of our tour. It is evoked in the pages of *El señor de Bembibre,* when don Álvaro and the Comendador Saldaña, Castellan of Cornatel, contemplate the land in silence from the battlements of the tower:

"Toward the west, the blue transparent lake of Carucedo seemed to serve as a mirror for the villages that adorn its shores and the softly-sloping hills that surround it. At the very edge of the water there grew corpulent oaks with pendulous branches, similar to the willows, also to be seen there. There were tall and supple poplars which swayed with the slightest wind; and round and robust chestnut trees. From time to time, gulls would circle spaciously in the air, descending to the reeds along the shore, or disappearing behind the stark peaks of Las Médulas."

Carucedo is still there, amid the mystery of its waters, where the outwash of the golden mud of the mines of Las Médulas came to rest, amid the lyrical vibration of the legend, of popular tradition, which the Romantic writer reconstructs, setting in this magic place an ambience of inspiration that was destined to accompany him always.

There is a mythic resonance, fed by the quiet power of legend, in the vision with which Gil y Carrasco commemorates the landscapes of the Bierzo, a vision frequently transcended by his dreaming of a land that, for him, came to be felt as a lost paradise which he always struggled to recover.

"Hills of soft and easy slope", he writes, "carefully cultivated gardens, meadows of eternal green, groves of chestnuts and fruit trees, the figs of Canaan, the olives of Athens and the vines of Chios..."

THE PLACES OF LAZARILLO

by

JOSÉ MARÍA MERINO

"LAZARILLO DE TORMES"

Printed at Burgos, Antwerp and Alcalá de Henares respectively, the three first editions that survive of La vida de Lazarillo de Tormes, de sus fortunas y adversidades *appeared in 1554; and it is supposed there was some earlier edition, never found. Such profusion of editions gives an idea of the popularity the work must have enjoyed. The choice of theme and characters, the raw and vivid style in which the adventures are narrated, the irony with which the book views the moral and social panorama of its epoch, all went to compose a formula that was a really revolutionary novelty in the literature of its day, inaugurating the modern novel.*

The anonymity of its author has given rise to endless controversy as to his identity. The strongest attribution seems to be the Hieronymite friar Juan de Ortega; but other names have been defended, such as that of the aristocrat Diego Hurtado de Mendoza, ambassador to Venice under Charles V; or one of the humanist brothers, Juan and Alfonso de Valdés. It has even been suggested the book was the collective effort of a group, composed as an entertainment in the course of a journey.

An interesting thesis is that offered by the scholar Francisco Rico, whose critical edition of the text is indispensable for those interested in Lazarillo. He suggests the anonymity is by no means accidental but is in fact another of the brilliant expedients the author employed to heighten the impact of his story. The writer, renouncing his own authorship in favour of the protagonist character Lazarillo, thus allowed the book to appear to its early public with all the force and weight of a true story related in the first person.

N

TEJARES
SALAMANCA

RIO TORMES

ALBA DE TORMES

PEÑARANDA DE BRACAMONTE

AVILA

PUERTO DEL BOQUERON

PUERTO DE LA PARAMERA

RIO ALBERCHE

SIERRA DE GREDOS

BARRACO

PUERTO DE ARREBATACAPAS

EL TIEMBLO

EMBALSE DE BURGUILLO

CEBREROS

TOROS DE GUISANDO ★

SAN MARTIN DE VALDEIGLESIAS

CADALSO DE LOS VIDRIOS

CENICIENTOS

ALMOROX

PAREDES DE ESCALONA

TO CACERES

N-V

RIO ALBERCHE

ESCALONA

TO MADRID

MAQUEDA

VAL DE SANTO DOMINGO

TORRIJOS

RIO TAJO

CASTILLO DE BARCIENCE

PLACES MENTIONED IN EL LAZARILLO

"LA SAGRA"

30 KILOMETRES

TOLEDO

THE PLACES OF LAZARILLO

Your Honour (as our friend Lazarillo might say) has asked me to write a description, be it short of long, of the places visited by Lázaro de Tormes four and a half centuries ago, where his "fortunes and adversities" befell him, telling what these spots are like today. Infinite and diverse shall be my pleasure in so doing; the enterprise of description being a manner of spiritually revisting these places once visited, and of living over again the sweet time once spent in journeying through that pleasant land.

Our journey, like the life of Lazarus himself, must commence at the village of Tejares, a huddle of low white houses by the river Tormes. The toponym Tejares proceeds from *tejas,* roofing tiles, which for many years were manufactured here. Of the old kilns, a chimney remains, on the upper outskirts of the village. Tejares lies between the river, by whose waters Lázaro said he had been born, and the highway leading from Salamanca to Portugal and La Fregeneda. Industrial strip development along the highway now connects Tejares with the *Arrabal,* where the old parish church of Santísima Trinidad remains closed, its services transferred to a new building close to the river and the Roman bridge.

From the solid bridge there is a fine urban panorama, lorded over by the Cathedral tower; and about halfway across the bridge we find a stone sculpture in the form of a bull, or so says Lázaro, who saw it when it was in better condition. Here he received his first lesson at the hands of the blind man. This statue, of prehistoric origin, had stood at the north end of the bridge since time immemorial. In the last century a provincial governor, for reasons we are not able to explain, had the statue's head smashed off and set on its present high pedestal, where a repetition of the blind man's brutal joke would be rather more difficult than it was in the sixteenth century.

The banks of the Tormes, of great natural beauty, have been left in a state of more or less benign neglect by the City Council, who might well do something positive with them. There still exists, near the bridge and across from the new church of Santísima Trinidad, a mill with its dam, now closed and abandoned, the old millstones resting in the yard, overgrown with weeds. This mill might be restored and conserved, not only as an example of a type of industrial plant common in past centuries, but because the parents of Lázaro worked in a similar mill, perhaps in this one.

As regards Salamanca itself, what can I tell your Honour of this famous city, that is not already common knowledge? A University town since the 13th century, it was already rich in fine and noble buildings when Lázaro knew it, above all the Old Cathedral, with its scale-roofed Torre del Gallo and splendid retable by Nicolás Florentín; and many later buildings, like the New Cathedral, were already under construction. Today, although the urbanism of recent decades does not offer many good examples, the city still possesses an ensemble of buildings in a splendid variety of styles and periods, a multitude of churches and palaces with their façades, towers and patios, all made of the

Roman bridge at Salamanca.

golden Villamayor stone, so amenable to the filigrees of the Plateresque style.

The youthful movement of the city is especially concentrated in the majestic and harmonious Plaza Mayor. Near the Plaza there are numerous places where the visitor may appreciate the cuisine of Salamanca; an experience, of course, hardly known to Lázaro. Sausages are no doubt an outstanding feature among regional products, especially the chorizo. However, judicious travellers of the past, such as Richard Ford, have opined that Salamanca has distinguished itself more for its production of scholars than for its production of cooks. There things being a matter of opinion, the visitor is invited to try for himself the *chanfaina*[1], the *hornazo*[2] or the meat *a la manera de Tejares.*

Of the wanderings of Lázaro immediately after his departure from Salamanca there is no mention; but from his later arrival at Ávila and crossing of the mountains, we may assume he went in the general direction of Ávila, in all probability by way of Peñaranda de Bracamonte. He could have taken two routes: direct across the plains, along the present Nacional 501 highway; or by way of Alba de Tormes.

The first of these routes is more or less that described by Alonso de Meneses in his *Repertorio de caminos* about the end of the 16th century. It crosses the bottom land of the Tormes by Santa Marta and Calvarrasa de Arriba, where the valley opens out into meadows and fields of maize. Further on is Encinas de Abajo, whose pompous tower dominates the steppes of wheat-fields and a few scattered villages. Finally there is Ventosa del Río Almar, where steppe, valley and oakwood define the landscape with their distinct patches of colour, with the Sierra de Ávila on the horizon.

---

[1] Meat stew.
[2] Baked egg dish.

The other route, which we recommend, follows mainly the local highway 510 to Alba de Tormes, through the similar wheat-field landscape of Calvarrasa de Arriba, with oakwoods and some pastures in gently rolling terrain. A grove of oaks and pines serves as portico to the spring of Fuente de Santa Teresa, six kilometres from Alba de Tormes. Very near to the *Vía de la Plata,* the western road that in Roman times connected Astorga, Mérida and Sevilla, this place was the scene of a prodigy. On a stormy night, St. Teresa and a party of her nuns had lost their way in these woods. An enigmatical youth suddenly appeared, bearing a light, who led them back to the desired road, at a point near the spring, then disappeared. A discreet, humble sort of miracle, so humble that it hardly seems a miracle at all; but food for contemplation as we approach the town of Alba, passing Terradillos and crossing the long Roman bridge over the wide river spread in shallow channels over the fertile valley bottom.

The escarpment at Alba de Tormes was no doubt a fortified site from very ancient times, but our first specific notice of it dates from the 12th century, when the original Alcázar was built, and later, through the centuries, enlarged by the Dukes of Alba. Most of it was blown up by the French during the Peninsular War, and the ruins used as a quarry for building stone; so that of the once vast castle all that now remains is the great keep or "homage tower", still an impressive mass, looming over the town with the frowning aspect typical of military buildings. There are other interesting monuments in the town. In the upper part, near the gracious Plaza Mayor with its iron columns, and palm trees unusual in this climate, we find the church of San Juan, a Romanesque brick building, its vault sustained by high arcades. Among other treasures, it contains images of Christ and his Apostles enthroned, in a fine ensemble of consistent Romanesque style.

The town contains several other churches, but by far the most famous of them is that of the Anunciación de Nuestra Señora, popularly known as "las madres". Here St. Teresa died, and her incorrupt body is kept, in a rich sepulchre that looms above the main altar: a type of ostentation not very consonant with the austere, frugal architectural style she preferred in her own conventual foundations. Her incorrupt body, or what remains of it: for at her death, clerics of several rival establishments fought for the privilege of cutting off a piece, so that bits of her are now venerated here and there in various shrines and chapels. Possession of the main bulk of her body was the object of long and bitter litigation between this convent and another one at Ávila. The church contains a varied collection of Teresiana, including an exact reproduction of the cell in which she died. Also there are several other sepulchres, the finest being those of the original patrons of the church.

I do not propose to wound your Honour's sensibilities by speaking at length of the hideous huge Neo-Gothic church perpetrated about the end of the last century, which has thankfully remained uncompleted. However I would like to recommend the curious ceramics they make at Alba, especially those known as *barriles de torre,* in which the potter's hand elaborates a simple pot with a high comb of iligree, the effect being somewhat that of a peacock made of terracota. And, for the visitor's delectation, there are the almonds known as *almendras garrapiñadas,* and the *yemas de Santa Teresa,* both local products.

The road to Peñaranda de Bracamonte proceeds through a landscape of rolling wheat-fields. First we come to Garcihernández, with fields of maize planted below bare hills, a three-arched belltower over flat bottom land of meadow and sugar beets; the Peñarandilla, and Coca de Alba. Far-off towns are seen on the horizon, and oak-woods near and far, then we come to Nava de Sotrobal, with the peculiar bonnet on its tower. Finally after crossing an inmense steppe, much of it planted with sunflowers, the flatness of the horizon is broken by the tall grain silos of Peñaranda de Bracamonte.

In the centre of Peñaranda there are two large, contiguous arcaded plazas, a bandstand and the church of San Miguel, infelicitously restored after successive fires, and wearing a grotesque cupola set atop its central nave. A speciality of the town in the edible department are the excellent roasts of crouton and kid, no mean attraction in the judgement of Lazarillo. From here, the road to Ávila, which only in the first fourteen kilometres follows the old route of the *Repertorio* of Meneses, crosses a plain scattered with ochre, earthy villages, bearing peculiar names, Cantaracillo, Gimialcón, Salvadíos; with decrepit carts and the occasional extravagant tower.

As we reach the Río Zapardiel, a sparse oakwood interrupts the monotony of the plain. Next come Chaherrero and Muñogrande, while the horizon becomes progressively more hilly. Pine-woods, sunflowers, poplars precede San Pedro del Arroyo. At Aveinte, a modest belltower features two bells whose dissimilar silhouettes suggest, perhaps, a bride and groom. The solitary landscape with fields of sunflowers continues to Muñoyerro; then oakwoods appear in ever more rolling land, and finally rocky crags make their appearance, abundant around La Alamedilla del Berrocal. Grazing land and rocky cliffs, walls of stone, undulating moorland denuded of trees. We are now approaching Ávila.

Seen from the roadside monument called Cuatro Postes, the highest city of Spain creeps down the hillside, within its circuit of walls, before the horizon of rolling mountains. Since Lázaro's time, Ávila has changed less than many other places. Of ancient origin, the town was repopulated by Alfonso VI with people from the kingdom of León. From its medieval period there remains a wealth of Romanesque and

Gothic architecture. Obligatory visits include the Cathedral and the Basílica de San Vicente. After a walk to view the many churches and civil buildings that give the city its exceptional old-world provincial air, the visitor may now feel it is time to seek out one of the many excellent restaurants, and sit down to a dish of the rich beans from El Barco, followed by the famous beef of the region. In hunting season, hare is recommended.

Two roads lead from Ávila to El Tiemblo; both of them coincide with the old itineraries described by Meneses and both are worth seeing. The first follows the Nacional 403 highway, between cliffs enclosing pastures and scrubby growth and great empty spaces; it crosses the pass of Alto de la Paramera (1395 m.) and El Barraco, then enters a region of vineyards and enormous oaks, dating perhaps from the time of Lázaro; crosses the reservoir of the río Alberche, a region with abundant chalets, and reaches a landscape of almost bare hills.

The second, more abrupt route leads through equally venerable oakwoods and rolling meadows to the pass of El Boquerón (1315 m.), then crosses Herradón de Pinares, hemmed into a narrow gorge between oaks and junipers, the San Bartolomé de Pinares, in a zone prodigal in springs and cliffs, and reaches the pass of Arrebatacapas (1065 m.) where the bent pines bear witness to the insistent power of the wind. A long mountainous cirque encloses a small plain, and here appears, below the huge crags, the town of Cebreros, out of which rises the mass of the church of Santiago, attributed to Juan de Herrera.

Both routes end at El Tiemblo, amig fig trees, cliffs, pines and vineyards, this being an area rich in production of strong wine, similar to that which tempted Lázaro and caused him the loss of his teeth, by the blind man's bashing them with the jug. Ten kilometers from the town we meet the "Bulls of Guisando", brothers to the statue on the

Roman bridge at Salamanca, worn and inscrutable witnesses to an ancient Iberian culture. Very near these bulls, a monument records the proclamation of Isabella the Catholic as heiress of Castile in 1468, made at the inn, now disappeared, called "Juradera" after the event.

From here on, we may return to the Nacional 403 highway and visit San Martín de Valdeiglesias, and continue on the same highway as far as Almorox; or follow another route which I will now describe. First we go to Cadalso de los Vidrios, at the foot of Peña Muñana. This town was once walled, and a few noble lineaments of that period are still to be seen. Charles III established a glass factory here. Cadalso stands amid a landscape of thick pine woods, but vineyards are also to be seen; and olives, the first of these on our route. Great cliffs loom around, and scrub-covered hills.

A small wooded pass, offering us an initial view of the valley of Alberche, leads to Cenicientos, amid hills and vineyards, with a church dedicated to St. Stephen, its nave sustained by hefty buttresses. From here we continue toward Almorox, by a hilly winding road in none too good condition, amid oaks, pastures, figs and moss-grown cliffs. This is good hunting country, and perhaps a band of partridges may cross the road. Rounding a curve, we come suddenly upon Almorox.

By now we are in the lands of Toledo, where the cunning blind man said that people were richer than at Salamanca, though not necessarily very generous. It was at Almorox, to be exact, that a harvester gave him a bunch of grapes, the sharpness of his malicious cunning being fully displayed in his manner of eating them. Arriving at the town on the road described, we first see the towers of its churches on the height of the hill, above extensive vineyards and a few plantations of olives. When Lázaro was here it was not yet termed a *villa,* or burgh: it was given that title by Philip II in 1566. From its past there remains the *rollo* or judicial column in a handsome plaza, and several churches. The shrine of Nuestra Señora de la Piedad is built on a peculiar site, a height dominating all its surroundings, as if maintaining in its present role a sacred condition that must date from very far back in time.

From Almorox, the ground becomes flatter, though seen from a distance it appears again undulating and hilly. The nature of these undulations may be better observed if we turn off toward Paredes de Escalona, where one of the hills has been deeply bitten into by a quarry. In the village there is a rough church, with a brick apse of Romanesque design, but disguised by whitewash. The rolling ground and oakwoods give way to a wide plain and, after a few recently built developments of villas, we arrive at Escalona, home of the Infante Juan Manuel, author of the story of Don Illán and the Deán de Santiago, which so fascinated Jorge Luis Borges.

Below the free-standing tower of the old collegiate church of San Miguel, an ogival arch gives entry to the town by way of the Calle de San Miguel, leading to the Plaza Mayor. In this place, under the same overhangs, Lázaro plotted his final vengeance on the vicious blind man, arranging for him to bash his own head against a pillar of stone; this incident is memorialized in a decorative plaque, one of several that adorn the sides of the bandstand here in the plaza.

The cobblers and saddlers shops that bordered the plaza, under the colonnades, in Lázaro's time have given way to hardware and other shops, and a few bars. The town, with its clean and well laid out streets, conserves parts of its medieval wall. The remains of square or cylindrical towers of brick or stone formed part of an enormous castle overlooking the ravine of the Río Alberche; this, like other castles, was ruined in the Napoleonic Wars.

We leave Escalona over a bridge, from which we see far off the poplars in the valley, a welcoming landscape to which the adjoining steppe forms a vivid contrast. On both sides of the road are towns with picturesque names, like Conejeras and Carrasquilla; occasionally we meet an incongruous plantation of eucalyptus in the plain preceding Maqueda.

From the heights of Maqueda we get a view of the castle, in its day a possession of the Order of Calatrava, and now a barracks of the Guardia Civil. In this town, where Lázaro nearly died, first of hunger and then of a beating, in the service of a miserable priest, was also the scene of the execution in 1354 of the Master of Calatrava by order of Peter I. There are a few remains of the historic past, such as the judicial column or *rollo,* the portal of the church of Santa María de los Alcázares, and the solitary tower called the "torre de la vela", where some remains of the old Arab wall may be seen.

The plain continues, planted with cereal grains, olive trees and vines. To the right of Val de Santo Domingo, a tree-lined road leads to the miraculous shrine of Santa Ana, painted yellow. Originating, it would seem, in the 13th century and built on the remains of a Templarian castle, the shrine stands atop a dominating height, perhaps a holy site since very remote antiquity. We may contemplate a while the vast panorama visible from here before proceeding toward Torrijos, leaving behind us the high chimneys of the tile works.

In this town, sometimes known as "Torrijos de los olivares" from the abundance of olive groves in its vicinity, doña Teresa Enríquez in 1509 founded a collegiate church endowed with copious rents and privileges. This lady's religious enthusiasm must have been somewhat bizarre, otherwise it is difficult to explain why Pope Julius II granted her the curious title of *Loca del Sacramento* (Mad Woman of the Sacrament), which to the modern ear sounds so ambiguous and not a little ridiculous. The city contains other exponents of traditional piety, such as the church of Cristo de la Sangre, presided by a figure of Christ with green skirts; flanked, in the inner nave, with images of the holy matrimony constituted by Isidro and María de la Cabeza. Af the feet of the latter, there are a number of ex-votos on display, mostly images of human heads: manifestations of the powerful and persistent belief in the efficacy of sympathetic magic.

Just after leaving Torrijos, we see on our left the castle of Barcience, above a cluster of buildings whence the breeze may bear strong odours proclaiming the existence of a meat-processing plant. It is said that its last heirs donated this castle, which looks better from afar than from close up, to Pope Leo XIII. Further on, at about kilometer 22, we first glimpse the outline of the Sierra de Yébenes. After Rielves, the river Guadarrama follows on its course through the tawny landscape and, at six or seven kilometres from Toledo, the singular spectacle of the Imperial City on its hill begins to come into view, of which the poet Rilke said that "the earth has become more grandiose since I knew of its existence".

As your Honour is aware, Lázaro in this city entered the service of a poor squire, undergoing here the worst hunger of his starved existence; later serving other masters, until reaching what seemed to him the height of ambition in his employment as town crier. This is the position he holds when he writes his book, dissimulating his wife's scandalous relations with the Archpriest of San Salvador.

This city also is very well known and much described; so I shall speak little of it except to say that many of the corners of it frequented by Lázaro are still there, often more or less unchanged, like the Cuatro Calles, or the tripe stands of the Tripería, now housed in the municipal mar-

Toledo.

ket next to the Cathedral; and that the Hebrew, Muslim and Christian strata of the city have been mixed to steep the atmosphere in a mysterious melancholy, through which walk the hurried, gawking tourists with their cameras and the indifferent locals with their daily shopping bags. In season, your Honour may well be tempted by a dish of partridge cooked in the local style, that is, stewed with abundant onions. And for desert, marzipan.

If, after exploring the city by day and by night savouring its intense flavour of the Middle Ages, the visitor should wish to visit that area of La Sagra where Lázaro assisted a dispenser of bulls (the ecclesiastical sort) in his performances, then he should follow the banks of the Tajo to Mocejón and pass through Añover de Tajo, Alameda and Numancia de la Sagra: stark open plains, hardly altered by a few dark hills, eroded and laid bare by the work of Time and Progress, where warehouses and factories rise among dusty craters, while across the river the industrial park shows the masses of its factories and residencial blocks.

But by no means should your Honour leave Toledo without going to contemplate, in the Cathedral choir, the smile of the Virgen Blanca. Perhaps this vision called up, in the chequered memory of Lázaro, an instant of peaceful nostalgia. And perhaps her smile, destined to outlive us as it did him, may bring a similar ray of peace to our hearts too. Amen.

THE CASTILLA
OF ANTONIO MACHADO

by

ANDRÉS SOREL

ANTONIO MACHADO
(Sevilla, 1875-Collioure, 1939)

After spending his early childhood in Sevilla, Machado moved wich his family to Madrid in 1883. He studied at the Instituto San Isidro and later at that of Cardenal Cisneros. In 1889 he first visited Paris; in 1893 his father died. In 1903, the press of A. Álvarez printed the first book, Soledades, *written between 1889 and 1902.*

On 4 May 1907, he took possession of the chair of French in Coria, and that same year published, in the Librería Pueyo in Madrid, his book of poems, Soledades, galerías y otros poemas. *He later published other books, principally:* Campos de Castilla *(1912),* Páginas escogidas *(1917),* Poesías completas, 1899-1917 *(1917),* Nuevas canciones *(1924), 3.ª edición de* Poesías completas y canciones a Guiomar *(1933),* Juan de Mairena, sentencias, donaires, apuntes, recuerdos de un profesor apócrifo *(1936),* La guerra *(1937).*

As a teacher, after a period in Soria, he moved to Baeza on 1 November 1912. There he occupied the chair of French until 1 December 1919 when he was transferred to the Institute of Segovia. On the 29th of the same month and year he also occupied the chair of Spanish Literature there. In 1932 he was tran-

ferred to Madrid. On 24 March 1927 he was elected member of the Real Academia de la Lengua.

On 30 July 1909 Machado had married Leonor Izquierdo, 19 years younger than he; she died of tuberculosis on 1 August 1912.

In November 1936 Machado was evacuated with his family from Madrid; and on 27 January 1939, upon the fall of Barcelona, from there to France, where he died on 22 February 1939 and was buried in the cemetery at Collioure.

By the mouth of his pseudonym Juan de Mairena, Machado called himself poeta del tiempo. *Dámaso Alonso has compared him to Fray Luis de León, "in depth, height and intensity of inspiration".*

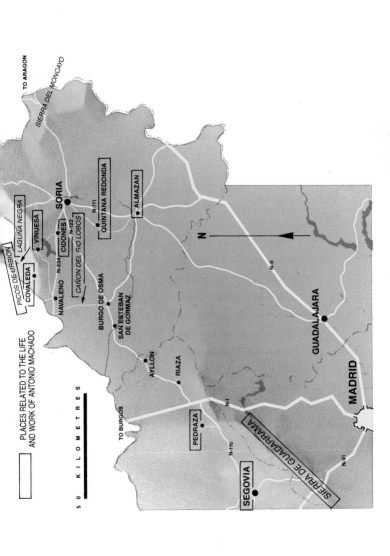

PLACES RELATED TO THE LIFE
AND WORK OF ANTONIO MACHADO

5 0   K I L O M E T R E S

TO ARAGON

SIERRA DEL MONCAYO

PICOS DE URBION

LAGUNA NEGRA

COVALEDA

VINUESA

CIDONES

NAVALENO

N-234

N-122

SORIA

N-111

QUINTANA REDONDA

ALMAZAN

CAÑON DEL RIO LOBOS

BURGO DE OSMA

SAN ESTEBAN
DE GORMAZ

AYLLON

RIAZA

N-I

TO BURGOS

PEDRAZA

N-110

SEGOVIA

SIERRA DE GUADARRAMA

N-VI

N

N-II

GUADALAJARA

MADRID

THE CASTILLA
OF ANTONIO MACHADO

It is not easy to travel through Castilla without seeing its physical and human landscape covered with quotations from Antonio Machado, especially in Soria and Segovia.

Continuity in time, for travelling to Soria, is given by the train. After Guadalajara the train rolls through the mist of September, between sown fields populated with stylized warriors, or escorts with green arms and grey legs.

Castilla is a land of ample horizons, of almost African deserts hemmed in by ridges and bare mountains; a land without rigid frontiers, where a person educated against prejudices may cleanly regard the past, a precondition without which it is indeed difficult to interpret the present itself. The sheep return here from Extremadura. And the Castilians, equally migratory, return to heir half-empty towns, even if only for a few days in summer, to satiate their eyes with the land and music of their childhood.

The río Duero wanders over the Meseta: the Mesta is the central axis of Castilla. And Soria is its gate bordering on the other high Spain. Also the "other fatherland" of Bécquer, the Sevillan poet most loved by Machado.

"Nobody chooses his love. My destiny one day brought

me to the grey hills where, with the falling of the cold snow, the shadows of the dead oaks flee... My heart is where it was born, not with life and love, near the Duero... the white wall, the erect cypress!"

Machado had arrived on 4 May 1907 at Soria to occupy the chair of French at the Institute there. He was to marry a daughter of the town and, above all, espouse the land itself. Now, some eighty years later, we return to Soria. The poplars still contemplate their reflection in the waters, silent and still, bordered with trees, a wavy mirror under the naked sun, waters which run down from the mountains to seek their death in the sea. It was springtime when Machado arrived, when the blood, like the plants in the fields, begins to quicken.

Now it is autumn. We are at 231 km. from Madrid, at 1063 metres altitude. He who wishes to see the curve of time, the dust of history, the traces of old Spain, must wander the fields and roads of Castilla, which b ʒan as a little corner and became an empire of lands and peoples. Now men and rivers emigrate from it. Those who love it however always seek it out again.

Let us enter quietly in Soria, having left behind "the pines of dawn, between Almazán and Quintana". The old city begins with the freshness of a park, at whose entrance old men from the last war offer you ice cream from a sleepy little wooden cart. In Soria not only the ruins sing, but the flavours too. And in this autumnal afternoon, without other music than the wind, the fountain and the birds zigzagging in the sky, the cars being blessedly far away, we may sit in the park of Cervantes next to the great elm, now ill and without its musical band. We close our eyes and dream, contemplating the people resting of the benches. People from the villages come to visit the doctor or to solicit permits from some bureaucrat. And forget for a moment the era of speed and television:

"My ballads do not emanate from heroic deeds, but from the people who composed them and the lands where they were sung; my ballads regard the elementally human, the country of Castilla and the first book of Moses, called Genesis."

Now let us walk. We are involved again in the asphyxiating noise on the modern city. Presently we arrive at the Calle de los Condes de Gómara, and the peace of centuries there, stopping before the arch that sustains the noble palace. The street, in its right-hand façade, gives on to the Plaza de Bernardo Robles, which conserves its mellow old flavour, and on a building with magnificent glasswork. An old woman, looking down from a balcony, seems to view us with surprise: Are there still people who admire these old things?, she thinks.

And at the end of the Calle Estudios (where there is still a pension where Machado stayed) we find Santo Domingo, with the colour of history, the shade and chiaroscuro of the Romanesque. At seven in the evening of late September, the nuns sing under the protective shade of the organ. Their voices are soft, their intonation warm. This is their body: the sensuality of their music. Between the rose window and the portal, we contemplate the seated figures of Alfonso VIII and doña Leonor. Our reading of the stones culminates with the Massacre of the Innocents. There was another Leonor, the girl Machado loved. On the way to El Mirón, the promenade beneath which the town reposes, caressed by the river, the writer or traveller may stop at the Palace, once a convent, of Nuestra Señora de la Merced, where Tirso de Molina once lodged, Now the highway roars; but silence was once to be heard. So much literature is hidden in Soria!

Machado's other promenade led to the cemetery of El Espino. At its entrance, the dead elm, now only a ruin, full of bricks, crucified with nails, all stone: once more, after

Nature dies, literature remains: "Only the river sounds in the bottom of the valley, under the high Espino." By the cloister of San Juan de Duero he might sleep the siesta. The scales of its waters reflect the veil the clouds have drawn across the sun. The cars thunder far off, while birds and children laugh at life beneath the trees. We contemplate the dance of golden leaves on the river, listen to the suave cadence of its music, and indulge our daydream that time's passage has stopped. When the wind rises and the waters of the river begin to murmur, the trees begin to tell a tale of terror that culminates in the deep night. The river opens in its embrace of the ravine and the roads: towards the ruins of the castle, the heights which lead to the promenade and to the shrine of Mirón, or, facing it, Las Ánimas and Santa Ana, towards Aragón. We travel along the banks with our eyes and with the verses:

"I have seen again the golden poplars, poplars of the road along the Duero banks, between San Polo and San Saturio, beyond the old walls of Soria, barbican facing Aragón, in Castilian lands."

From the hill of San Saturio, with its chapel of 1559 and triptych of the Crucifixión, we watch the ball of the Sun fall into the water under the lichened eaves. The hills seem to lead nowhere: although only in point of colour, edges of the city are confounded with them, and with the winding, empty roads. Pure Soria, Soria the noble; though few nobles remain and civilisation is corrupting its purity.

The road of art must yet lead us to the church of San Juan de Rabanera, of the 12th century, and to the sepulchral silence of the cloister of San Pedro. To take our leave of the city of Soria, let us visit the Plaza Mayor. The sound of our own footsteps accompanies us along the Calle Real, while our eyes roam over escutcheons, balconies, porticos. To the right and left of El Collado, traditional promenade of the city, is the zone of bars. We walk among old pensiones; cafés once called El Recreo or El Desengaño; confectioneries whose names were logically La Delicia, La Azucena. And conversations: the Casino de Numancia, Círculo Mercantil, Círculo de la Amistad... Today, the elderly go up the hill to the Mirón to play at cards. Perhaps today you may find yourself alone in the Plaza. A wolf-dog sniffs at you, lifts his snout to the moon and howls. Four trickles of water ignore you in their constant flow, facing the city hall. The clock of the Audiencia, under restoration, does not give the time. Almost hidden and in shadow is the church where the girl Leonor and the poet were married. The *mesones* are closed by now. Someone's hurried footsteps fall in quick rhythym of the paving stones. The moon, in the geometrical centre of the Plaza, seems to feed the dreams of the loiterers in it.

Machado travelled to Laguna Negra and composed *La tierra de Alvargonzález*. He went to a rendezvous there, not only with the Laguna, but also with the cliffs on the canyon of the río Lobos, tributary to the Ucero.

"We took the wide Burgos highway, leaving the road to Osma on our left, bordered with poplars that had begun to turn gold with autumn. Soria was left behind us, among grey hills and bare ridges. The Duero forms a wide curve around Soria, like that of a crossbow. We were moving in the direction of the arrow."

Cidones, at 17 km. from the capital. A rock bastion guards our route. The town, at this hour of the morning, seems deserted. Chickens lord it in the Plaza Mayor, next the church, where birds sing, and the fountain murmurs, constructed in 1913 by the Philanthropic Society of Sons of Cidones, founded at Buenos Aires: the exile, always nostalgic for his childhood. The air smells clean, and it seems as if past the rock there were only vacant space. The inn is modern, where old men play at cards. Like a framed poem of Machado.

The Laguna Negra.

Next, Vinuesa, at 1107 metres altitude. In Vinuesa the crow caws, the cowbells tinkle, the roofs rise stepped in a clustered huddle, with lordly poplars casting shadows on them. The houses are robust, the streets clean and well laid out. It seems a fortress of stone. We take the Calle Ramos Calonge and follow it to the end, where the fields and hills gladden our eyes and the odour of a far-off cooking fire arrives on the wind. Plazas: summer nights with barefoot dancing on the coals at San Pedro Manrique. And Covaleda, 41 kilometres from Soria. Laguna Negra, at 1800 metres altitude. Pine and beech groves. Wolves used to come down to the water to drink. Now excursionists and tourists seek dreams and legends in the nights of the full moon. Baroja says: "The Laguna Negra seems a round blot of ink on a white paper." He was speaking of the snow. Now the stone organs point at a blue sky. The ferns rest in carpets, from which the vertical pines shoot up. The path (how many footsteps wore it) winds between dead trunks which open the skeleton of their bony fingers, long and twisted, to the earth that imprisons them. Here, silence speaks. There are two Lagunas Negras, two Black Lagoons: that of Machado and Baroja, of the winter; and that which may be seen under the sun of late spring or early autumn: this is a peaceable, soft, green, almost intimate ovaloid pool watched over by the peaks, jealous guardians of its seclusion. Light, climate, solitude, even tourism all metamorphose this place. The poet elects the winter, the tourist the summer. And from Burgo de Osma —the Uxama of the Celtiberians, where the 12th century Gothic cathedral conserves a retable by Juan de Juni and an old pendulum clock "with display of hours, minutes, seconds, days, and mooons, with sectors and sounds for twelve toccatas"— some twenty kilometres to the north bring us to the natural park of Río Lobos. There the Knights Templars evoke the age of chivalry. Men and forests: they sought the unknown. The animals fled from their approach. Eagles and vultures soared overhead. Rocks like castles of protohistoric ages. They cleared a meadow by the mountain, and built a shrine. Escorted by birds, lizards, butterflies. The birds squawk for pity. At three in the afternoon, with the Sun still strong, one renounces the written word in this solitude: poetry and art are but pallid images of what one sees. Guardians of the 12th-century shrine, four elms with their branches intertwined, with branches bare and trunks cracked, caressed only by the eagles.

Let us now leave Soria, though not Castilla, and take the road to Segovia. Passing Cerezo de Abajo we take the turnoff to Riaza. The highway parallels the edge of the Duero basin. And we stop, as Machado did, at Pedraza de la Sierra, where the houses perpetuate the image of the past. The benches built against the walls between the doorways are like mirrors set for people to appear in the street, to see, speak and feel. The plaza, or the bar that gives on to the plaza, with its heavy wooden counter, casts a spell. We ascend the slope of the Calle Real to the landscape painted by Zuloaga. Remains of town walls. Roads of sand. Barking dogs. The flight of the crows follows the undulations of the land. And low in the sky, over the blue silhouette of the Sierra, the great disc of a satin-coloured moon. Pedraza is settled like an eagle's nest on its rock. On its vertex in the castle that belong to the Constable of Castilla, don Pedro Fernández de Velasco. The odour of roast lamb drifts through the colonnades of the Plaza. Nowadays an excellent and modern inn lodges the traveller, who reads by night:

"It was afternoon, when the land flees from the Sun; and to the astonishment of the planet, as a beloved globe the beautiful moon appeared, beloved of the poet."

We arrive at Segovia. The journey has left us memories of roads, of towns and people. "In these old cities of Castilla, saturated in tradition, with a Gothic cathedral and

Plaza of Pedraza.

twenty Romanesque churches, where there is hardly a corner without its legend or a house without a coat of arms, beauty nevertheless always resides in —take heed, brother poets!— the living present, that which is not written nor can ever be written in stone: from the children who play in the streets —village children, twice childish— and the swallows that swoop around the towers, to the grass in the plazas and the moss on the roofs."

Segovia was the last, impassioned life of the poet. One day in the summer of 1928, in the old hotel Comercio, he met Guiomar. They ate at his restaurant, and walked to the Alcázar, down the Calle Daoíz on a night of full moon. The Alcázar. How many days, and evenings, would he not return here, in the absence of Guiomar?

"Autumn with two rivers has gilded the circuit of the giant sentinel of stone and light, towered prodigy modelled against the spotless blue."

For the Institute where Machado imparted classes, to the Alcázar, in an easy walk, we may cross the vertebral column that has formed Segovia. We descend to the Calle Ochoa Ondátegui, stopping before the church of San Justo, closed these many years, but now the scene of select musical concerts. Machado did not see the 12th-century Romanesque paintings that cover its apse and vault; but he did see, as we also may, the tower, and knew of the Cristo de los Gascones, drawn in silence by gentlemen of the city in the frequent rain of Holy Week. By narrow stairs we descend —on the right is the cemetery, facing the walls, and in the background the bare rock that now shelters the Parador— to the wondrous structure of the Aqueduct, 29 metres high here at the Azoguejo, 167 arches in all. Between these granite pillars united by arches to a length of 728 metres, Roman legions have passed, and Arab warriors; Visigothic legislators, converted Jews, Christian knights, Flemish merchants. People from all over the world pass under its arches today. People who then congregate to eat in the city's *mesones,* the most famous of them being Cándido. A special pleasure is the small dining room whose windows look out on the Roman arches. The walls are crowded with photos and autographs of celebrities who have eaten here. One table, for example, has a marked American connotation with photos of Hemingway and several Roosevelts above it.

We climb the steep Calle Real toward the Plaza. Resting in front of the Teatro Cervantes, we can see beneath us the Romanesque jewel of San Millán, and on the distant mountain horizon, the ridge known as La Mujer Muerta. We stop again at the Casa de los Picos: the façade of large ashlars shaped in diamond points tempts us to visit the interior patio, and remember that on 6 April 1922 —it was then the Círculo Mercantil— Machado gave a lecture here on Russian literature. And a few metres more bring us to two plazas united by history and beauty: those of San Martín and Medina del Campo. In its centre Juan Bravo proudly harangues his Comuneros, inciting us to rest on the pleasant steps, to shelter ourselves in the porticos of the church whose sculptures serve as columns, or to seek refuge in the tower of the Lozoyas. But time presses. Segovia is one of the most medieval cities of Spain. Of thirty Romanesque churches that were, sixteen remain. And if we wish to drink our fill of the art on view, yet we cannot neglect another side of it, that is to walk amid the silence of its alleys at night. Now we have arrived at the Plaza Mayor, dominated by the "great lady of cathedrals", the last great work of Spanish Gothic, designed by Juan Gil de Hontañón, and containing paintings by Morales, Berruguete, Van Eyck, Valdés Leal, etc. By the Calle Daoíz or the Calle Velarde we may descend toward the Alcázar. Between these streets winds the narrow alley of Desamparados, where Machado lived at N.º 11 (now 13). We may stop at night before the iron grille through which we glimpse the courtyard. As if the poet were still working, reading. The bells of the Cathethedral and of nearby San Esteban —a tower whose beauty is beyond adjectives— ring the hours. The cold deepens. The city rests.

Sleepless ourselves, we may continue to the Alcázar. No matter that it is closed. We can see the façade, the gardens. From the parapet we seek out the lights of Zamarramala, or the stars twinkling between the towers. Some water channel gurgles in the silence. We recite:

"O land ungrateful and strong, my country! Castilla, thy decrepit cities! The sour melancholy that peoples thy shadowy solitudes! Castile, manly sunburnt land; Castilla of the contempt for Fate, Castilla of pain and war; immortal land, Castilla of death!"

Dawn is approaching. Let us skirt, next to the walls, the northern edge of the upper city. As far as Fuencisla. We pass arches and convents. In March of 1574, Teresa de Jesús and Juan de la Cruz arrived at Segovia, to found here one of many monasteries. We seek the Templar church of Vera Cruz near San Marcos, whose single nave is curiously disposed in an oval, round a stone table where a Vigil of Arms initiated knights to the Order.

Finally, we leave the city to visit one of its most beautiful suburbs: that of San Lorenzo, whose church features the only brick tower in Segovia, and which is the geometric centre of an octagonal plaza, sagely reconstructed, that still smells of ancient trades, chiefly baking. It also recalls one of its most illustrious inhabitants, the Dominican Domingo Soto. San Lorenzo is lost in the mist of a valley watered by the sluggish stream of the Eresma; the gardens being ever more devoured by development. "Today I walked through the outskirts of Segovia, the groves along the Eresma, San Marcos, La Fuencisla, the Camino Nuevo. I hope the storks will soon arrive: an unmistakeable sign that winter is almost gone", the poet writes to Guiomar. And then: "And I dreamt we were together in Segovia, walking by night in the cloisters of El Parral. There we found don Miguel de Unamuno dressed as a friar, and singing the Marseillaise."

A city of dreams, of legend. How many tears in history have fallen on its stones, its convents, its Jewries! We take the train. Through the windows there enters an aroma of firewood burning far off. The valleys climb through pine woods toward the peaks of Navacerrada, gilded by the sun of the early morning, or turned violet by the sunset under a rising moon. Between tunnels the train winds along the rails with their hundred years of history. Its lurching makes it difficult for the traveller, Machado, you, me, to read the book in our hands. The number of stops seems infinite, their duration eternal. Cows graze on the blue skirts of the Sierra. The wheat fields are turning brown. The great tower of the Cathedral, which bids greeting or farewell to the traveller in the burnt land where the city is set, recedes from view. Time seems not to run anymore. Castilla lies behind us.

"The train devours, devours, daylight and rails. The brush passes in shadow; up rushes the air of Guadarrama... The air of the storm breaks the iris, and the mountain in planetary sadness. Sun and bells in the old tower.» The rocks in Soria, in Segovia, seem still to be dreaming. Every man traveller in Castilla, cannot help but be a man in some wise poet. Or as says Mairena: «It is in the solitude of the land that Man leaves his mirrors behind."

ROADS AND ABODES
OF TERESA SÁNCHEZ

by

JOSÉ JIMÉNEZ LOZANO

SANTA TERESA DE JESÚS
(Ávila, 1515-Alba de Tormes, 1582)

When Teresa de Cepeda y Ahumada was born in 1515, it was 22 years since the Jews had been expelled from Spain; and when she died in 1582, there remained only 18 years until the expulsion of the moriscos. Her life took place, then, exactly in the period of time in which Spanish society was becoming closed and monolithic in the political, racial, cultural and religious aspects; and she was deeply involved in this process. Teresa was a descendant of converted Jews: "mean cattle and generation of endless affront", in the words of Fray Luis de León, another of them. A restless and literate woman in a world and church of men, among whom she had to play up her feminine ignorance, we see her living her interior religion amid a Christianity of superficial ceremony.

The life and writings of Teresa —brought to the altars in 1614, and declared Patroness of Spain, not without acrid polemic, 45 years after her death, by a society and Christendom that had tried to crush her and her followers— are seen to possess a double dimension. A dialectical dimension in the face of a hostile reality, against which she defended herself by various or subtle ironies; sometimes swimming with the current, adopting stereotypes and attitudes as if she believed in them; sometimes, when necessary, confronting persons and deeds. And another profounder dimension: that of interior or mystical life, the radical experience of the spirit where "there seemed not to be a world", expressed in a literary style at once simple and colloquial and characterized by violent grammatical transgression, with which she speaks both of "the unspeakable" and of daily reality.

This is indeed what she does in all her books: the Libro de mi vida *(Salamanca, 1588),* Camino de perfección *(Évora, 1583),* Las fundaciones *(Brussels, 1610),* Las moradas, o castillo interior *(Salamanca, 1588),* Relaciones, o mercedes, o cuentas de conciencia *(Salamanca, 1588), real writer's notes, and several other small books. And her superb* Epistolario *(Madrid, 1658), comprising almost five hundred letters in the later editions, full of lucidity, psychological penetration and charm.*

Teresa de Ávila was declared a Doctor of the Church in 1970.

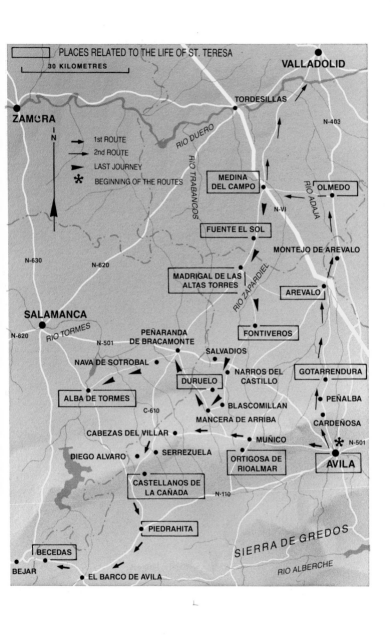

PLACES RELATED TO THE LIFE OF ST. TERESA

30 KILOMETRES

VALLADOLID

TORDESILLAS

ZAMORA

RIO DUERO

RIO TRABANCOS

N-403

N
↑

→ 1st ROUTE
→ 2nd ROUTE
▸ LAST JOURNEY
✳ BEGINNING OF THE ROUTES

MEDINA DEL CAMPO

OLMEDO

RIO ADAJA

N-VI

FUENTE EL SOL

MONTEJO DE AREVALO

N-630

N-620

MADRIGAL DE LAS ALTAS TORRES

RIO ZAPARDIEL

AREVALO

SALAMANCA

FONTIVEROS

N-620

RIO TORMES

N-501

PEÑARANDA DE BRACAMONTE

SALVADIOS

NAVA DE SOTROBAL

DURUELO

NARROS DEL CASTILLO

GOTARRENDURA

PEÑALBA

ALBA DE TORMES

BLASCOMILLAN

C-610

MANCERA DE ARRIBA

CARDEÑOSA

CABEZAS DEL VILLAR

MUÑICO

DIEGO ALVARO

SERREZUELA

ORTIGOSA DE RIOALMAR

AVILA

N-501

CASTELLANOS DE LA CAÑADA

N-110

PIEDRAHITA

SIERRA DE GREDOS

BECEDAS

BEJAR

EL BARCO DE AVILA

RIO ALBERCHE

L

ROADS AND ABODES
OF TERESA SÁNCHEZ

I

Ávila, the acropolis

Ávila is almost like a "Bois de Boulogne" on the outskirts of Madrid, though a wood not of trees but of stones and dreams. It is visible from far off, situated on a height, at 1126 metres above sea level; the highest city in Spain, the country's acropolis so to speak. Also it has three unequivocal marks of identity: it is walled; the cold there in winter is extreme, and referred to with perverse pride; and it is the birthplace of Teresa. Ávila, icon and figure of the interior castle of Teresa is, no doubt, the highest and deepest symbol of her writings.

Teresa de Jesús was named Teresa de Cepeda y Ahumada, and would have been named Teresa Sánchez if her father, don Alonso, had not changed the surname of the grandfather: the merchant Juan Sánchez, a converted Jew who had been "reconciled" by the Inquisition and obliged to wear the *sambenito* or penitential robe for some time. To put ground between him and this memory, the merchant moved to Ávila with his family, here opening a mercer's shop in the Calle de Andrín: then as now the principal street of the city, now bearing the name of Reyes Católicos, and which had been the Cardo Maximus of the Roman town. This was the axis of civic life in the Middle Ages: the Cathedral, the Market, the main Plaza were all on or near it. Today the Plaza is the site of the City Hall and the Friday market.

Precisely across from the City Hall stands the church in which Teresa was baptised, and where her parents are buried, though their tomb is not marked. And a few steps away, we find the house where she was born, now a church and convent of discalced Carmelite friars; in the space of the alcove where, according to tradition, she was born, there is a chapel in a gilded and overworked Baroque style, somewhat sad. To console himself the visitor, looking from the same church, may rest his eyes on a small almost romantic garden, all that remains of the garden of the house where Teresa and her brother Rodrigo devoured books about the lives of the saints: the literature of heroes and adventures of those days, inspiring in them a desire to go to Africa and be martyred by the Moors. But "the moors" were in reality there a few paces from the house, if they had left by the gate in the city wall, and, from the balcony or terrace of the Paseo del Rastro, had looked down on the little houses of tapia or adobe, perhaps whitewashed with their mouldings of brick and painting of indigo, and a glazed tile above the door, for here there was still a Moorish quarter. A few years earlier, there would also have been Jews, this time much closer to her house, to be reached by simply turning right and going down the Calle de Telares to the Puerta de Mala Dicha or Mala Ventura, in the most

Ávila.

sombre corner of the city. But she and Rodrigo went out of the city toward the río Adaja by the gate of the same name until, on the old Roman bridge still there, they were brought back to reality by a gentleman, an uncle of theirs, who made them return home to a world that is not in books or dreams nor in the interior of the soul. For this very reason the world seemed to have little weight for Teresa, and reality for her had a strong admixture of dream.

Later she passed through all the illusions and enthusiasms, but also the sufferings, of adolescence, including falling in love, and internment in a severe convent school, Nuestra Señora de Gracia, whence she had to be taken out by her father. In those days, she confessed in the Dominican convent of Santo Tomás, where the confessional she used may still be viewed. Also in this church, a work of melancholy Renaissance beauty awaits the visitor: the sepulchre of the prince don Juan, son of the Catholic Kings, who died "of love", according to popular rumour and the opinion of his physicians too, reading the "divine Aristotle" to reconcile himself to death at such an early age. Everyone in those days seemed preoccupied with the fragility of human life, a life which Teresa for some time already had esteemed as "nothing", so that on All Sous Day of 1535, she ran away from her father's house to the monastery of Encarnación outside the city, to become a nun. And so she did; and here invented her reforms, and faced the problems bringing them into practice, and became prioress. Here she became acquainted with St. John of the Cross, for whom she prepared a cell in the convent garden, a place which, it was said, had been a cemetery for Jewish heretics, and in which had been buried Moshé de León, author of *Zohar* or the *Libro de Esplendor,* a key text of Jewish mysticism.

When the reform of the Order began, Teresa was also

to invent a "habitat" or room —the Carmelite cell— which epitomizes her spirit and her esthetic complicity with the tranquil and profound spaces of Spinoza and Port-Royal, or with the Cistercian or Islamic simplicity and the simple dwellings of the poor: a whitewashed room, with ceiling of dark wood and red brick floor; perhaps a table or a single rush chair, a cot for a bed, a hempen mat, a water jug and washbasin, perhaps a book on a shelf; and the empty space inhabited by light entering through a window perforated in thick walls, partner to shade and silence. Beauty here resides in what is absent. As in the verse of Rimbaud, but in an even more profound way: "Beauty is always absent".. Reality cannot sustain itself here, a beauty flashes in like lightning.

In the monastery of Encarnación, the visitor may view Teresa's own cell, and many other rooms and mementos; similarly in the convent of San José, the first foundation of Discalced Carmelites if there is one, we may see the rooms El Cohombro and Los Candiles, real triumphs of the the esthetic of the bare and minuscule. But the entire city is saturated with her memory and that of her times; and we cannot neglect to visit the Cathedral, where she went for consolation on the death of her mother; and there, of course, remember Tomás Luis de Victoria, who was a choirboy there; or, in the ambulatory see the statue of Bishop Tostado eternally reading in his book of alabaster like Dante in Ravena, and admire the crystal walls broken by the shock wave of the Lisbon earthquake of 1755. But by that time Teresa had long since constructed in the air her mansion of diamond and incorruptible crystal, her "enchanted castle", as she referred to her book *Las moradas* in the edition of 1610.

To this end she worked; to this end she worried and travelled the roads from inn to inn, stubbornly dealing with

Monastery of La Encarnación.

notables and bishops, undergoing heat and cold, seeking water or the shade of trees.

II

The roads

Teresa was no vagabond or globetrotter by nature, and travel for her was always a torture. Thinking of the road ahead and, above all, of the inns and hostelries awaiting her, she finds no more dreadful image for the portrayal of Hell than "living in an inn forever and ever, without end". And of one of the hostelries between Beas and Sevilla, she wrote: "I judged it better to get up and be on the road; better to suffer the weather in the fields than that awful bed."

The vehicle Teresa habitually used in her travels was a small covered cart: "this was always our manner of travelling"; but she sometimes went by carriage, often on a mule or donkey. And on her last journey, between Medina del Campo and Alba, she travelled in a coach, sent to her by the Duchess of Alba. But she was half dead by then.

The Teresian itinerary outside Ávila has two main branches: one relating to travels of her younger years; and another seeking out the memories of her foundations, which were the motive for her journeys. These took her to Toledo and even to Andalucía, but it was the roads of Castilla that she crossed and recrossed most constantly.

III

The three Castilian routes

Teresa's first journey, apart from her visits to the house at Gotarrendura in winter, or to the house of her maternal grandparents at Olmedo, was in 1533 at eighteen years of age, some five leagues out of Ávila: to the house of her uncle, Pedro Sánchez de Cepeda, in Ortigosa de Rioalmar. There she went to rest from an attack of nervous exhaustion, produced by the severe discipline at the convent of Nuestra Señora de Gracia.

Don Pedro Sánchez de Cepeda, a melancholy widower, lived in a large house, still known in the village as "El Palacio", with a round-arched doorway, now half filled in, surmounted by an escutcheon featuring a lion and an eagle: a coat of arms more or less invented, like many others of that period, to promote the prestige of the family. The building faces east, toward a hill covered with oaks: the "Costalpié", around whose base there is a grove of trees. And the church is a few paces away. Here Teresa again the sensation that "everything in the world was but nothing", and this feeling of vacuity of the world must have echoed powerfully amid this rural solitude.

The traveller who nowadays leaves Ávila may follow practically the same route she did, and contemplate the same austere, calm landscape: great rocks of grey granite, holm-oaks, cistus; small groves of poplars. Leaving the city by the bridge over the Adaja and taking the Salamanca road, we pass the Cuatro Postes, an old roadside shrine from which there is a panoramic view of the city, spreading down the hillside from the Cathedral to the river, as in an old engraving. Soon we find a turnoff to the left, towards Muñico, thirty kilometres away. From this village another road takes us over the remaining four kilometres to Ortigosa; and if the traveller, instead of entering the village, follows the highway beside the poplar grove, soon he will find himself by the church and the house of the Cepedas.

On that occasion, Teresa spent only a few days here, and from here went to Castellanos de la Cañada, a small hamlet and land holding where her sister María lived, married to don Martín de Guzmán, a country hidalgo. It is not far. Returning to Muñico, we continue to Cabezas de Villar, then take the higway from Peñaranda to Piedrahíta in the direction of Piedrahíta. Having passed, on our left, San Miguel de Serrezuela, we shall do well to slow down in order to notice a little village to the right of the road, Diegoálvaro. Just past this village the traveller will see, to the left of the road, a typical entrance wall of a country estate, before which a small sign reads: "Castellanos". And the visitor may pass this entryway to the very gateway of a private property: "Castellanos de la Cañada". But even if he ventures through this second gate and arrives at the buildings in the oakwood, they will not show him anything. This memorial of Teresa, like that of "La Serna", another estate very near to Ávila, is in "private hands". What can we do about it?

Five years later, in the autumn of 1538, Teresa repeated this journey to Ortigosa and Castellanos de la Cañada. Ill again, she had to leave the Encarnación, on the way to Becedas. Her uncle Pedro offered her on this occasion "strong books", which were not of Chivalry or Romance but of prayer and inner life; among them was the *Tercer abecedario* of Osuna. Teresa devoured these books, and says that from then on she was most fond of reading. She continued her reading that winter in Castellanos de la Cañada, and in mid-April set out for Becedas, to consult a healer.

In Piedrahíta, as she was a nun and travelled accompa-

nied by another, she was offered lodging at the convent of
her Order there and it is recorded that to nourish her in
her infirmity, they bought her a hen. Also worth a look in
Piedrahíta is the Palace of the Dukes of Alba, bringing to
mind Goya and the "enlightened" adventures of the duchess Cayetana who, it is said, is represented in Goya's *Ma-
jas.* Another memory may come to mind in the colonnades
of the Plaza Mayor: this is the romantic figure of don José
Somoza, a man astride the divide between the 18th and
19th centuries, a small-town Montaigne. From Piedrahíta
we proceed to Barco de Ávila, not far away; and from there,
leaving on our left the obscure castle of the Albas by the
Tormes, we pass between oaks and fruit trees, apples especially, to Becedes, which lies between a mountain and two
low hills called the Neila and the Gilbuena. It is a peac-
ful spot.

The church is atop the knoll. Behind it, in the street
that now bears the name of Teresa, some Franciscan nuns
maintain a chapel on the site of the old inn where Teresa
stayed three months; they will be glad to show it to the
visitor, upon request made at the door of the school run
by the nuns. And descending this street, there is a quiet,
neglected park with a fountain which also bears Teresa's
name, because of a tradition that she was wont to fetch
water there. Here we may remember the episode of the
village priest, bewitched by a lady-friend, who had hung a
little idol around his neck, until one day the cleric gave
the amulet to Teresa and she threw in in the river, which
may well have been the little stream that runs near the
fountain. And if we have the same sort of intuition Unamuno had on contemplating these little vegetable gardens
with their cabbage, apples and walnuts, we may also see in
them "what is the interior garden of the soul, a walled garden with its humble well", one of the loveliest metaphors
in Teresa's writings.

IV

Second route

Our second route evokes Teresa as a foundress of convents, and a writer; it lies to the north of Ávila. First we proceed some fifty kilometres to Arévalo. Again we leave Ávila by the bridge over the Adaja and the Salamanca highway, but now we take a turnoff to the right, which leads to Cardeñosa, Peñalba and Gotarrendura. In the last mentioned village was the hacienda of Teresa's maternal grandparents, Juan de Ahumada and Teresa de las Cuevas; later she was in the house of her parents in the winter, where several of her brothers were born, and her mother died. There still remains the old dovecote with its wooden niches, which Teresa always remembered.

Inquiry at any house will lead the visitor to someone who might show him these sights, but it is not certain that he would do so. The family that owned the building donated it to the Pope in 1982, and it is unavoidable to reflect on a certain irony in this, that now the house of Teresa's grandparents is the property of the Papal nunciature; for among the hardest of Teresa's struggles were those with the Papal Nuncios. She described one of them as "Methuselah", perhaps because he had continued living too long for her liking.

At Arévalo, where Teresa was at least twice, she once arrived on the night of 13 August 1567, on the way to Medina del Campo, and stayed in a house or lodging in the Plaza de la Villa, next to the church of Santa María, now under restoration. It is one of the most evocative and lovely plazas in Spain. In its church of San Martín, with two doors, one of them with a Romanesque portico, and two admirable towers, one of which has the look of a minaret, there occurred, during a period in the Middle Ages, the curious circumstance of both Christian and Islamic services being held in the same building. St. John of the Cross played in this plaza as a child, for he lived in a street nearby.

We take now the highway to Palacios Rubios, and turn off onto a small road (it is well to ask someone, for the road signs may be deficient). Here the visitor must go to some effort to see "La Lugareja", now fenced in as private land. The key may be requested from anyone met in the vicinity, for example in the houses grouped to the left as we arrive at the building. The church is a wonder of Romanesque-Cistercian-Mudéjar, a shady mosque, an oratory of bare brick and whitewash: without adornment, exactly to the traste of Bernard of Clairvaux.

Then we return to the town and, just as we pass before the portico of San Martín, we take a little street that leads us to the Madrid-Coruña highway, which we cross to proceed to Montejo de Arévalo; and from this little willage, following the signs toward Valladolid, come out on the Madrid-Gijón highway in the direction toward Olmedo.

From Arévalo, Teresa went to a nearby village, Fuente del Sol, to deal with the owner of the house at Medina that she and her nuns were to occupy, and then passed through Olmedo for a meeting with the Bishop of Ávila, who spent the summer here; but Teresa only spent a few hours in the town, and the traveller will also have to settle for a brief look at the town wall with its excellent Mudéjar gates, in front of which the highway passes.

Teresa moved so quickly that by midnight of the same day, the 14th, she had arrived at Medina del Campo. She entered the town unnoticed, as a fiesta with bullrunning was in progress. Pride of place among the town's Teresian monuments of course belongs to the convent of Discalced Carmelites that she founded here. In it is the tomb of the enigmatical mother of St. John of the Cross, Catalina Álvarez. Nobody in the town has come forward to save the house of the Yepes. The visitor, after seeing the church of the Carmelite convent, where Juan de la Cruz preached, may contemplate other memories: the fair of Medina del Campo, so famous throughout the Middle Ages; the death here of Isabella I; or Cesar Borgia, Duke of Valentinois, escaping one night from the castle of La Mota, climbing down a rope from the tower, with a veil to cover his face, for it was made hideous with bubos, the result of syphilis. St. John of the Cross consoled many patients of this disease when he worked at the Hospital de las Bubas in this same town.

Valladolid is less than an hour away. In the convent of Discalced Carmelites of this city, there is kept one of the manuscripts of the *Camino de perfección;* also there are admirable rooms such as the refectory. But none of this may be visited, so that Valladolid is excluded from our route, as are the convents of Soria, Segovia, Palencia, Burgos and Salamanca, though the foundings of these were episodes so wonderfully described by Teresa.

V

The last journey

From Medina del Campo, on the highway to Peñaranda, we proceed 26 kilometres to reach Madrigal de las Altas Torres. In this town there is a monument only indirectly related to Teresa, but with a profound and intense flavour of her time. This is the convent of Augustinian nuns, formerly the palace of don Juan II; to which convent belonged doña María Briceño, who had been Teresa's teacher at the school of Santa María de Gracia. Here there is an old Court salon, and another salon of Ambassadors, now the refectory; both of them noble rooms; also there is a patio and a gilded hall, splendid also, but closed to the public. A visitor here was Fray Luis de León, who died in this town and was such an ardent admirer of Teresa's writings, seeking a cure for his "melancholies and passions of the heart".

A few metres outside the Mudéjar gate in the city wall in the direction of Arévalo, a turnoff on the left leads to Fontiveros. Here, in the superb church of somewhat synagogal aspect, is the tomb of Gonzalo de Yepes, father of San Juan de la Cruz, and that of his brother Luis, who died of hunger. And in the Calle de Cantiveros, the old Barrio Nuevo, the humble house of Yepes was converted to a church in the 17th century. A project for maintenance and restoration of these buildings is now under way.

From Fontiveros, in the direction of Salvadiós, by way of Narros del Castillo, we reach Blascomillán; and continuing between rolling hills where wheat or sunflowers alternate with oak or poplar trees, arrive at Duruelo. When Teresa first came here, she lost her way and had some problem in finding the place: "I still remember how tired we were of tramping this way and that." She arrived shortly before nightfall. It was a house of "too little cleanliness", and she did not care to sleep in it; but in any case the smallness and poorness of the house were to her taste: "It had a reasonable doorway and a chamber communicating with its loft, and a kitchen. This was the building for our monastery», the first foundation of Discalced Friars. And here arrived Juan de la Cruz, we might say as architect, to remodel and accomodate it to the bare Carmelite esthetic. To Teresa the result seemd a marvel: "The loft served as choir, for it was raised and suitable for chanting of the hours; but you had to come down a great flight of stairs to enter and hear Mass. In the two corners toward the church, there were two little rooms, so low of ceiling you could only sit or lie in them; full of hay (for the place was cold) with two little windows giving on the altar and two stones for head-boards."

In the 17th century a convent was built here, which had to be abandoned in the last century; nowadays there is a small building which serves as a chapel. It has great charm on account of its small dimensions, with its little belfry containing a single small bell. The visitor sees it immediately he enters the village and the street widens to the left of the road. There is another convent of Discalced Carmelites at Duruelo, but of more recent foundation. Retracing our footsteps, about two hundred metres outside the town, on the left side of the road by which we arrived, there is a little fountain out of which comes a bare trickle of water; but it is very closely tied to the memory of Juan de la Cruz. This is the "crystalline fountain" of his *Cántico,* the water that Teresa always viewed "with more perception" than others did.

And finally we go to Alba de Tormes. Returning to Blascomillán by way of Mancera de Arriba, almost reaching Peñaranda, and then pasing through Nava de Sotrobal. Teresa made her last journey along other roads, from Medina del Campo, and arrived at Alba exhausted, on 20 September 1582, saying to the nuns: "How tired I am; how many years since I went to sleep so early!" She died on the 4th of October, which in that year was the 15th, due to the reform of the calendar. Alba offers the visitor some singular sights such as the Romanesque Apostolate around the Judgement at the church of San Juan, reminiscent of the great art of Moissac. But the entire town is full of memories of Teresa. Even the río Tormes, running under the medieval bridge of twenty-two arches which she could see from her cell. There is the castle of the Dukes of Alba, of which only the keep remains, with frescos of the battle of Mühlberg, where Teresa had seen so much ornament and luxury it made her head spin. But she is above all remembered in the convent where she died: a veritable reliquary of Teresiana, though perhaps it is too rich a celebration of her memory for her own tastes; and to rediscover the real Teresa, the reader must return to the "interior life" portrayed in her *Castillo* or *Morada,* filled «high and low and on either side, with pretty gardens and fountains, labyrinths and delightful things». This is the end of our road.

CATALUNYA/CATALUÑA

ROUTE OF JOAN MARAGALL

by

JOSÉ MARÍA GIRONELLA

JOAN MARAGALL
(Barcelona, 1860-1911)

The personality of Joan Maragall is inimitable, as much in his facet as translator as in that of essayist, journalist and, above all, poet. According to a popular saying, Catalunya, thanks to Joan Maragall, "has reached the stars". Maragall, who figures in the Gallery of Illustrious Catalans, is one of the patriarchs of Catalan letters, together with Jacint Verdaguer, Josep Plà, Eugenio d'Ors, Carles Riba and others.

Joan Maragall i Gorina was born in Barcelona on 10 October 1860. The same house he was born in was his hime until 1875; that is, for the first fifteen years of his existence. His career though productive was short; he died, also in Barcelona, at the age of 51.

A bilingual writer, in Castilian prose he was the equal of the best figures of his time; and as a poet in Catalan he contributed to the renaissance of Catalan literature. Among his compositions some of the most notable are La vaca cega *(1893), one of the masterpieces of Catalan poetry, and* Cant espiritual, *which appeared in the collection of lyrics* Seqüencies *(1911). Also in this collection there appeared the third and last part of* El comte Arnau, *his most ambitious poem.*

The impression that Maragall produced on Azorín was that of "a man who is in ecstasy in the face of things. Not a man who tries to explain things to himself; a man however who admires the spectacle of the world and puts his spirit effusively in communication with it".

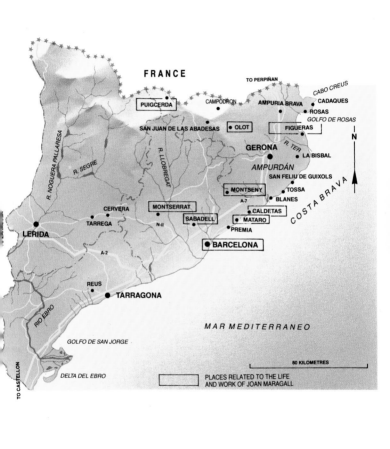

FRANCE

TO PERPIÑAN

CABO CREUS

PUIGCERDA

CAMPODRON

AMPURIA BRAVA

CADAQUES

ROSAS

GOLFO DE ROSAS

SAN JUAN DE LAS ABADESAS

OLOT

FIGUERAS

GERONA

R. TER

LA BISBAL

AMPURDÁN

SAN FELIU DE GUIXOLS

R. SEGRE

R. NOGUERA PALLARESA

R. LLOBREGAT

MONTSENY

TOSSA

A-7

BLANES

CERVERA

MONTSERRAT

CALDETAS

COSTA BRAVA

TARREGA

N-II

SABADELL

MATARO

LERIDA

PREMIA

A-2

BARCELONA

REUS

TARRAGONA

RIO EBRO

MAR MEDITERRANEO

GOLFO DE SAN JORGE

80 KILOMETRES

TO CASTELLON

DELTA DEL EBRO

PLACES RELATED TO THE LIFE
AND WORK OF JOAN MARAGALL

ROUTE OF JOAN MARAGALL

Since we are to travel the ways of Joan Maragall, and accompany him on his itinerary through the cities and countryside that nourished his mind and heart, let us begin in Barcelona, where he was born at Calle Jaime Giralt, number 14, first floor. This house is presently almost abandoned, although the structure still retains a certain lordly appearance. Here, surprisingly, there is no plaque commemorative of his birth, though there is one on the house where he died. It seems that in Catalonia —other examples might be found— we give more importance to the place of death than to that of birth.

When Joan Maragall was fifteen, his father, owner of a textile factory at Sabadell, in the days of the economic boom purchased a house at number 15 of the Calle Trafalgar, on the corner with Urquinaona. Later, the family moved to the Calle Consejo de Ciento, number 344. Yet later, from 1895, they resided in Paseo de Gracia, number 564, second floor. Finally, Joan Maragall resided and died in the Calle Alfonso XII, N.º 79, a house which has been conserved intact and, in fact, converted to a museum, for here we may see the rooms in which the poet wrote, and met his friends in many fruitful conversations.

Few alterations have been made in the house, where a sister of the poet, 90 years of age, still lives, and kindly attends to the inquiries of curious visitors. Thanks to the loving care of our poet's family, we may still view, in this museum-house, the library of the poet, the dining room, the piano on which Joan Maragall played splendidly (he also sang well, with a firm voice), the archive and a multitude of souvenirs and mementos, awards, personal effects such as his pocket watch and pipe, with its vague odour of tobacco still about it. On the walls are numerous photographs of Maragall, his family his friends, and of personalities he admired. Few paintings of any value, which is somewhat of a surprise. But although there is no evidence of his interest in painting, there is plenty that evokes his passion for music. Also on display are a series of manuscript versions of his most inspired works, many written in school notebooks, some in pencil, some in pen and ink.

Great impact is caused by a wooden triptych, which being opened reveals a photograph of the poet in his coffin. Resting in it, Joan Maragall is seen in the habit of a Franciscan friar. This photograph is wrapped in an air of sanctity. The triptych might be the resume of his life. A scale of values that he respected since childhood, balanced between love, friendship and duty. The theme of friendship is a constant factor in his work and in his life.

We see period furniture, curtains, divans, chairs upholstered in red plush, rich carpets, the desk at which he worked so many years. In contrast to the tortured Dostoevsky, upon whose desk in Leningrad the visitor may see the little box of poison he kept ready to hand, the desk of Maragall always featured a modest wooden crucifix, carved probably in some workshop at San Hilario Sacalm, a municipality of the Selva near the Guillerías. Visitors, always at pre-arranged hours, enter the house-museum of Maragall as if entering a sanctuary. Néstor Luján wrote that, on crossing the threshold, he felt an emotion like that he felt on entering the house at Bonn, where Beethoven was born.

At the age of seven, while still living in the Calle Jaime Giralt, Joan Maragall began his primary studies at the school of "señor Nicolau" in the Calle Calders. His *bachillerato,* according to the archives, he began and finished at the Instituto de San Isidoro, together with studies of piano, English and German. Joan Maragall was the last of four children of José Maragall, and the only male.

Between the ages of 14 and 18 (1874-1878) he spent the worst years of his life. His father was determined to channel Joan into the textile business. Joan resisted, finally obtaining permission to begin studying Law at the University of Barcelona, where he finished in 1884. He then began his literary dabblings, mostly verse, which appeared in minority publications, as he was still a complete unknown.

At the age of thirteen, he married doña Clara Noble. A fecund marriage: thirteen children, the first five being girls, with two sets of twins, and the rest boys. His attachment to the traditional conception of the family was total, as was his passion for poetry. After his marriage he lived a while with his wife in the Plaza Urquinaona, N.º 2, 1.º, 2.ª.

The career of Law did not much interest him and, according to contemporary accounts, the only client of his legal practice was his father. But his literary activity was already intense. He translated the *Werther* and the *Faust* of Goethe. He spent long evenings with his University friends and companions, at the Ateneo Barcelonés (Calle Canuda, 6), at the Liceo (Ramblas) and at the Café Suizo. On 7 November 1893 the famous bomb exploded in the Liceo; Maragall was present, in box N.º 7. with his wife, parents and various brothers. Fortunately all of them escaped safe and sound. However, being then a writer for the *Diario de Barcelona* (Brusi), he wrote several articles centred on the theme of human aggression. He also wrote *La vaca cega,* a poem considered immortal, which Unamuno translated into Castilian. According his family, he wrote it all at once —one might say "at one sitting", but it seems that he was standing up all the time; with the exception of the last two lines.

The family spent the summers at different spots in Cataluña. There is a plaque in the Calle Mayor, N.º 11, in San Juan de las Abadesas, marking where he spent the summer of 1898. This coincided with Spain's colonial disaster in America, which inspired several fervent patriotic articles, among them his well-known *Oda a España.*

Joan Maragall was an enthusiastic walker. On foot or on horseback he travelled many regions of Cataluña. Among his most frequented areas was Cerdaña —Puigcerdá is its capital, bordering on France— from which he visited the French towns of Cauterets and Pau. In Puigcerdá he stayed with his family at the Hotel Europa (where, years before, he had met his wife, a native of Jerez de la Frontera). Near the Hotel Europa there was once a commemorative plaque, which disappeared in the Civil War. However there is still a plaque on the main façade of the City Hall of Puigcerdá.

From 1902 to 1904, he spent the summers at Caldetas (Caldes d'Estrach), in the are of the Maresme. In this town, reached by way of Mataró, there still exists a bronze bust of the poet, at a place immemorially named "bosque de pinos" (pine woods). Maragall resided there in a tower in the Paseo de los Ingleses, now destroyed by a development of chalets. In Caldetas there were thermal springs and a casino. The thermal springs are still there, though abandoned, and the place of the casino is now occupied by the Hotel Colón.

Maragall returned ofthe to Caldetas. From here he would climb Montseny, from whose peak there is a tremendous view: Serralada with its 1707 metres of altitude and fertile vegetation. Maragall made frequent excursions to the Turó de l'Home, Matagall, where there is a fountain —Font d'en Vila— dedicated to the poet. By then he had been named President of the Ateneo Barcelonés, a post in which he took great pride. He won "Englantine" prizes in Floral Games and wrote *Elogi de la paraula,* one of his most inspired and original works.

In 1904 he spent the summer, as in other occasions, on the Costa Brava. The Costa Brava, then almost entirely unknown as a resort coast, took him to Blanes, San Feliu de Guixols, Lloret de Mar, Palamós, Rosas and the very frontier of France. We know that he covered much distance this way on foot or horseback, but there is no plaque or monument marking where he stayed. From this period date more translations of Goethe, Nietzsche, Novalis and Homer (this, directly from Latin).

In the Costa Brava the poetry of Maragall was read with enthusiasm by the people, and many of his verses became part of the popular repertoire.

Especially notable are the lyrics of the *sardana* of L'Empordá (Ampurdán), the homeland of Dalí, who was later to make an excellent drawing dedicated to the poet, and conserved in the Palacete Municipal de Montjuich. The lyrics of this sardana call up such a deep resonance of Catalan feeling that often, hen the first notes of it are played, the audience breaks into applause.

There were many visits to Olot in the province of Gerona, where he wrote numerous articles for *L'Avenç, Catalònia, La Renaixença* and *La Veu de Catalunya.* Olot was one of his favourite towns; and the town has responded by raising a monolith in his honour, at the place called La Fageda d'en Jordà (Beechwood of En Jordà), easily found, and which schoolchildren occasionally approach to kiss those austere stones pointing at the sky. It is not uncommon to find bunches of wild flowers at the base of the monolith. Olot especially inspired Maragall, as it has inspired a Pleiade of landscape painters, such as Urgell, Vayreda and others. The population of this fertile volcanic terrain maintains a traditional manufacture, that of religious imagery, exported to many places you would hardly suspect. I personally have seen them in Colombia, India and the Holy Land.

In 1909 Barcelona collided with the Semana Trágica (Tragic Week) of catastrophic social tumult. The patriotism of Joan Maragall showed itself once more in a series of articles in which he lays a great part of the blame on the Catalan bourgeoisie, of which he, of course, formed part. Joan Maragall was never a political man; he once refused a candidacy offered him in the Lliga Catalana party founded by Camó. At that time his principal friends were Cambó, Pijoán, Roura, Rubio y Lluch, the architect Gaudí and, above all, the bishop Torres y Bages. His admiration for Gaudí and for his portentous project of the Sagrada Familia, now a practically obligatory visit for every tourist who arrives in Barcelona, was unconditional. In an impassioned article entitled *En la Sagrada Familia,* we may read: "Observe now what is going on inside this circuit... there are trees within the temple, and birds in flight, and the tender green of the grass at this season; and children playing, men resting, women busy, and old men contemplating in the sun; there are poor people, the first thing that a temple needs... And what else is a church, if not a place where all is filled with meaning, from the stones and fire to the bread and wine and words?"

He stayed too at Monserrat. The monks of the "Sacred Mountain", heart of Cataluña and guardian of the Catalan identity, received him as an illustrious guest. The mountain and the monastery had always fascinated the poet. Excursiones into the surroundings —a geological miracle of venerable stones— suggested many poems. In memory of his

Church of the Sagrada Familia.

visit, of the Vespers, the Gregorian, the chants of Escola-
nía, there is today a monolith with his name in the so-
called Paseo de los Artistas. A place of unique grandeur
and peace. Here he began one day the writing of his classic *Cant espiritual.* At Montserrat there is also a bust of the
poet, work of the sculptor Federico Marés.

His poem *La vaca cega,* which was the occasion of a
lengthy correspondence between Maragall and Unamuno,
is also commemorated in Sabadell, in the plazoleta del Pe-
dregar, with a bust by Manolo Hugué. In 1904 Maragall
won the Flor Natural prize in the "Floral Games" of all
the recognitions and honours he received, gave him perhaps the most satisfaction.

In 1910 he published *Oda nova a Barcelona, Nausica,
Himnes homèrics, Notes autobiogràfiques.* In these notes, as if
with foreknowledge of his own death, he writes: "I am
married to the best of women, who loves me passionately.
I have twelve children fine and sound, my own house, fortune sufficient to maintain my family, a name honoured by
my fellow countrymen, a poet's glory and a spiritual health
which allows me not to yearn for the days when I was
twenty-five. On the contrary, just a minute ago I was re-
reading something I wrote in those days, and I give thanks
to God that it was his wish to convert that morally decrepit young creature into the man I feel myself to be
today."

At three in the morning on 20 December 1911, Joan
Maragall died in Barcelona, after receiving the Sacraments,
in N.º 79 of the Calle Alfonso XII, near the Plaza Molina.
Around him was all his extensive family. At his own request, he was shrouded in the habit of St. Francis of Assisi,
for whom he had always felt profound devotion. His last
words were: *Amunt, amunt...* (Arriba, arriba...).

He was buried in the cemetery of San Gervasio, in a
family pantheon which says briefly: *Joan Maragall i els seus*

Monistrol with Montserrat in background.

(Joan Maragall and his own). Each year on the second Sunday in February, the members of the Peña Soler and of Poesía Viva. The pantheon is always adorned with bunches of flowers.

His death was a shock throughout Cataluña. Many of the places where he rad resided or even visited decided to remember him in monuments, monoliths or street names. Among these, we may single out for mention the monument erected in Ampuria Brava, on the Gulf of Rosas, at the intersection of two principal avenues: a rectangular slab of stone, with the text of his poem *El pastor y la sirena*. On the reverse, an iron profile of the poet's face, with a strophe of the sardana *L'Empordà* (The Ampurdán), with his signature beneath.

THE AMPURDÁN:
THE CHALDEAN UNIVERSE
OF JOSEP PLÀ

by

MANUEL VÁZQUEZ MONTALBÁN

JOSEP PLÀ
(Palafrugell, 1897-Llofriú, 1981)

With his ample production as journalist, literary chronicler, writer of memoirs, biographer, Josep Plà is one of the major Peninsular writers of the 20th century. He may be said to be esentially a Catalan writer, though he used Castilian in much of his journalistic work. Journeys often form the raw material of his writings, travel being for him a pretext for his capacity of looking and of proposing ways of looking; without ever losing his fundamental cultural identity, which was that of a well-off peasant of the Ampurdán, who just happened to be a reader of Montaigne and Spinoza. Among his principal works we may mention: El quadern gris, Els pagessos, Cartes de lluny *(1928),* Carta d'Italia, Viatge a Catalunya *(1934),* De l'Ampordanet a Andorra, Vida de Manolo *(1928),* Cambò *(1928),* Homenots, Notes del capvespre, *and* El viatge s'acaba.

He has also published various books in Castilian: Historia de la segunda república española *(1940-41, four vols.);* Rusiñol y su tiempo *(1942);* Viaje en autobús *(1942);* La huida del tiempo *(1945);* Viaje a pie *(1949); and* Guía de la Costa Brava,

His complete works occupy forty volumes.

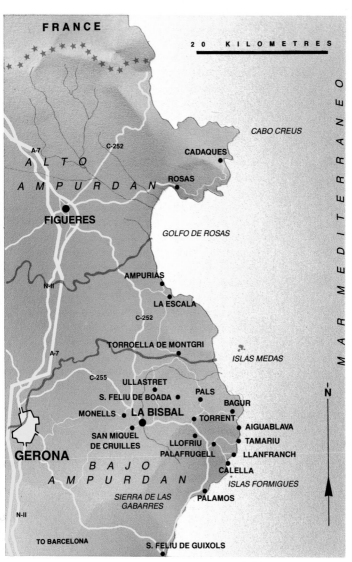

PLACES RELATED TO THE LIFE AND WORK OF JOSEP PLA

THE AMPURDÁN:
THE CHALDEAN UNIVERSE OF JOSEP PLÀ

The centre of the world (why not?) may well be in Llofriú, a small municipality of Palafrugell, in the region of Bajo Ampurdán (Baix Empordà, also popularly known as *Empordanet*). Here Josep Plà began his principal and universal voyages, starting from his old house, *mas Plà,* a noble old house, golden ochre in colour like most of the *masías* of the Ampurdán, with its ivy and its sundial that seems to lend a special stubborn slowness to the passage of time. Plà said that he had been born in a humanized landscape, where ploughed fields and groves of cork oaks and pines surround ridges where houses had clustered through the centuries, as if from these modest heights the people had intended to avoid the raids of turks or the threats of the Spaniards or the French. The towns are spaced at distances of a few kilometres and, until the tourist hordes arrived and, with them, the architectural corruption of the landscape, they preserved their airy isolation, with the Medas and Formigues islands sprinkled along the line of the sea, hardly an obstacle to conquerors and pirates, and which Plà's friends the fishermen used as a source of small fish,

sometimes so small as the gathering of rock clams, a black
diamond with the soul of rosy seas. Wherever he travelled,
Plà always kept his farmer's beret on, and his viewpoint of
the Ampurdanese, half farmer, half fisherman; it is even
possible to trace all his Catalan, Spanish or universal journeys from this starting point of Llofriú; or perhaps from a
circle only slightly wider, taking in Palafrugell and its coastal towns, especially Calella. There, in Calella, the fishermen "gave him the task of a man", letting him take a boat
down the Costa Brava as far as Tossa and Lloret de Mar.
In the ketchens of Llofriú he picked up his considerable
knowledge of cooking and time, in an age when there was
a season for the pea and another for the apple, when one
might still speak of spring fruit and summer fruit: before
the refrigerator disoriented the textures and the palate.
And in Calella, on the boats that calmly dot the silhouette
of the coast, Plà learned what he later wrote about seafood: squids, meagres, red sea scorpions and lobsters, survivors of the sea which Plà was as familiar with as if he
had descended with them to the coldest waters. From Llofriú his land routes began, and from Calella his routes by
boat: towards the north, Cabo Bagur and its coves, like an
obscure button at the beginning of the long beaches of
Pals; and towards the south, slow rowing: Cabo de San Sebastián, Tamariú, Llafranc, Aiguablava, or even the risk of
crossing the bay of Palamós with its decor of mediterranean
architecture, to caress the curves of San Feliu de Guixols,
Tossa and Lloret.

By sea the boats, and by land the *carriage,* the railway
or the bus line, of which Plà was an important customer
since when, from the 1940s onward, he began to travel
more in his own country than in a Europe he had already
covered in his youth as a correspondent. By sea the boat
allowed him to enjoy from afar the diversity of geology
and vegetation on the land; then stop for a while, cook a

Calas de Llafranc and Calella de Palafrugell.

meal among the pines and under them enjoy a siesta in the breeze, like Ulysses and his band in a moment of rest between his two returns: "We of Palafrugell all our lives carry with us a dream floating in our minds: that of the marvellous life of the free man on the sea. The sea satisfies our contemplative tendency. It is the grain of sand we are always talking of. The sea, a fugitive element without continuity, variable, contradictory, undulating, complements perfectly our manner of being, and connects with our *insouciance*. Also the sea excites the tastes of our palate, colours our cuisine in the most vivid manner, and we cannot understand what a good meal might be, if not beside the sea and with the products of the sea. Thus the tendency of Palafrugell people toward the sea is ancient, permanent, constant: Calella, Llanfranc, Tamariú, Aigua-sellida, Aigua-blava and Fornells are not mere geographical places for us or toponyms of the littoral; they are forms of our spirit, pieces of our intimate personality."

This enlightened "kulak", reader of Montaigne and Spinoza, distrusted wide horizons. In fact he was a participant of the world-view of the ancient Chaldeans, convinced there was nothing beyond the mountains at the border of their known territory. Plà was aware of the earth's immensity, but he loved above all the human journeys that began at Llofriú, Palafrugell or Calella. The Ampurdán for him is a landscape not spectacular but "discreet, elegant, svelte", and to demonstrate as much he made continuous, systematic tours through the Bajo Ampurdán, the vital centre of the territory, and the Alto Ampurdán, beyond the barrier of the Montgrí mountains, toward Figueras, the French frontier and the rough littoral of the Cap de Creus. "The Ampurdán has its precise, well-marked natural limits. In countries as profoundly Romanized as this, that is, where it has been many centuries since nomadism was abandoned, and the population has grown deep roots in the soil, the fixity of limits and the elimination of vagueness in them, is very satisfactory and agreeable." If Llofriú was his cradle and Calella his pier on the Costa Brava, the Ampurdán is his Chaldean universe, limited by the Pyrenees on the north and by the massif of the Gabarras on the south. Land of Greeks and Romans, not passed through by Hannibal, to the relief of Plà, no friend to the Robespierre of any age. The writer stopped in Ullastret, an Iberian village; at Ampurias, with Greek archaeology; at Rosas with its Roman remains hidden under apartment buildings of both high and low standing, like a homage to the anthropological roots of the people, to which must be added some drops of the blood of Turkish pirates, one of whose hobbies in their raids was the sowing of their eastern mediterranean chromosomes.

The writer sets out to visit the markets of Gerona: each important nucleus has a fixed day of the week: Besalú, La Bisbal, Palafrugell, Palamós... and he sees in them the shadow of the Middle Ages, as perceived in the stones of ancient houses, whose stuccoing and whitewash has not been able to annul the soul of the quarry. Sometimes he gets off the bus and goes on foot, from village to village, each with its walls, its central plaza with an inn, and a bell-tower in which perhaps the bell-slots have been abandoned to the use of birds of passage on their way to the swamps of Pals, at the mouths of the rivers Daro, Ter and Fluvià. "Torrent is a little village of peasants, recondite, silent, with the cemetery in the centre of the habitat..." «Sant Feliu de Boada is no more than a street with a few tentacles branching off it. On one of the first houses as you enter town, you may see this inscription on a stone: "I have a donkey like this (after this phrase appears the figure of an ass, scratched on the stone). In the stable, there is another; that makes two. And with you who are looking at this stone, that adds up to three." In Palausator: "... the infiltration of the Baroque into the serious and grave intimacy of the Romanesque is a distasteful phenomenon that sets the nerves on edge." Plá also saw towns between the memory of their past and the devastation caused by the abandonment of the peasants, or the invasion of the first colonies of tourists. Now many of these towns of the interior of the Ampurdán have been saved thanks to an "enlightened" tourism, often readers of Plà, who have rescued houses and estatues suitable to the bigamous condition of second residences. Behind this effort of recuperation there is usually a curious tourist, somewhat different from the predator of sun and paellas; marvelling at the Pals which Plà saw half ruined, or the Monells saved in its Gothic essence, or Sant Miguel de Cruilles, where the only Romanesque monastery of the Bajo Ampurdán resists bureaucratic abandon.

Extreme cardinal points of his travels in "his land" are Figueras, a commercial city whose frontier spirit was captured by Plà; Gerona, scene of the formation of his sentimentality, so finely described in *El cuaderno gris;* finally Barcelona, capital to which Plà devoted as much irony as curiosity. For Plà, neither Figueras nor Gerona had abandoned their country identity. Barcelona, on the other hand, was a half-baked attempt at a metropolis, degraded by demographic pressure and by the bad taste of the bourgeoisie. Plà did not like it, did not like even the Ensanche, a boring grid in his judgement; nor did he like the modernist style, fruit of a rapture of esthetic madness (*rauxa* in Catalan), in contradiction with the sense of measure, almost Neoclassical, that Plà demanded of the life and history of the Catalans.

A judicious taster of deep flavours linked to the cycles of the earth, Plà's palate was equally judicious with regard to the physionomy of landscape, of towns, of men. But of course he exercised it also on cuisine, so much so that he

Street in the Jewish quarter of Gerona.

may be said to be the initiator of the recuperation of the gastronomic culture of Catalonia, always from the initial starting point of his Chaldean world: Llofriú, Calella, the Ampurdán. There was no inn or kitchen unvisited by Plà in that countryside; he distinguished with his attentions all sorts of dishes, from the stew *El niu* (fruit of the delirium of some Ampurdanese fisherman fleeing from the Northern Lights) to the prodigies of the *nouvelle cuisine* of Ampurdán, initiated at the Motel del Ampurdán by the great chef Mercader. Plà often came to this splendid restaurant in the last lustra of his life, to delight his palate with the dishes, and delight those present at his table with his repertoire of anecdote and his capacity for disconcerting people. Part of his *persona* was the peasant ingenuousness which allowed him to leave 100 pesetas on the table, as the only payment for a Trimalchian meal. It is curious that the balanced follower of Montaigne and of the schizophrenic virtues of "l'honnête home" was able to enjoy a high repast like *El niu,* composed of died codfish, squids, thrushes, tripe of cod, peas, potatos, peppers and garlic mayonnaise. Plà describes it as a foundation dish, to lay a stable substructure in the stomach, upon which later, more fanciful constructions of a meal may be built. In his days it was to be found in all the restaurants of Palafrugell; now it is pure archaeology, made nowhere else but at the restaurant Gipcelle, and even then only on request. In conjunction with this savage culinary experience, Plà proposed the sobriety of natural products with the exact metaphysical flavour they were intended to have. "I have never been a partisan of exotic cuisine, or of remote or strange dishes. Sometimes, during my visits to one city or another, my friends have vished to take me to a Chinese, Jewish of Polynesian restaurant. I have never set foot in such outlandish places. I have never felt the last curiosity about Arabic, Semitic or Far Eastern cuisine. I have always liked to east with a spoon, fork and knife — not with my fingers, or with chopsticks. I am a frank partisan of the varied cuisine of this continent or of North America. Perhaps, you may say, boring and monotonous. This monotony enchants me, because I do not believe that novelty as a system helps us to live our lives."

This philosophy is also present in the repetition of landscapes familiar to him since the day he opened his eyes in the little centre of his universe. But if there is anything prodigious in the Ampurdán, it is that the reiterations of its landscape always carry with them a variant factor, which converts the reiteration into a way of reconsidering what one has seen. Sometimes this will be tower that corrects the flatness of a building's silhouette, other times the rotundity of the habitat, soon violated by the lightneas of arches and porticos. Then, in an agrarian landscape, the emergence of the antique world here and there, beyond the summer, beyond the flood of tourism: the parsimony of people with their berets and their memories, as if out of Plà's anthropological observations. To walk the Ampurdán is to walk with Plà. Arriving at the line of the seacoast, we find that construction can be destruction. The writer's landscape has disappeared, and vestiges of it must be sought in holes or corners, or under the asphalt of parking lots. But with patience and with Plà's works as breviary, it is still possible to explore his Chaldean universe, and even acquire, perhaps with the help of a beret on one's head, his "kulak" world-view, with one eye on the shadow of a storm over the Gabarras, and the other on the fury of the sea when the Tramontana is blowing.

EXTREMADURA

THE EXTREMADURAN ROUTE OF GABRIEL Y GALÁN

by

JOSÉ ANTONIO GABRIEL Y GALÁN

JOSÉ MARÍA GABRIEL Y GALÁN
(Frades de la Sierra, 1870-Guijo de Granadilla, 1905)

Gabriel y Galán was born at Frades de la Sierra, Salamanca, on 28 June 1870, to a family of agricultural labourers.

He studied to be a teacher, and obtained his diploma at the Escuela Normal Central in Madrid. He worked as a teacher at Piedrahíta from 1892 to 1898. That same year he married Desideria García Gascón, a young Extremaduran from the town of Guijo de Granadilla, Cáceres, where he then moved, occupying himself in managing the family's lands there.

In 1898 he wrote a poem in Extremaduran dialect, called El Cristu Benditu, *immediately appreciated by personalities such as Unamuno, Balart, Salvador Rueda, etc. In 1901 he won the Flor Natural at the Floral Games of Salamanca, with a jury presided by Unamuno; the festival being sponsored by Joaquín Costa. The poem thus prized,* El ama, *became enormously popular and, at the same time, its author, who was awarded further prizes in Zaragoza, Murcia, Lugo, Buenos Aires, etc. His poetical production (brief, for he died at the age of 34, on 6 January 1905) includes the books* Castellanas *(1902),* Nuevas castellanas *(1905),* Extremeñas *(1902),* Campesinas *(1904), and* Religiosas, *published separately. His complete works, first published as such in 1910, have been reprinted in almost a hundred editions.*

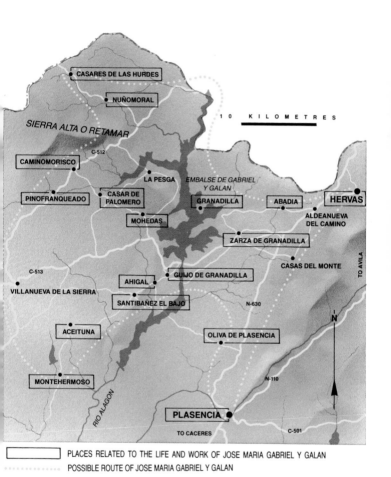

PLACES RELATED TO THE LIFE AND WORK OF JOSE MARIA GABRIEL Y GALAN
POSSIBLE ROUTE OF JOSE MARIA GABRIEL Y GALAN

EXTREMADURAN ROUTE
OF GABRIEL Y GALÁN

In the summer of 1892 José María Gabriel y Galán for the first time crossed the dividing line between the provinces of Salamanca and Cáceres, moved by a rare intuition which led him to visit, in the village of Guijo de Granadilla, an uncle of whose daughter he had heard generous praise.

On horseback, as they say, upright and gallant, this Salmantine of Frades de la Sierra appeared in Guijo, a village some thirty kilometres from the venerable city of Plasencia, with a population of under 2,000 inhabitants and situated at the gates of Las Hurdes. Little did the schoolteacher José María Gabriel y Galán imagine that this town of fig trees, acorns and pastures was to become the centre of his life and inspiration, not to mention his final resting place.

The fact is that in his cousin Desideria he found the woman he was looking for and, after several years of engagement, married her at Plasencia in January 1898. This event was to mean a radical change in the life of Gabriel y Galán, who left school and classes to devote himself to agriculture and stock-raising in the "burnt land of Extremadura". He adopted these fields of oak-woods and heaths with the naturalness of one who had been predestined to them. "She (his wife) and these fields, made me a poet", he writes in one of his verses.

Plasencia will be the capital of our Extremaduran route of Gabriel y Galán, for here was the birth of his Extremaduran existence, his marriage to Desideria García Gascón. Plasencia, crown of the valley of the Jerte, is a city still largely walled, with an ensemble of monuments some of them superbly individual, such as the Cathedral or the palace of the Marquesses of Mirabel. But its main attraction is its ambiental harmony, its omnipresent historical resonance.

Plasencia has been linked with the name of Gabriel y Galán. He dedicated several poems to the city, particularly one which he read at a function organized by the Red Cross, to celebrate the granting of the title "Muy Benéfica" given to the city for its humanitarian reception of those returning from the wars of Cuba and the Philippines. Gabriel y Galán read a poem in Extremaduran, full of patriotism and irony, called *La Cenéfica,* parodying the title of Benéfica given the city.

> *Cuando los yanquisis*
> *nos robaron las tierras aquellas,*
> *p'allá estuvon estos*
> *pasando las penas.*
> *N'más que de oílos contar sus trabajos*
> *se queaba aginao cualisquiera*[1].

From Plasencia to Guijo de Granadilla, to begin a new life as apprentice farmer, devoted to his family, to his writing, to his love for the fields and the hunt, and to learn to know and love his new social surroundings.

---

[1] "When the yankees / Robbed us of those lands, / living through all that trouble, / Just to hear them tell of it / Anyone would be petrified."

Plasencia. Convent of San Vicente and Palace of Mirabel.

The Galanian traveller must follow the highway that leads to Hervás, and turn off to the left, taking a secondary road, which leads him in a few minutes to Guijo de Granadilla. However it is well worth the trouble to turn off from Oliva a few hundred metres and see the interesting Roman ruins of Cáparra, with some notable pieces, including an arch which is still in good condition. The landscape we pass through in apparently arid; but if we look closely we may appreciate a number of nuances. It is not all wasteland and rocks; there are cork oaks and olives, and a pretty stream called Ambroz with a Roman bridge; and there is, of course a Nature that is hard, dry, rocky, of wide spaces; its colours picturesque but finally impossible to reproduce.

This must have been exactly the landscape José María was looking for, because this melancholy personality, schoolteacher in Piedrahíta and Guijuelo, when transplanted to the land of Extremadura, seems to undergo a transformation of his character, which becomes strong and open, without losing a bit of his extraordinary sensibility. One would say he was another person, more happy and reflective, who gradually gains the confidence of the people till he becomes a sort of patriarch of the place, to whom many came in search of aid, advice or conversation.

The poet is at home in his new life, and manifests this in the simple manner in which he tells his sentiments:

> *Qué bien se vive así! Pasan los días*
> *sin dejar en el alma sedimentos*
> *de insanas alegrías*
> *ni de amargos tormentos*[2].

Here he found moments of fullness, as if internal natural forces were welling up and had to be given an outlet:

---

[2] "How fine this life! the days pass / leaving no sediment in the soul / of insane joys / nor of bitter torments."

Yo no sé qué tieni,
qué tieni esta tierra
de la Extremaúra
que cuantis que llegan
estos emprincipios
de la primavera
se me poni la sangre encendía
que cuasi me quema
se me jincha la caja del pecho
se me jaci más grande la juerza,
se me poni la frente möora
y barruntu que asina me entra
como un jormiguillo
que me jormiguea [3]...

At the entrance to Guijo, on a modest height there stands the shrine of the Cristu Benditu, a little church surrounded by ilex and olive, of no great architectural value, but great sentimental value for the people of the village; a sentiment which has grown since Gabriel y Galán in 1899 published the poem, *El Cristu Benditu,* on the occasion of the birth of his first son, as an act exalting paternity. José María, though conscious of having written a great poem, kept it to himself for months, until he sent it to his brother Baldomero, a lawyer in Salamanca, who showed it to Unamuno. The rector liked it so much he proposed to publish it in "La Ilustración Española y Americana" and, on trips to Madrid, would read it to poet friends like Federico Balart or Salvador Rueda.

The simple and discreet church that receives the voyager

---

[3] "I don't know what it's got / what it's got, this country / of Extremadura / that when there comes round / this early period / of springtime / my blood so catches fire / it just about burns me / my rib cage swells out on me / and my strength increases / my forehead gets heavier / and I can feel the approach / of a sort of itch / that makes me itchy..."

Shrine of Cristu Benditu.

at the entrance to the town is now permanently identified with the poem of Gabriel y Galán, who exultantly wished to present his new-born son to the "Christ of that shrine". For the Galanian pilgrim, this is a fane of the first magnitude.

Early in the morning José María would go out on horseback to the fields. He would usually wear an open-necked linen shirt, a corduroy jacket with large pockets, into which everything he needed would be stuffed; and what he most needed was his notebook. This contained the names of cows, bulls and other beasts, *Primorosa, Colegiala, Arrogante, Lucero,* and their dates of birth, weaning, shoeing, etc., mixed with verses, first drafts, corrections, finished versions. With shotgun on shoulder, he toured the lands, watched that the cows were well attended and vaccinated, sought out newborn calves, and above all rode and rode from one place to another, then sat down under an oak to write in his oilcloth-covered notebook.

Less than three kilometres from the village is *El Tejar,* a spread of land much favoured by José María Gabriel y Galán, a solitary place of rough and austere terrain, where the poet would come and go, and converse with farmhands and drovers. It was precisely here that he liked to sit down and write, or take notes without getting off his horse. Here he composed, upon the death of his mother in 1901, his most famous poem: *El ama,* awarded the Flor Natural at the competition in Salamanca, by a jury presided by Miguel de Unamuno, and whose act of proclamation was sponsored by Joaquín Costa.

Perhaps this land, a pure Extremaduran paradise, quintessence of the *guijarreño,* has inherent in it all the plastic, ambiental and sentimental elements that form the literary space of Gabriel y Galán. However, El Tejar was drowned by the waters of a reservoir created in the 1950s and named after the poet.

José María Gabriel y Galán, now totally integrated in Guijo de Granadilla, was in a way the soul of the village, its great witness and great giver of name. His knowledge of people, events, ambience, places seems to have been total. He must have possessed a great capacity of communication, a great aptitude for generating confidence. El Guijo was his microcosmos; in describing it he described the world entire. The rural poetry of Gabriel y Galán is made of small insights into this microcosmos, significant pictures of customs, situations, sentiments, characters, all of it from a *social* perspective (based on a Utopia of concord) unusual in those last years of the nineteenth and first of the twentieth century.

To express himself, he expedites a passport of literary legitimacy on behalf of the *fabla del lugar,* in its peculiar Extremaduran form, with such fortune that before long, specialists were talking of its language as a separate dialect, which some called *extremeño,* others *castúo;* some have not hesitated to describe it as "Castillian hoarsened and abused by its passage through the gorge of Las Hurdes". But in any case the Extremaduran speech, incorporated by Gabriel y Galán in most of his work, *functions* perfectly in the literary sense, producing a surprising effect of rhythym, precision and vigour.

The Salmantine poet after 1901, date of *El ama,* acquired a fame that deprived him, in his few remaining years of life (he died at 34) of that absolute peace he had hoped to find in Extremadura. In 1902 he had to travel to Madrid to give a reading of his poems, an event which was a great success, allowing him to meet most of the official poets of the Madrilenian Parnassus. Gabriel y Galán returned from the party disillusioned, as he relates in his poem *Regreso,* where he opts definitively for the authenticity of rural life. However, the originality of his poetic forms excited the interest of important persons of the period, with whom he maintained a plentiful correspondence: Unamuno, Pardo Bazán, Menéndez Pidal, Pereda, Miguel and many others.

A visit to the village of Guijo today, almost a century later, presents us with the vestiges of a society that was, but which still conserves some of the emotional keys of those times; more than we may think. And in any case, the persistence of the lyrical and vital spirit of the poet is appreciable everywhere; a sort of moving act of social fidelity toward an ambivalent figure, half myth, half physical person, whose life and miracles are known to the guijarreños by tradition from father to son.

In the centre of the village plaza there is a statue of the poet (as there is also in Salamanca, Plasencia, Cáceres, etc.). Also in this plaza is the house where José María Gabriel y Galán, now converted to museum use. Remodelled a few years ago, its interior preserves furniture, objects, photographs, books and texts of the poet, amid a Galanian atmosphere conserved with skill and devotion.

Another obligatory visit is the cemetery, on the edge of the town. Here is the poet's grave. The site is singular, for the impression one has is that of walking in an untended garden full of high grown grass, a rural space far removed from the solemn darkness of cemeteries. The tomb of Gabriel y Galán is a plain, simple slab of stone, upon which flowers are not wanting, especially on the 5th of January of every year, when the anniversary of his death is commemorated, with moving homages at the best-known Galanian sites. And they always return to that classic strophe where the poet writes, as if by premonition, a few days before his death:

> *¡Quiero vivir! A Dios voy*
> *y a Dios no se va muriendo,*
> *se va al Oriente subiendo*

por la breve noche de hoy.
De luz y de sombras soy
y quiero darme a las dos[4].

The death of the poet on 6 January 1905, the chroniclers tell us, was a stunning blow to the region, and above
all to Guijo de Granadilla. The village remained in silence
for several days, while each of the inhabitants passed to
kneel before the cadaver of don José María, amid the wail-
ing of the women. It appears that when the coffin was borne
out the door of the house, a general moan was heard over
all the plaza. It is also said there were attempts on the part
of Salamanca to take the cadaver of the poet for burial in
the chapel of the University, next the remains of Fray Luis
de León. The reaction of the people of Guijo was blunt,
manifested by groups of villagers with shotguns, keeping
watch at the cemetery for many days and many nights.

But the Galanian route cannot end at Guijo de Granadilla. We must proceed to the neighboring villages, bordering already on Las Hurdes: Ahigal, Granadilla, Zarza de
Granadilla, Abadía, Hervás.

Granadilla was an historic town, closed and architectu-
rally coherent, now cut off by waters of the Gabriel y Galán reservoir. But it may be reached by boat, to appreciate
its magnificent 15th-century castle and other works in process of restoration. It is a curious town and in a very real
sense a ghost town, because its former inhabitants return
each year on All Hallows day to render respects to their
ancestors. In Granadilla Gabriel y Galán had close relatives, and it was a place much loved and visited by him. A
few kilometres further on, near to Hervás, is Abadía, a village where, surprisingly, there rises an extraordinary palace

---

[4] "I want to live! I go to God / And to God one does not go by dying, /
We go to the Orient Sun by rising / through the brief night of present
time. / I am of light and shadow both / and wish to partake of the two."

of Templarian origin, with Mudéjar patio of the 13th century and some exquisite gardens in the Italian style, made at the bidding of the Duke of Alba in the 16th century. Continuing to Hervás, this town is an oasis, with its mountain landscape, its waterfalls and ruperb chestnut trees; and within the town, the ancient Jewish quarter.

All these towns, by their proximity to Guijo, were well known to José María in his continual journeys. But obviously he wandered further and had ample occasion to explore Las Hurdes; entering, for example, by Mohedas. Significant towns like Pinofranqueado, Caminomorisco, Casares de Las Hurdes, Nuñomoral, etc. from that polemical conglomerate of villages, object of so much attention and disagreement in cinema, literature and science.

We cannot doubt that in the time of Gabriel y Galán, Las Hurdes was indeed that territory of extreme misery that he paints for us in various poems. The descriptions he makes of that land are hard and unmistakeable. He speaks of "a solitary hill country, miserable huts of stone and mud, and dried-up springs; a world without life, a country like a cemetery; madroños, cistus, brushwood, ferns, stones, nettles, thorns; a landscape without wheat, or gardens, or trees, nor bridge, nor river".

In 1904, on the occasion of the visit made by Alfonso XIII to Las Hurdes, the now famous Gabriel y Galán wrote a simple, blunt poem dedicated to the King, denouncing the situation of those people:

> *Dolor de cuantos los vieren,*
> *mentís de los que mintieren,*
> *aquí los parias están...*
> *De hambre del alma se mueren,*
> *se mueren de hambre de pan*[5].

---

[5] "Giving pain to whoever sees them, / Giving the lie to the liars, / Here the pariahs are... / Of the soul's hunger they die, / They die of hunger for bread."

Im another poem he portrays in melodramatic colours a *jurdana,* a mother —"hungry she-wolf"— who comes down out of the mountains in mid-winter, with her half-wit son on her back, to try and find some food to eat. A text in which the poet perhaps overdoes the description of the tragedy, but which demonstrates the sensitivity of Gabriel y Galán to the terrible reality of Las Hurdes. Here he begins a vein which he had not time to work, but was to grow in importance as the new century progressed, of verse with a social purpose, intended to move the conscience of the public and produce concrete results.

In reality, the Extremaduran geography of José María Gabriel y Galán comprises practically all the province of Cáceres, though the places we have mentioned are the most significant ones in a real, beautiful and austere landscape, which Gabriel y Galán adopted as his own, into his poetic world.

The traveller may, then, initiate his route at Plasencia, moving through Guijo de Granadilla, Ahigal, Santibáñez as far as Montehermoso, then going up into what are Las Hurdes proper. And from Casares, Nuñomoral and other mountain villages he returns down, bordering the reservoir of Gabriel y Galán, to Hervás on the Nacional 630 road. From Hervás he returns to the same road to Plasencia, the starting point.

GALICIA

PLACES
OF ROSALÍA DE CASTRO

by

RUBÉN CABA

ROSALÍA DE CASTRO
(Santiago de Compostela, 1837-Padrón, 1885)

Rosalía de Castro studied music, drawing and Freench in the halls at Compostela of the Sociedad Económica de Amigos del País. In April 1856 she moved to Madrid, where she published a handful of poems title La flor, *which the Coruñese Manuel Martínez Murguía, future historian of Galicia, praised in the newspaper* La Iberia, *of Madrid. The indulgent critic and the poetess were married in Madrid on 10 October 1858. They travelled in Extremadura, La Mancha and the eastern coast; then returned to Santiago, where they resided for some years. For a short time, they lived at Simancas and, again, at Madrid. From 1871, Rosalía never left her homeland again; but her husband did, and resided in Madrid between 1879 and 1882. Rosalía retired with the children to the house of Hermida, in Lestrove, and later to another large house called La Martanza, in Padrón, where she died of cancer.*

Her lyrical work, the best known and celebrated part of her writings, includes, as well as the leaflet La flor *and the poem* A mi madre, *three books:* Cantares gallegos *(1863),* Follas novas *(1880) —two of its pieces in vernacular— and* En las orillas del Sar *(1884), which is her masterpiece in Castilian.*

She is also the author of various novels: La hija del mar *(1859),* Flavio *(1861),* Ruinas *(1866),* El caballero de las botas azules *(1867), and* El primer loco *(1881).*

In Azorín's opinion Rosalía is "one of the most delicate, most intense, of the many originals that Spain" has produced. Perhaps the secret of the persistence of Rosalía is that —as writes Enrique Díez Cañedo—"when others declaimed or sang, she dared to simply speak".

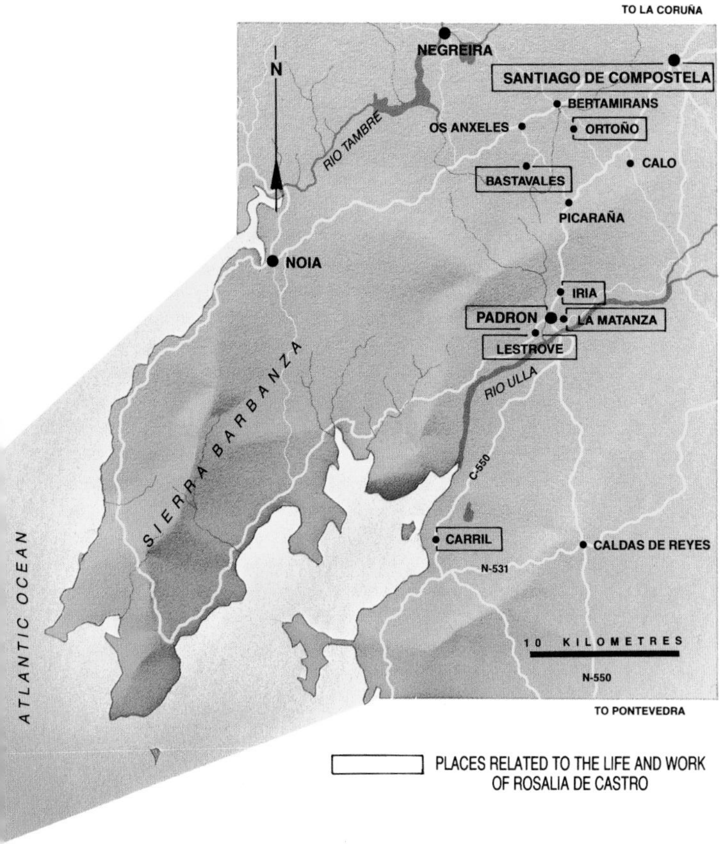

TO LA CORUÑA

N

NEGREIRA

SANTIAGO DE COMPOSTELA

BERTAMIRANS

RIO TAMBRE

OS ANXELES

ORTOÑO

CALO

BASTAVALES

PICARAÑA

NOIA

IRIA

PADRON   LA MATANZA

LESTROVE

RIO ULLA

S I E R R A   B A R B A N Z A

C-550

A T L A N T I C   O C E A N

CARRIL

CALDAS DE REYES

N-531

10   KILOMETRES

N-550

TO PONTEVEDRA

PLACES RELATED TO THE LIFE AND WORK
OF ROSALIA DE CASTRO

PLACES OF ROSALÍA DE CASTRO

The culture of walking and seeing justifies itself. But if anyone needed motives for visiting Santiago de Compostela, he could find a good number of them: religious, artistic, historic, scientific, gastronomic. For centuries it was the goal of the *pilgrims,* for this was the proper name for those who went to Santiago, to distinguish them from those who went to the Holy Land (palmers) or those who chose Rome (romers). In his *Vita Nuova,* Dante Alighieri enumerates these three modes of referring to "those who walk in the service of the Highest".

In Santiago, one of the most spectacular architectural ensembles in Europe, it is possible not only to venerate relics, contemplate carved stone, evoke legends, admire knowledge, taste viands; the addict of literature may also give loose rein to his confessable passion in the many and well-stocked libraries. This kind of visitor will not be long in finding a sign on some wall, on a lecture hall, a building, a street, or the seminary of the Faculty, bearing the name of a great artificer of the written word: Rosalía de Castro.

In the Paseo de la Herradura her compatriots have immortalized her in a sitting, doubtful position, with chin in hand, like the Thinker of Rodin, but with less muscles and more dreams. This sculpture of Rosalía has tried to give form to the two poles of her tense personality. From her father —the presbyter José Martínez Vioxo, of a peasant family settled in the place called Ortoño— Rosalía inherited a robust body and wide face, solid and sensual. And from her mother —señorita María Teresa de la Cruz de Castro y Abadía, of hidalgo birth, who inhabited the house at Arretén— she inherited a fragile spirit and refined sensibility.

Rosalía de Castro is, on first view, a landmark in Spanish poetry. She was a forerunner of the metrical innovations to be developed and perfected by Rubén Darío, and inspirer, in no slight measure, of the sober, essential poetry of Antonio Machado. Machado's admiration for Rosalía extended to the paraphrasing of some of her verses. Thus the poem *Follas novas,* which begins: "Unha vez tiven un cravo / cravado no corazón" ("Once I had a nail, nailed in my heart") is re-created by Machado in his book *Soledades:* "In my heart I had the thorn of a passion; I managed to pull it out one day: I no longer feel my heart." And Federico García Lorca, carried away by his veneration, composed in Galician a "lullaby for Rosalía Castro, dead". However, Rosalía did not in her lifetime obtain the sort of recognition enjoyed by her contemporaries Carolina Coronado and Gertrudis Gómez de Avellaneda. This neglect Rosalía repaid with her disdain for society life and literary circles.

In Galicia today, Rosalía de Castro is much more than a writer; she has crossed the frontier of literary values to settle in the world of myths. Not the ironical Manuel Curros Enríquez, nor the stylist Castelao, not even the melancholic Eduardo Pondal, whose poem *Los pinos* has become the Galician anthem, represent the spirit of their people with the same fidelity as the figure of Rosalía.

Monument to Rosalía de Castro in Santiago de Compostela.

Our future myth could not have proceeded from more obscure origins. She was born at Santiago de Compostela on 24 February 1837, and was christened in the sole presence of her godmother, as the child was, according to her baptismal certificate, "daughter of unknown parents". Rosalía spent her childhood with paternal aunts in Ortoño, a village on the banks of the Sar near Santiago. We must suppose that here she visited her father who, being a priest, could not recognize or legitimize her. Nor is it known exactly when her mother, Teresa de Castro, who had given her name to the child, assumed her care; but it must have been when she was eleven or twelve years old. Mother and daughter lived first at Padrón and, later, about 1850, in Santiago, near the Porta Faxeiras, probably in the Calle de Bautizados. At fifteen, Rosalía underwent a spiritual upset, perhaps on learning of her condition of illegitimate child, which developed into a chronic "pain of living".

Although she resided for two periods in Madrid (there she began writing her *Cantares gallegos,* and married the journalist Nurguía), during some time at Simancas (where she composed almoat all the verses of the *Follas novas*), and also at Corunna (where her daughter Amara was born), most of her life was spent in the neighborhood of Santiago-Padrón-Carril, an axis formed by the basin of two rivers, the Sar and the Ulla, whose waters having joined, enter the sea in the Ría de Arosa. No wonder the work of Rosalía is full of references to the rivers and the sea.

The house where she was born has disappeared, situated in the Camino Novo, at the corner with the Conxo road. But the literary pilgrim may begin his route at the Porta Faxeiras, starting point also of the Way of St. James, followed by Rosalía in the poem *Santa Escolástica,* in her last book *En las orillas del Sar.* Rosalía —we must imagine her with her melancholy gait and pained expression which carned her, among her sensible and merry neighbours, the

nickname of *A Tola* (the Mad)— set out walking one afternoon in April on the Calle del Franco and, "on crossing
the silent plazas", remembered the glorious past of the city,
until the "the graceful gate of Fonseca" (the portal of the
College of Fonseca) offered her its "exquisite statues and
reliefs", and the Plateresque façade of the "Gran Hospital"
(now, Hostal de los Reyes Católicos) before her "sad eyes,
traced its proud form in space". After admiring "the Ca-
thedral-mystical palace of daring Romanesque arcades" she
turned her eyes toward where "there rose the celestial
image of the Zebedee" (that of St. James Apostle, crown-
ing the building of the present City Hall). She left behind
the "severe street" (Calle San Francisco) and, "like a fugitive deer", passed "under the dark arch, where the eternal
hidden torrent of water sounds" (the subterranean current
that ran under the arch of the Archbishop's Palace). She
walked "with insecure feet" when she saw "open the church,
deserted of the faithful" (the church of the Benedictine
monastery of San Martín Pinario, now Conciliar Seminary).
She entered there and saw how a ray of light entered the
shadowy space and illuminated "the divine contours of an
angel and a saint" (the sculptures of the Transit of Santa
Escolástica). Impressed by the beauty of this sight, she
knelt and exclaimed, not unlike Bécquer: "There is Art!
There is Poetry...! There must be a Heaven. There is God!"

Also in Santiago is the tomb of Rosalía. The visitor to
it, in the church of Santo Domingo de Bonaval, a chapel
dedicated as "Pantheon of Illustrious Galicians", will find
a mausoleum of white marble, not only uncharacteristic of
the modesty in which Rosalía always lived, but which con-
travenes her express desires as, shortly before her death,
she asked her children to have her buried in the cemetery
of Adina, in Iria, a quarter of Padrón. Rosalía might have
been saved the disturbance of her remains if she had done
as Shakespeare, who put a warning verse on his tomb:

"GOOD FREND FOR IESUS SAKE FORBEARE
TO DIGG THE DUST ENCLOASED HEARE.
BLESE BE YE MAN YT SPARES THES STONES
AND CURST BE HE YT MOVES MY BONES."

The traveller will encounter the town of Padrón at 18
kilometres from Santiago, unless perhaps he eschews mo-
torized transport, and prefers to accompany the river Sar
by means of forest paths that wind along the valley,
shaded by pines and perfumed by eucalyptus. A river that
Rosalía wrote of:

> *Cual niño que plácido duerme,*
> *reflejando el azul de los cielos,*
> *lento corre en la fronda a esconderse*[1].

If we choose this fluvial route to Padrón, we pass near
the village or Ortoño, which of course my also be reached
by road, from Bertamiráns. In Ortoño Rosalía played as a
child, while she heard the bells of San Julián de Bastavales:

> *Campanas de Bastabales,*
> *cando vos oyo tocar,*
> *mórrome de soidades*[2].

The traveller enters Padrón through the Iria quarter,
the birthplace of Camilo José Cela, who won the Nobel
Prize for Literature in 1989. This quarter occupies the site
of a Roman mansion called Iria Flavia, which figures in
the Itinerary of Antoninus, and of the medieval city of the
same name; in whose vicinity, in a sylvan grove there was

---

[1] "Like a child sleeping placidly, / reflecting the blue of the sky, / it
runs slowly under the fronds."

[2] "Bells of Bastavales, / when I hear you chimes, / I am heavy with
nostalgia."

an ancient fortress, later to become the city of Santiago de Compostela. Here, early in the ninth century, by angelic revelation and to the accompaniment of lights and celestial music, the sepulchre was found that contained the body of St. James Apostle.

In the Iria quarter, beside the highway and across from the museum devoted to the life and work of Camilo José Cela, is the cemetery of Adina. Here, next to the wall, reposed the remains of Rosalía for six years, until in 1891, some local worthies came up with the idea of disinterring her remains and installing them, as we have said, in a grandiose sepulchre in Santiago, with total disregard for own wishes, expressed to her children on her deathbed, and given poetic form in some verses of *Follas novas:*

> *O simiterio de Adina*
> *no hay duda que é encantador,*
> *c'os seus olivos escuros*
> *de vella recordaçón;*
> *c'o seu chan de herbas e frores lindas,*
> *cal no outras dou Dios;*
> *(...)*
> *Moito te quixen un tempo,*
> *simiterio encantador*[3].

At the end of her life, after spending two years in the house known as Torres de Hermida, which her relatives possesed in Lestrove, a place incorporated in the municipality of Dodro though it is only one kilometre distant from Padrón, she took refuge (with the occasional trip to the sea at Carril) in the house of La Matanza, in Padrón,

---

[3] "The cemetery of Adina is beyond doubt enchanting, with its dark olive trees of ancient memory, with its masses of grass and lovely flowers, like the garden of God... May I rest in thee some day, enchanting cemetery."

Padrón. Casa de la Matanza.

now occupied by a museum dedicated to her memory. Facing the principal door, a fig tree Rosalía planted still bears fruit; near it, under a vine-grown pergola, are the seat and table of stone, where Rosalía liked to write on hot days. And in the garden there grow, in brotherly company, the plum, the pear, the olive, along with various exotic species brought from beyond the seas by American readers of Rosalía.

COMUNIDAD DE MADRID

THE MADRID OF GALDÓS

by

JOSÉ ESTEBAN

BENITO PÉREZ GALDÓS
(Las Palmas de Gran Canaria, 1843-Madrid, 1920)

Considered the greatest Spanish novelist since Cervantes, Galdós was the tireless creator of a world of personalities full of life, who reappear in various perspectives, assuming different roles, in many of his novels, almost all united by a common world: the Madrid of the 19th century, especially the second half of it.

A prolific writer: forty-six episodios nacionales, *thirty-four novels, twenty-four plays, five volumes of articles and various other productions, constitute a mass of work seldom equalled by writers of his quality. Madrid, for Galdós, is not a city but rather a residence for Galdosian characters, the ambit in which they move. Perhaps* Fortunata y Jacinta (1886-87) *and* Misericordia (1897) *are his greatest masterpieces. They are high points of the Galdosian novel, and high points of Madrid as a novelistic character.*

He was the inventor of the so-called Episodios nacionales: *a peculiar from of novel, in which an historical thread leads the reader through the atmosphere and events of nineteenth-century Spanish history, from Trafalgar to the Restoration.*

In 1892 Galdós began his theatrical career with Reality;

but it was Electra, *first represented in 1901, that yielded him the greatest recognition as a writer for the stage, in both the literary and political senses.*

A deputy in various legislatures, Galdós represented the Republican party. His candidacy for the Nobel Prize for Literature in 1912 was blocked and boycotted by the "live forces" of the country. Blind and poor, he died in "his Madrid" in January 1920.

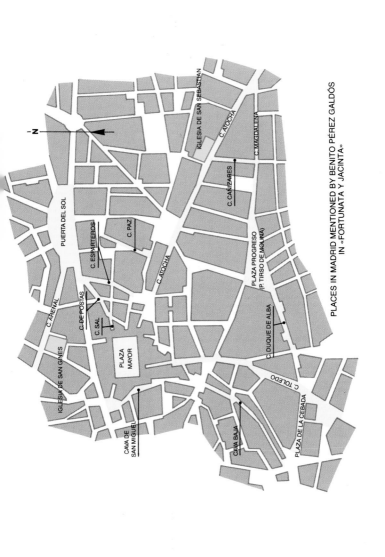

PLACES IN MADRID MENTIONED BY BENITO PÉREZ GALDÓS
IN «FORTUNATA Y JACINTA»

THE MADRID OF GALDÓS

"Es mucho Madrid éste"[1]
(B. P. Galdós, *La de Bringas*)

Benito Pérez Galdós arrived at Madrid when he was nineteen, in 1862, and lived there until his death in January 1920.

Between these two dates almost sixty years went by, during which the beloved city passed through an intense period of transformation and growth, which took in from 300,000 inhabitants at the beginning to some 650,000 at the end. Thus, "Isabeline" Spain, the "Gloriosa" and the Restoration were the historical periods lived by the writer in Madrid, periods which mark a definitive passage from a Court of the Ancien Regime to a modern city, run and formed to the tastes of a new-born bourgueoisie, of which Galdós was the major interpreter.

Let us hear how the novelist narrates his arrival at the *Corte*. "In that epoch so productive of serious political events, precursors of the Revolution, I was present, in-

---

[1] "This is so much Madrid."

volved in a crowd of students, at the riot on the night of San Daniel, 10 April 1865, and in the Puerta del Sol a few of the whacks with a lantern, distributed by members of the Guardia Veterana, were received by me; and the next year, on 22 June, memorable for the rising of the sergeants in the San Gil barracks, from the windows of the boarding house in the Calle del Olivo, where I lived with some friends, I could observe the tremendous happenings of that mournful day." This is from his *Memorias de un desmemoriado* and refers to the days when Galdós, a mediocre student of Law, "loitered in the streets, plazas and alleys, delighting in the observation of the bustling life of this huge and motley capital". He adds that he "frequented the Teatro Real and a café in the Puerta del Sol, where a fair number of my compatriots gathered".

This urban scene, these streets, plazas and alleys which surround the Puerta del Sol as far as the Puerta de Toledo and the Palacio Real, appear in many of his pages, with thousands of personalities who live their own lives while living, at the same time, the life of the city. In his first novel, *La Fontana de Oro,* Galdós already evokes that celebrated café, beloved redoubt of the liberals in 1820, and brings back to life before our eyes the Carrera de San Jerónimo itself, with its convents, palaces and political cafés.

We may say that it was with Galdós that the urban novel of Madrid was really born; and to the city's memory and with its inestimable aid, the novelist raised that incomparable madrilenian monument which are the pages of *Fortunata y Jacinta,* which at the same time as an object of it: that is to say, as a foundation on which to base his novel, and also as a human hive. A hive that is to be both analysed and endowed with organic sense in the same novel.

Thus, of all Galdó's novels, *Fortunata y Jacinta* is that

which exploits the literary possibilities of Madrid in the most detailed manner, completing its structure as a city at the same time as it draws the structure of so complex a novel.

An unrivalled chronicler, then, of the Villa y Corte, Galdós needs the presence of Madrid, to lead his many personalities around the labyrinth of its streets and the labyrinth of their lives, which has given us the so-called "Galdosian Madrid" or "Madrid of Galdós". But owing to the extension of this Madrid that he portrayed and inhabited so passionately, we are going to reduce it to the Madrid portrayed in *Fortunata y Jacinta,* masterpiece of the Canarian writer and classic novel of Madrid, which leaves us still with a lot of Madrid to describe.

Well, this Madrid of Galdosian literary route based on the novel has its centre at the Plaza Mayor, to whose right we find the upper world of commerce, with its aristocratic and banking premises in the quarter of Pontejos; and on the other side, the left, we find the popular world (in the time of Galdós and now) of Las Cavas and the quarter of Puerta Cerrada and the Calle de Toledo, which leads off to South Madrid, poor and proletarian.

The starting point of our route, the Plaza Mayor, was a place of meeting and of confrontation between those two married women, Fortunata and Jacinta, taken as symbols of social class. Let us not forget that the subtitle of the novel, with a certain sensational flavour, was "Stories of two married women".

It is true that in the long course of the narrative, there is a clear advance toward the north of the city, to that area which represented, and still represents, a rise in social or economic class; while the dispossessed and outcast persons, so abundant in Galdós, tend to drift south, to the popular quarter of Lavapiés and its surroundings, or to the vicinity of Las Vistillas.

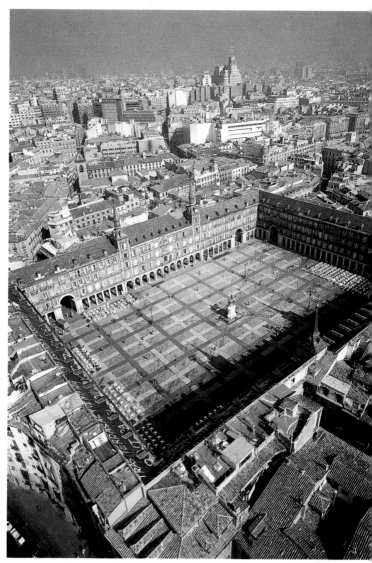

Plaza Mayor and surroundings.

The novel, seen in this perspective, contains 710 references to streets, plazas and quarters of Madrid, and to buildings or institutions whose location may be identified.

Galdós reflects and describes all the Madrid existing about 1870 after, the years when the action takes place. The old Madrid, seat of the aristocracy, which is beginning to move, along with the upper bourgeoisie, to the modern Salamanca quarter. The mainly artisan Madrid which is born and develops in the Chamberí quarter. The commercial life, so cordially liked by the artist, with its traditional establishments in the Calle Mayor and, especially, in the Calle de Toledo, a street much loved and sung by Galdós and where, according to the writer, the money of Madrid was concentrated, and most of its alcohol too: this impertinent explorer once counted over eighty taverns in this street. To this commercial Madrid we may add the first part of the Calle de Atocha, and Pontejos. However all the luxury shops were in the Calle de la Montera, and also the old Ateneo, so frequented by Galdós, along with the Carrera de San Jerónimo and the streets of Caballero de Gracia and Arenal. Nor does the writer forget the existence of a Madrid of small artisan industries situated in the old nucleus of the city, which already in those days was losing its traditional physiognomy.

GALDOSIAN ITINERARY

Calle de Postas

This street begins in the Calle de Esparteros, next to Sol, and ends in that of Zaragoza, leaving to one side the short Calle de la Sal. This is one of the most "Galdosian" streets of draper's shops, shops of ecclesiastical habits, military and waiter's uniform. It borders the east side of the

Plaza Mayor, the balconies of its last section having a direct view onto the impressive principal agora of Madrid.

A street of legend and story, there is a typical corner where it crosses the Calle del Marqués Viudo de Pontejos. Here is the old and famous inn called Posada del Peine, shelter and refuge of countrymen from the region ("Isidros") arriving at the Corte. Galdós describes a certain pocket of squalour that existed in this street. "You could touch the ceilings with your hand; the stairs were to be climbed only with the Creed on your lips, and the rooms seemed places destined for the premeditation of some bloody crime. Some of these dens were entered from the kitchen. Others had a sloping floor, and in all of them, you could hear the breathing of your neighbours. Some of them had shoddy little arches in them to support the stairs above. Wood and iron were abundant. So were doors you had to stoop through, floor tiles decaying into dust, unusable locks and broken leaded windows."

Calle de la Sal

This is a short street between Postas and the Plaza Mayor, in the Madrilenian mercantile quarter, where the predominant surnames are of Basques or converted Jews. A gracious street, now access to the underground parking beneath the Plaza Mayor. In Galdós' time there existed a café, "El Gato Negro", where Benavente often held forth in conversation.

Plaza Mayor

This great plaza is the centre of Galdosian Madrid. In old times it was a knot of alleys where a market existed;

Cava de San Miguel

in the seventeenth century this gave way to the present impressive rectangle, in a sober architectural style. On one of its longer sides is the so-called Casa de la Panadería, whose clock atop its tower, told time to the personalities of *Fortunata y Jacinta.* Beside this famous building, Estupiña had her draper's shop; from the imposing central balcony, kings viewed bullfights and other, less enjoyable, spectacles.

Fortunata could view this fine building from the balcony of her garret; inhabitants of the quarter made rendezvous under its colonnade; and all of them heard, and ordered their timetables by the solemn bell of its clock.

Calle de Toledo

An arch on the south side of the Plaza Mayor is the starting point of this famous street, which connects the old Madrid with the southern quarters of the capital. An eminently commercial street, it is mentioned numberless times in Galdós' works. In his old age the novelist said that "there is no street in the world more beautiful or more picturesque than this one".In the time of *Fortunata y Jacinta* a saying attributed all the money in Madrid to this street. Various personalities of the novel have commercial establishments on it.

Cava de San Miguel

Now a street of student bars, the so-called Cava, from the Plazuela de San Miguel to the Calle de Cuchilleros, with its celebrated arch, was the address (at N.º 11, then and now) of none less than Fortunata and Estupiña. A house with small windows on the Cava, and with Austrian balconies on the Plaza Mayor. This was the scene of the meeting of Fortunata and Juanito Santa Cruz, Gordian knot of all the novel's action. Fortunata, at that very moment, was about to eat a raw egg in her uncle's poultry shop in the ground floor of the house. From this building, by way of the shop that gives on the Plaza Mayor, Fortunata went off in 1870 to live with Juanito in a house in the Calle Concepción Jerónima.

Calle de Cuchilleros

From the stairs under the arch, to the Plaza de Puerta Cerrada. In this street we find *Botín,* a tavern in the seventeenth century and now a restaurant, mentioned by Galdós in several of his novels.

Calle Imperial

This descends in a tight curve, from the Plaza de la Provincia, with the façade of the Ministerio de Asuntos Exteriores (Ministerio de Ultramar, in Fortunata's time) to the Calle de Toledo. There is a corner here, now a fire hall, which formerly housed the school attended by Barbarita, the mother of Juanito Santa Cruz.

Cava Baja

From the Calle de Segovia to the Plaza de la Cebada. This is a street of inns, which has managed to conserve much of its popular flavour. Here is the famous Mesón del Segoviano; here, visitors from the region south of Madrid found lodging. The Cava Baja supplied the town with spring vegetables, with the wines of Arganda and Tarancón and the Manchegan regions of Toledo. There is a saying that refers to the sharpness of eye necessary for making purchases of these products: "In the Cava Baja it is the sight that does the work."

Plaza de la Cebada

Site of the most popular market in the south of Madrid. Between 1872-75 there was built in the plaza a metal structure, demolished a few decades ago to be subsituted by a more ample one of brick. The young Galdós often wandered through this plaza, where the famous Café de Naranjeros was. The plaza was also the site of executions; here the liberal Riego and the bandit Luis Candelas lost their lives. Galdós has much to say about this plaza in Episodio Nacional, *El terror de 1824,* and exclaims, "Plaza de la Cebada, out of my sight!".

From the famous Plaza de la Cebada, by San Millán and Duque de Alba, we arrive at the Plaza del Progreso, now Tirso de Molina. Here begins the Calle de La Magdalena, mentioned in various Episodios. Going up Cañizares, we reach the famous parish church of San Sebastián, on the Calle de Atocha, described at the beginning of *Misericordia.* "The parish of San Sebastián, like some persons, has two faces... the church, it were better to say... two faces with are surely more amusing than pretty. One of them looks toward the lower quarters, down the Calle de Cañizares; the other, toward the domain of the Plaza del Ángel." Its origin dates from 1550; it took the advocation of St. Sebastian from a shrine of that saint which existed a bit lower down Atocha, near the Plazuela de Antón Martín. The building itself is somewhat mediocre, we are told in a Madrilenian book of curiosities of that epoch: but in the interior there is a chapel remodelled by the famous Ventura Rodríguez, and in its vault the playwright Lope de Vega was buried.

At the door of this church Benigna begged for alms; one of the best-painted heroines in the immense Galdosian census. She appears in the novel *Misericordia.*

Not far from San Sebastián, crossing the commercial Plaza del Ángel, now more or less a meeting place of the Calle de la Cruz and the Calle de Carretas, we arrive at the long narrow Calle de la Paz, which starts from the alley of San Ricardo, by the rear façade of the former Post Office building, later Ministerio de Gobernación, and now seat of the Community of Madrid, and ascends to the Plazuela de la Leña, now Plaza de Jacinto Benavente or Plaza de la Bolsa. A steep little street, with shops of antique books and religious objects, and an old tavern.

Descending, on our left we find the Plaza de Pontejos. Here at N.º 1, lived the Santa Cruz family, the children being Juan and Jacinta. This large house retains the same appearance it had in those days. It was built in 1845, situated behind the famous N.º 1 of the Calle Mayor, where one might hear "the tolling of the bell of the Calle de Correos, as clear as if it were inside the house".

Our Galdosian route through Old Madrid ends at the church of San Ginés, in the very Madrilenian Calle del Arenal, which inherited the status of local parish church in 1872 when the church of Santa Cruz was demolished, an event of which we are told in the novel.

Estupiña and Barbarita heard Mass daily in this church, before doing their shopping in the nearby markets.

In its crypt devotional ceremonies were held, famous throughout Madrid and well attended.

Its handsome patio and tower appear in many of the novels of Galdós, among them *Fortunada and Jacinta.* Together with the now disappeared church of Santa Cruz, it is the one most frequently mentioned.

This has been only one of the possible Madrids of Galdós. The Madrid of the middle classes, of employees, of small merchants and a good portion of the people.

The route still conserves much of the savour which the novelist managed to capture so well and, as often happens with great writers, these streets retain part of his spirit, his personalities and his stories. These streets, plazas and alleys have since been known as "Galdosian Madrid".

REGIÓN DE MURCIA

IN SEARCH OF THE MURCIAN AIRS OF VICENTE MEDINA

by

SALVADOR GARCÍA JIMÉNEZ

VICENTE MEDINA
(Archena, 1866-Rosario de Santa Fe, 1937)

Those who have studied the work of Vicente Medina usually class him, together with Gabriel y Galán, as the other *generation of '98, perhaps because of his adherence to the sweet speech of the Murcian* huerta. *Regarding his relation to the group, apart from his experience as a volunteer in the Philippines, he won praise from Unamuno and Azorín. His poem* Cansera, *and all the considerations on Spain that he offers in his* patria chica *(1920) after the rotund quote from Saavedra Fajardo ("It is better to govern well than to expand an empire") are an authentic sample of regenerationism. When it comes to defining the character of his work, there is also a certain hesitancy, which ends by pigeonholing him in the genre of popular realism, as does Manuel Alvar. To avoid reiterations on these themes, we only need to read his extensive production, which the poet himself published with no small effort.*

Proud in his humility, as a close friend defined him, he published, apart from his poems and theatre in panocho *dialect, 26 volumes of work, in rich bindings. Published at Rosario de Santa Fe, Argentina, between 1919 and 1927, he called these his Colección de las Obras Completas. His autobiography may be dis-*

cerned especially in the introduction to La canción de la huerta
(1905), *in the above mentioned* Patria chica, *and in* Humo
(1921), *which exude a fragrance of simplicity. The Academia Alfonso X el Sabio, of Murcia, apart from having published the
most illuminating* Estudios sobre Vicente Medina *(1987),*
Mariano de Paco's edition of his Teatro *(1987), and the* Aires
murcianos *(1985), has announced the coming publication of a*
Biography *written by Manuel Enrique Medina Tornero, present
depositary of his whole work, including unpublished material.*

*Vicente Medina is the poet of Murcia, as Salcillo was her
sculptor; and the latter has never been compared with Miche-
langelo. From his birth at Archena on 27 October 1866 till his
death in Argentina on 17 August 1937, Medina, amid his various sufferings and joys at the whim of Fortune, had the recur-
rent dream of being a classic writer; Juan Maragall among others
tended to encourage him in this view of himself.*

*The existence of Medina is that of a literary persona. In the
riches he hoarded up while running a luxury hotel in the land
of the tango where, like the young Rosmann in the* America *of*
Kafka, *he lived through a story like* The Trial *on account of an
embezzlement in "Remonda, Montserrat & Cía", a story published by the chiefs of that same company. Once in prison, though
nothing has been written yet about this period of his life, he became, like Alberto Moravia in our days, an elderly lecher given
to erotic writing. Of the nine typewritten volumes from this
period, all of them apparently attributable to his hand, only three
are so far accessible to readers.*

*Like Melville, he was an apprentice to modest trades, and
wrote a book on the sea. Although he would seem to have all
the features of a Utopian anarchist, he wrote a fair number of
pages on Communism. There has been a project in recent years
to have his remains exhumed from the cemetery of La Piedad,
in the Argentine city of Rosario de Santa Fe, where they now
repose, and bring them to his birthplace of Archena, but this has
not yet come to pass.*

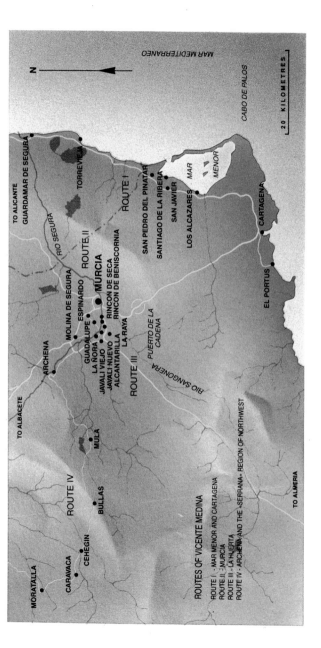

ROUTES OF VICENTE MEDINA

ROUTE I - MAR MENOR AND CARTAGENA
ROUTE II - MURCIA
ROUTE III - LA HUERTA
ROUTE IV - ARCHENA AND THE "SERRANA" REGION OF NORTHWEST

MORATALLA

CARAVACA

CEHEGIN

BULLAS

ROUTE IV

MULA

TO ALBACETE

ARCHENA

TO ALICANTE

GUARDAMAR DE SEGURA

RIO SEGURA

TORREVIEJA

MOLINA DE SEGURA

ESPINARDO

ROUTE II

MURCIA

GUADALUPE

LA ÑORA

JAVALI VIEJO

JAVALI NUEVO

ALCANTARILLA

RINCON DE SECA

RINCON DE BENISCORNIA

LA RAYA

ROUTE III

PUERTO DE LA
CADENA

RIO SANGONERA

ROUTE I

SAN PEDRO DEL PINATAR

SANTIAGO DE LA RIBERA

SAN JAVIER

LOS ALCAZARES

MAR
MENOR

CABO DE PALOS

MAR MEDITERRANEO

N

EL PORTUS

CARTAGENA

TO ALMERIA

20 KILOMETRES

IN SEARCH OF THE MURCIAN AIRS
OF VICENTE MEDINA

I

A reading of the works of Vicente Medina takes us from one end to another of the Murcian Region, so that we have asked ourselves a hundred times where to begin, and have traced a hundred times the routes of his *Aires murcianos,* and have finally settled for the following solution: to begin at Guardamar del Segura in Alicante, a retreat that Medina and his family much needed, far from the bad feelings produced by his speeches in favour of the Popular Front, where he could write, accompanied by the sound of waves, the work that he concluded during his brief stay in Mallorca: *El mar,* a book of poems not yet published. For Guardamar and Orihuela were, for him, part of Murcia; blues and greens especially preferred. Gardamar in the old age of the poet, and the Manriquan music of the Segura oblige us to exceed the limits of the Region by a few kilometres upriver, following the tango and the nostalgia of an elderly nightingale:

> *Ya cansado y agotado...*
> *a ti llego, Guardamar...*
> *a ti llego, como el río...*
> *Los ríos van a la mar*[1].

Vicente Medina, due to political circumstances, had to tear himself away from the land of Murcia, where he later returned to die. Sadly, he then crossed the ocean again to Argentina, where one morning in August he said goodbye to the world at the age of 71. His poignant verses come to our lips:

> *Cuando mi horica me llegue*
> *quiero morir en mi tierra,*
> *verla al cerrarse mis ojos*
> *y tener mi hoyico en ella*[2].

From Guardamar, let us proceed to that humble but smiling string of beaches on the Mar Menor that he used to frequent:

> *Blanco sobre azul de añil,*
> *pueblecitos de la mar:*
> *La Ribera, San Javier,*
> *San Pedro del Pinatar...*
>
> *Pueblecitos de la mar:*
> *Torrevieja, Los Alcázares...*
> *la mar... blancos pueblecillos*
> *entre palmeras... ¡oasis!*[3].

---

[1] "How tired and exhausted... / I reach thee, Guardamar... / I reach thee as does the river... / The rivers go to the sea."

[2] "When my hour arrives / I want to die in my homeland / To see it as my eyes close / And have my little grave there."

[3] "White on aniline blue / Little towns of the sea: / La Ribera, San Javier, / San Pedro del Pinatar... / Little towns of the sea: / Torrevieja, Los Alcázares... / the sea... White little towns / among palms... oasis!"

At a short distance from Cartagena, the visitor may enter El Portús, a compact bunch of houses where our poet lived for three months. The diminutive beach is now occupied by nudists, as if foreseen by the poet in the erotic *Plaie lascive* that he wrote in the Argentine prison. From Portús we continue, as he did, to Cartagena, aspurred by our curiosity in the echoes of his adolescence, of the newly married poet, of febrile writing in spite of his several jobs. The Calle Mayor, which the visitor inevitably passes along, gives us the feeling we are being watched through the jalousies by eyes of the poet's epoch. In the Café de la Marina, long since swallowed by the invasion of bank premises, the poet participated in a literary circle called the Peña del Abanico. It was probably also in this street that he had his rented second residence —the first, in the well-known and central Calle de San Francisco, has not been identified either— as we may deduce from the address he supplies us in *La canción de la huerta: Pedidos al autor: Calle Mayor, 5, 3.º.* From this house he would leave hurriedly, passing in front of the Casa de Cervantes —behind whose façade, still perfectly preserved, the Caja de Ahorros del Mediterráneo now offers its services— before entering the Casino, former property of the Marquesses of Casa Tilly, to inspect the Cartagena press in search of his latest articles. At the end of a slight descent in the street, the City Hall which, like the Palacio de Aguirre in the Calle de la Merced, is a fine example of early art-nouveau style. Across from its doorway, the narrow street of the Subida de las Monjas. Following this to its end, we arrive at another souvenir of Vicente Molina, which has so far survived the passage of time: a printing shop with the sign IMPRENTA DE LA TIERRA, where the writer spent many an hour in his work for the daily newspaper printed there, of the same name. Let us now go back and, behind the City Hall, feel the breeze of the port on our faces. Sung by

Virgil in his *Aeneid* as he seeks the ideal site for the land-
ing of Aeneas, the port of Cartagena was coveted by all sai-
lors. By our side there rises, like a desiccated whale, the
huge submarine of Isaac Peral. We stop where the autumnal gaze of a man returned from a foreign prison evoked
his youth, stolen by the sea: here he was assigned at the
age of twenty-two, as a corporal of Marine Infantry; from
here he left for Mahón and the Philippines, assignments
he himself requested. Much later, at the age of forty-two,
he again left Cartagena aboard the steamship Sagunto for
Barcelona, there to re-embark for Montevideo. Near here,
the Calle Real takes us toward the Arsenal, in whose ad-
ministrative offices Vicente Medina worked as an accoun-
tant. The tiled fountain this building had in the Twenties
has been faithfully reconstructed. Resuming our movement
back along the same street, we come out on the road to
Murcia. The poet, especially in his twilight period, turned
his back on the sea as we now do, in his yearning for the
valleys of Murcia and Archena.

II

By the motorway now being finished, we shall arrive at
Murcia in less than an hour; and on crossing the bridge
called Puente Viejo, near the City Hall and the Glorieta,
we encounter a rich field of Medinan memories in this
quarter which features four of his great loves: the Cathedral, the Paseo del Malecón, the Teatro Romea and the
Plaza de las Flores. Too obvious for inclusion in this list is
the Río Segura itself, which passes beneath the Virgen de
los Peligros like a serpent, moribund and evil-smelling, like
a bad dream for the Murcians, who live with this lesson in
ecology underneath their eyes and noses. Climbing the Cathedral tower, we admire its nests of angels, and its lights

Teatro Romea in Murcia.

and shades of the Baroque. The view extends far. Unamuno described Murcia as the "most rural city of Spain"; and the verdure of the surrounding market gardens is still in fairly close contact with the golden stone of the city, for the zone of vague suburbias that choke most cities off from immediate contact with the countryside have been kept to a minimun here. On the north, the hills of Churra, Cabezo de Torres and Monteagudo, reverberate with rabid thirst; on the south, the Sierra de Carrascoy, with Fuensanta and La Alberca at its feet. The pollens flower and flower round about on the irrigated plain.

By his flower-pot of mallows —he called them mal-vaseda (silk mallow) for the softness of their leaves— in an Argentine afternoon, the herald of this valley must have felt the completest solitude, for there are no nightingales in America, though Colón thought he had heard them. There the Murcian writer, struggling like a firefly to repro-duce the sun of Murcia, must have wept like a tree in a dewy night. At the feet of the Andes, he would like to have brought his river with him too:

> *Dulce es el agua que corre,*
> *verde la orillica está...*
> *Un no sé qué del Segura*
> *tiene el río Tunuyán*[4].

Now we descend from our Cathedral height, and take a short walk to the Malecón. We note the disappearance of the Biblical rows of palm trees immortalized by Vicente Medina in his illuminated photos. Next, returning down the Gran Vía and turning right by the Hotel Internacional, we discover the recently restored grace of the Teatro Romea, where Vicente Medina presented on 10 March 1901 his

---

[4] "Sweet is the water running, / Green the bank is, indeed... / An I-know-not-what of the Segura / Belongs to the río Tunuyán."

play *En lo oscuro,* and on 5 April 1931, presiding the festival of Gay-Saber upon his return from Argentina, advertised his love for the valley: "And I will confess that, in this poet that you have before you, Nature rolled together in one a sentimentalist and a Phoenician whose eyes, enchanted by the whiteness of the orange blossoms, dream with the eyes of the oranges." Let us walk past the Hotel Victoria, now a shopping centre; and behind it, advancing to the nearby Plaza de las Flores, walk in front of the old building of the daily *Línea,* which four centuries earlier was the seat of the Inquisition. The flower-sellers with their products of the eternal springtime of the greenhouse greet us in the plaza. Surprisingly, we may still repeat the rite common to so many visitors to Murcia in Medina's day and ours, that of buying meat pastries at the Confitería de Bonache. Then we proceed along Platería to the four corners, and in Trapería, in the opposite direction to the Cathedral rising in the distance, advance to the Santo Domingo Garden, where shade is cast by the same rubber tree that shielded our poet sometimes from the sun. If it is springtime, we can admire how Murcia opens out like all the books of the poet: *La barraca, La reina de la huerta, Murcia, la de las flores...* The four seasons and the hundred dreams of Vicente Medina meet here in Murcia, between these four corners.

III

Before heading for Archena, the *patria chica* of our poet, let us briefly perambulate the green environs of Murcia, leaving the city by the Madrid highway toward Espinardo, whose outskirts, having dust as their only fruit, have become the city's industrial zone. On his way out the visitor will note how almost all the avenues of Murcia have been planted with mulberry, the mythical tree of the silkworm, symbol of resurrection and spring. Taking the turnoff to Madrid and passing the San Basilio quarter and the Escuela de Maestría Industrial, we shall have to imagine what the garden zone of Huerta de las Bombas was like, now swallowed by development. Its great coat of arms, with savages carved in stone, of the 16th century, may now be seen on the Paseo del Malecón in the centre of Murcia. In Espinardo, famous for its red peppers, we may admire a gracious 16th-century tower, that of the Palacio Marquesal de los Vélez, where Polo de Medina held his learned Academies of the Garden. It now houses nuns and students of the Colegio de la Consolación. The neighboring orchards of Guadalupe burn their orange-blossom incense in the sun. Soon we come to La Ñora, crowned by bare ochre ridges, kneeling before the Monastery of Los Jerónimos, whose silhouette has a certain air of El Escorial. Founded in 1579, its exterior is in a severe and sober style; but ornament breaks through in the patio and the decoration of the church.

In La Ñora —a deformation of *noria,* water-wheel, in the dialect— the main attraction is the water-wheel itself, which its name to the place and to the peppers grown there. The huge wheel raises water from the river Aljufía in buckets, supported by a great brick arch of Gothic design. This famous artifice of 1396, of which a copy exists next to the Museum of the Huerta de Alcantarilla, is a key to this valley, where water murmurs endlessly. Medina froze its movement in one of his photographs, and in his notebooks reduced it to a toy to illustrate the cruelty of children:

> *Poquicas comparanzas*
> *hallara pa mi vida, como aquella:*
> *una ñorica hicieron los zagales*
> *en el mismo quijero de la cieca,*
> *   y a un pajarico de esos,*

alegría y encanto de la huerta,
a estilo de una mula
lo engancharon a ella⁵.

At the edge of the groves that extend towards Javalí Viejo, among the jasmine plants that still climb the balconies, and made a perfumer of our author, we will find the old *Fábrica de Pólvora* (Gunpowder Works) acquired by the State in 1747 to house the Artillery Arm. In these groves, his *Aires murcianos* picked petals from the chrysanthemums of elegy. Around us, villages and hamlets with mysterious Arab names, a landscape of quiet harmony that returns a lost peace to our souls. Above our heads, the twittering of the birds brings to mind a sample of Medina's style when he was temporarily infected by a passing Becquerian fever:

¡En el fondo de los valles y en los altos de las lomas
de flor llenos
ostentaban su blancura
como galas virginales de la tierra, los almendros!⁶.

Javalí Viejo and Javalí Nuevo, separated by the trough of the river, bring us on the right side to the cicadas of Alcantarilla, where the writer Pedro Jara Carrillo has a shade of marble, and the Blessed Franciscan Andrés Himbernón a street sign. The hagiographers tell us that this holy man wore out his habits with the constant flapping as he flew through the air in his frequent levitations over the moun-

---

⁵ "Few comparisons / will be found for my life, like that one: / the boys made a toy water-wheel / at the corner of the garden, / and one of those little birds, / the joy and charm of the valley, / in the manner of a mule / they tied to it."

⁶ "In the bottom of the valleys and on the heights of the hills, / in full flower, / their whiteness they exhibited, / like the earth's wedding dres, the almonds!"

tain of Santa Ana. Above the canal of La Barrera, another water wheel refreshes our sight; and twenty steps further on the museum of La Huerta: a profound homage to Medinism, though no plaque affirms his. Everything in this paradise named by the son of Juan de Dios "he of the romances" is found here embalmed under the brilliant light; silk looms, skirts, agricultural implements, pitchers... and the *barraca,* like the one the poet built as his nest in Argentina, as if only in such a building could he feel warmth:

> *A la orillica del río*
> *y mirándose en el agua,*
> *está como satisfecha*
> *y orgullosa mi barraca...*
> ....
> *Yo no envidio los palacios*
> *que en las ciudades levantan,*
> *que en ellos, con ser tan grandes,*
> *el corazón se me aplana.*
> *Y, en cambio, en mi barraquica,*
> *que es tan pequeña, se ensancha*[7].

Returning to Murcia after this short tour on the Granada road, at a half-kilometre after Alcantarilla, we may turn off to the left through the outlying villages —La Raya, Rincón de Beniscornia and Rincón de la Seca— to enjoy the scenery that Vicente Medina employed in *¡Lorenzo!, La sombra del hijo* or *El alma del molino,* dramas which begin with a common notice: "the scene is in the Vega de Murcia". As the traveller enters deeper into these orange and peach orchards, he may imagine Vicente Medina by the

---

[7] "On the bank of the river / Looking at itself in the water / As satisfied stands / And proud, my barraca... / .... / I envy not the palaces / That they raise in the cities, / In which, they being so great, / my heart feels flattened. / While in my little barraca / which is so small, it expands."

canals, under the shade of the grapevines, with cats and chickens wandering about; writing here with the facility of a swift's flight.

Before again taking, by Rincón de Seca, the highway leading to Murcia which we have left, let us mention that here resides the most famous *campana de auroros* of the region, belonging historically to the Brotherhood of the Virgen del Rosario de la Aurora. This band of singing musicians normally comes out on Saturdays and certain other customary days, though in the time of our writer they did so from twelve midnight until six in the morning. Vicente Medina, who as a child often followed them, has left us a portrait of them in *Patria chica:*

> The shrine in the fields is well known, it is called Casa de la Virgen... Its auroras, melancholy, pious songs, can make the pure waters of simple faith spring from the hardest souls.

Let us move further from Murcia along the Espinardo highway that we know already. Passing it, we find the University campus. Further on, the industrial town of Molina del Segura and, at 12 kilometres, Archena.

IV

In Archena, the traveller will soon see, at some hundred metres from the church, in the Plaza del Príncipe, house N.º 9, a plaque on the wall, commemorating the birthplace of the poet. Leaving the same engraved in the stone, letting ourselves be guided by the street names mentioned in *Mi pueblecito,* one of the poems of *¡Allá lejicos!...,* we soon meet his image in bronze, facing the flowers of the Villarías Garden. Bidding him farewell, we proceed to the charming spa where our poet, as a child, sold newspapers and books, before he practised, like a character from Dickens, various

Spa at Archena.

humble trades. The splendid colours of these places invite mention of Inocencio Medina Vera, who with brush portrayed the ways and life of the valley with the same tenderness and inspiration as his cousin Vicente Medina with his pen. Both were to emigrate to America like twin souls, anxious for laurels and fortune; but the painter died in poverty.

The visitor must now begin on foot the climb up the hill of Los Intes, and there shall find the house in ruins, built by the poet with the money he had gained from the lands he cultivated at the feet of the Andes, before selling them to a railway company. He called it "Jeja"; from it we get a privileged view of all the river valley. We return to the edge of the highway, and on the way to Ceutí, before reaching Los Torraos, we have an opportunity to take the same route as did Vicente Medina: some three and a half kilometres from the Río Segura to the Río Muerto. With the sound and the poplars, we will have an unforgettable memory of Archena.

Let us now undertake a trip to the mountain region of the northwest, on the Mula highway, retracing, thanks to the signs left us in *Patria chica,* the footsteps of our apprentice writer:

> I accompanied my father in his rounds through the villages to sell Zaragozan calendars and romances. We went on foot, from Archena, to Mula, Bullas, Cehegín, Caravaca and Moratalla.

At the inns in these towns, before the fire of vine twigs, his father, like a jongleur of old, would read the romances aloud, to sell them printed to the audience. If night fell when they were far from an inn, they slept under the stars. The romances sowed the seeds of poetry in the child's heart.

In Mula we motive the recently restored castle, from which Vicente liked to contemplate his beloved valley.

Nearby are the Baths of Mula, famous as the nest of love the people have made of them. Embroidery and ceramic proclaim the Moorish origin of its artisan skills. *La plaza de Mula* was another of the many poems that Vicente Medina wrote, like El Tostado.

In Bullas he hardly need to stop. Like the sellers of romances ("The twelve Peers of France", "Lisardo the Student", "Diego Corrientes"), we need only stop to buy the wine of Carrascalejo, and the exquisite *torrijas,* made according to a secret formula at a pastry shop in the Plaza del Ayuntamiento. Its cemetery, now forgotten, enjoyed some notice twenty years ago, when it was dreamed of by certain theatre directors as a setting for the *Tenorio.*

The climb to Cehegín through its steep streets shall give the best treasures of light to the lover of photography. And at the top, next to the 15th-century church of La Magdalena, we shall be astonished at how the Moorish quarter of Puntarrón falls in a cascade of roofs to the Río Argos. Cehegín is a nest of heraldic escutcheons, where one may feel nostalgia for the alpargata-maker, now only a metal statue beside the road, or for the herbs put inside chest to perfume the clothes. The pear of Cehegín, cousin to the apple, which made better propaganda for the town than its marble, succumbed in favour of the peach and apricot demanded by the markers of conserves.

Of Caravaca de la Cruz, Medina in a poem of his old age and somewhat inclined to credulity, published in his last book *Belén de pastores,* describes the miracle of the apparition of the True Cross to the captive Father Chirinos during the Mass held before the Moorish king and his court. Caravaca still turns upon this event in its festival of Moors and Christians, the first week in every May. Here are two stanzas:

> *Parece que Caravaca*
> *debió la CARCA llamarse...*

Puede ser que Moratalla
no tuviera nombre antes.

Lo cierto es que viene bien
de la reina el "¡Cara vaca!"
y el "mórate allá" del rey...
Moratalla[8].

Between the merlons of its castle which guards the two-armed cross, we may view the cluster of the medieval quarter on the slopes, the Carmelite convents which brought San Juan de la Cruz from Andalucía on seven occasions, the pavilion with escutcheons of Carlos III to bathe his cross, at the end of the Calle de la Corredera, near the magnificent sculpture that Pi Belda made of the Patron of Poets.

Moratalla, the last stop on our route, receives our approach like Cehegín and Mula, draped over a hill, proud of its 961 square kilometres of territory, which extend along the Granada road as far as Revolcadores, the highest peak in the region at 2001 metres. This is land for hunters, of vast panoramas like the Campo de San Juan, el Sabinar or Cañada de la Cruz, beautiful whether the almonds are opening their flowers of the snow is closing the high passes. After the silence of this whiteness in the Sierra de Segura, we contemplate in the headwaters of our river the splendour of the setting sun.

---

[8] "It seems that Caravaca / must have been called the CARCA... / It may be that Moratalla / had no name before. / In fact it suits it well / The 'Cara vaca!' of the Queen / And the King's 'mórate allá'... / Moratalla."

COMUNIDAD FORAL
DE NAVARRA

THE ROUTE OF TEODOSIO DE GOÑI, ACCORDING
TO FRANCISCO NAVARRO VILLOSLADA

by

MIGUEL SÁNCHEZ-OSTIZ

FRANCISCO NAVARRO VILLOSLADA
(Viana, Navarra, 1818-1895)

Navarro Villoslada studied Law, and was employed as an official in the Ministerio de la Gobernación. From 1860 to 1871 he was private secretary to Carlos VII, the Carlist Pretender. His political activity led him to be deputy in three legislatures, senator for Barcelona, and chief of the Tradicionalist Communion of Spain. He was an assiduous contributor to the press of his day, in defense of his traditionalist ideas.

As a novelist we may mention his works Doña Blanca de Navarra *(1847),* Doña Urraca de Castilla *(1849),* Historia de muchos Pepes *and* Amaya o los vascos en el siglo VIII, *his most famous work, in which he narrates the union of Basques and Visigoths by Christianity in the struggle against Islam.*

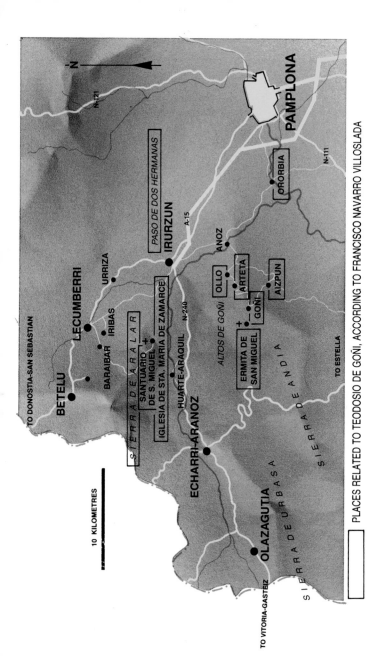

PLACES RELATED TO TEODOSIO DE GOÑI, ACCORDING TO FRANCISCO NAVARRO VILLOSLADA

THE ROUTE OF TEODOSIO DE GOÑI ACCORDING TO FRANCISCO NAVARRO VILLOSLADA

The natural scenery of the most outstanding episodes of the historical novel of Francisco Navarro Villoslada, *Amaya o los vascos en el siglo VIII*, are to be found in areas close to Pamplona, capital of the old Kingdom of Navarra. These are rocky, wild, lonely valleys, surrounded by bare rock ridges or closed by woods of beech or oak, scenes of other legends and other wars; valleys no doubt visited, in the capacity either of a Romantic or a forced traveller, by Navarro Villoslada. In any case, they are painted with considerable precision in his novel: Val de Ollo and Val de Goñi, the Burunda and the Sierra de Aralar, the Paso de las Dos Hermanas... These places are isolated from each other only by the abrupt topography.

A first route in the footsteps of Teodosio de Goñi would take are traveller from Pamplona to the entrance to the Val de Ollo, by the road passing through Olza and reaching Irurzun along the course of the río Araquil.

The legend of Teodosio de Goñi, closely associated with the sanctuary of San Miguel Excelsis, and enjoying

an ancient popularity in the popular literature and ico-
nography of Navarra, was used by Navarro Villoslada in
Amaya o los vascos en el siglo VIII to give substance to his
vision of the Basque leader who stood against the Goths
in their attempt to conquer the city of Iruña (Pamplona)
and the last redoubts of the Basques, among them Val de
Goñi.

Before entering the Val de Ollo, in the church of Oror-
bia, the oldest parts of whose structure date from the 13th
century, the visitor may view a Navarrese-Romanist retable of the 16th century, work of the so-called Oror-
bia Master, one of the best retables of this period existing in Navarra. In the central nave there is the image of
San Julián el Hospitalario, represented as a hunter of the
epoch, with falcon and mastiff, and in another nave there
are four scenes relating the main episodes in the story of
San Julián el Hospitalario or San Julián "the Parricide",
whose story parallels that of Teodosio de Goñi: the meeting with the deer, the discovery that the victims of his
fury were his parents, the construction of the hospital on
the banks of the river, and the ailing pilgrim given hospitality by San Julián, and who announces to him that he
has been pardoned.

Upon arriving at the village of Anoz, the traveller must
leave the local highway, cross the río Araquil and gradually enter the Val de Ollo, crossing several rough medieval bridges, some or them with a large round arch, half
covered with ivy in the shadier parts, next to groves of oak,
as in a Romantic engraving, under which the río Udarbe
runs. The valley comprises ten villages, where there have
always been numerous healers, herbalists and miracle-wor-
kers, and it is surrounded at the head by the great limestone walls of the Sierra de Andía and the crests of the
Sierra de Saldise.

According to a geographical dictionary of the last century, the valley is "surrounded by unequal mountains". And in fact Navarro Villoslada thus describes it, a valley surrounded by precipitous peaks, which was, until the early tenth century, one of the principal bulwarks of the nascent Kingdom of Navarra. Here stood the fortress of Peña Quays, the ultimate objective of Abd-al-Rahman III in his attempt to conquer the entirety of the Kingdom of Navarra, and which no doubt inspired the author of *Amaya.*

At the end of the valley, within a depp gorge into which twe waters from the Val de Goñi fall, is the spring of Arteta. A place of rare beauty with its closed mass of vegetation, the walls that rise covered with ivy and massy moss, the song of the blackbird and thrush, and above all the sound of the water gushing from the rock of falling from the heights of the gorge.

After leaving behind us the village of Arteta, where we may visit a curious ethnographic museum created by the sculptor José Ulibarrena, and surmounting the Sierra de Andía by the pass of the same name, we enter the Val de Goñi. The curious traveller here may wish to climb up from the road at one of the tight curves in the last part, and will be rewarded with a splendid panorama over the valley and the whole Pamplona basin. In Navarro Villoslada's novel, it was at this very spot that the lord of Cazteluzar, Miguel de Goñi, stationed his watchmen.

Having crossed the pass of Arteta, the traveller finds himself in the Val de Goñi, scene of many of the most relevant episodes in Navarro Villoslada's novel. Here the lords of Goñi had their palace Gazteluzar; and the wife of Teodosio, Constanza de Butrón, her palace of Jaureguía; here took place the tragedy of Teodosio, the jealousy induced by a diabolical hermit and the error which led him to parricide. And on the outskirts of the village of Goñi is the shrine of San Miguel, where popular belief situates the first apparition of the Archangel to Lord Teodosio de Goñi, and the fall of the first links of the chain that he was condemned to drag behind him. The shrine was built by Teodosio himself, according to the author of *Amaya*. But of all this, there is no trace but legend.

In the old church of Goñi some popular mural paintings, in ruinous condition, recall the story of Teodosio de Goñi and the Archangel Michael, the dragon, the hermit and the crime. The shrine of San Miguel, or San Migueltxo, was used in the last century, during the Franch occupation, as a powder magazine, and blown up by the guerilla chief Mina; and reconstructed in 1956. Only in Aizpún is there a palatial house of the 15th century, with tower and ogival windows.

Navarro Villoslada said of these valleys that they had a Romantic beauty. He said it with good reason: great crags of bare rock, deep woods, streams that drop from one valley to another, autumnal mists, beeches or solitary oaks growing twisted between the rocks, and vast panoramas. The visitor cannot help but think of the paintings of Caspar David Friedrich. Desolate places, small silent villages, woods, meadows and a far-off sound of cowbells. It is rare to meet anybody.

The second route takes us to the sanctuary of San Miguel Excelsis, on the heights of the Sierra de Aralar. For this we must again take the road at Aznoz, descending again to Val de Ollo by a road through majestic beech woods, leading to one of the medieval bridges already mentioned, and continue on the way to Irzurzun, then going up again in the valley of the Araquil and through the gorge of Osquía.

Now in Irzurzun, the traveller continues on the way to San Sebastián, and soon crosses the Paso de las Dos Hermanas, another of the scenes in which Navarro Villoslada, moved by his fantasy and the awesome gorge, sets

Irurzun. Pass of Dos Hermanas.

deeds of arms and valour in *Amaya o los vascos en el si-glo VIII;* here is where Teodosio of Goñi saves Amaya's life, whose crazed house rushes toward the precipice, and is stopped by an arrow accurately shot from the other side of the gorge.

Further on up the river Larraun the traveller arrives at Lecumberri, passing the inn of Urriza. On his right he may see the remains of one of the early paper mills that supplied the presses of the Old Kingdom. Once in Lecumberri we take on the left a road that leads us, after 16 kilometres, to the sanctuary of San Miguel Excelsis. The traveller will pass through two towns, Iribas and Baraibar, from which he may see an ample panorama of the valley of Larraun, and may reach the dolmens of the platform of Albia, not far from the road. Now we pass through meadows and woods with undergrowth of ferns, until we enter some beech woods not far from the top of the Sierra de Aralar. When the woods become thicker and carpeted with fallen leaves in autumn, they acquire a rare depth and silence. Only the isolated sound of a cowbell in the bush, or the whistle of the wind between the trees and over the dead leaves, breaks the silence of the day.

These places, especially those of the Sierra de Aralar, are also the scene of much of the Basque mythology and of not a few of their legends, which the author of *Amaya* echoes in his novel, as in the case of Basajaun, lord of the woods and the depths, and of treasures hidden in the crevices; and among the legends, of course, is that of Lord Teodosio de Goñi who, dragging his chains, wandered through these murmuring woods, where crevices, fountains with medicinal properties and prehistoric remains abound, until his final liberation, according to legends far antedating the novel of Navarro Villoslada, who knew them well and recreated them with the enthusiasm of the Romantic writer.

The origins of the Sanctuary, whence we get an ample panorama of the mass of Monte San Donato, la Barranca and the Sierra de Andía, are lost in legend. It is not unlikely that on the same site there was a Roman altar that protected the route of la Barranca, just as it is not impossible that such an altar would have been placed on the site of earlier rituals pertaining to a Neolithic pastoral culture, genuinely Basque. It is not for nothing that over sixty dolmens have been found in the Sierra de Aralar.

The present sanctuary seems to have been built, on earlier foundations of course, beginning early in 11th century and ending in 1143, the date of its consecration in the presence of King García Ramírez, who made abundant donations.

Thus, in the structure of the sanctuary we may discern remains of pre-Romanesque, Carolingian and Romanesque architecture. Our attention is drawn to the Romanesque interior chapel built, says Navarro Villoslada, by Teodosio himself, as is narrated in the last chapter of the novel, where the opening is found that, according to popular tradition gives, or grave, onto the chasm by which the dragon fled, that had appeared to Teodosio as an ultimate proof —another of the elements corresponding to the Basque mythology of the region— and from which he was saved by the intercession of the Archangel, St. Michael. On the outside of this small chapel we find, always according to popular tradition, the chains that, as papal penitence for the parricide committed, Teodosio had to drag. These chains, as much as the opening in the wall, have played an important role in the rites of popular medicine in the País Vasco and Navarra. The novelist also speaks of a hostelry that existed, was destroyed by fire and finally reconstructed, as the traveller finds it now.

But, setting aside these legends so difficult to prove, the jewel of the Sanctuary of San Miguel Excelsis is the

Church of San Miguel at Aralar.

altar front commonly called "retablo de Aralar", which
has been kept here for eight centuries. This is a spectacular front of enamels, made with Limoges technique, but of
Navarrese manufacture, composed of a central mandorla
representing the Virgin and Child; other enamels represent the Hagi, St. Joseph, the Virgin of the Annunciation,
the Angel of the Annunciation, the Apostles, the Eagle and
Lion of the Tetramorphos... also important is the image-
reliquary of St. Michael, which at Easter is carried on a
long circuit through towns and valleys as far as Pamplona,
blessing the fields on its way.

However the history of the Sanctuary, which depends
on the Cathedral of Pamplona through the monastery of
Zamarce, and which was generously endowed by the kings
of Navarra, has not been without vicissitudes. The early
hostelry was destroyed by fire, and the retable and other
precious objects of the sanctuary robbed various times,
occasioning a certain dark episode, remembered every
year with the arrival of the Angel at Pamplona, when a response is recited at the spot where three thieves were ex-
ecuted who had stolen it in 1797. The last robbery took
place in 1979, and the enamelled retable disappeared.
However, after a long and improbable search in the international market of stolen art works, almost all of the pieces
have been recovered.

A new and steep road, which follows the old road of
access to the Sanctuary from Huarte Araquil, will take the
traveller to the church of Santa María de Zamarce, also
the scene of some episodes in *Amaya,* those preceding the
pardon of Teodosio. Before this road was constructed the
way to the Sanctuary was, in the words of Navarro Villoslada, "difficult and painful, nowadays, by the trees, roots
and bushes that interrupt it; stones and slippery ground
that often inclines to a precipice. It was much more dan-

gerous then, when there was hardly an open path". This church is of Romanesque style, the only visible vestige of the old monastery.

The traveller leaves this church behind him, and after passing through the town of Huarte Araquil, may take the N-240 highway, either to Vitoria or to Pamplona.

LA RIOJA

THE PLACES
OF GONZALO DE BERCEO

by

RUBÉN CABA

GONZALO DE BERCEO
(c. 1195-after 1264)

The approximate date of Berceo's birth at Madriz, in the quarter of Berceo, is deduced from the scarce facts we possess relative to his life. In the year 1220 he was a deacon; and in 1237, presbyter. He appears as witness in documents of 1240, 1242 and 1246. He figures for the last time in a testament of 1264, as master of confession of the testator. In his books he tells us his name, that he was born at Berceo and brought up in San Millán de Suso: strophe 757 of La vida del Santo Domingo de Silos *and strophe 489 of the* Historia del señor San Millán. *In his old age, and tired, he began to write the* Vida de Santa Oria, virgen, *as he tells us in the second strophe. He also composed three Marian works,* Milagros de Nuestra Señora, Loores de Nuestra Señora *and* Duelo de la Virgen el día de la Pasión de su Hijo; *and other religious poems:* El martirio de San Lorenzo, El Sacrificio de la Misa *and* Los signos que aparecerán antes del Juicio.

His work, ignored or disdained until the 19th century, has been praised in our times for its simplicity and candour; though commentators such as Américo Castro have not been lacking, who see beneath his apparent ingenuousness a "propagandistic spirit in favour of the monasteries in which he had a personal interest". But for Rubén Darío, Berceo's verse "has freedom with decorum; and returns, like the gyrfalcon to the wrist, bringing golden rhymes from the blue sky". Antonio Machado declares that, among his poets "the first is Gonzalo de Berceo called", whose verse "is sweet and grave". And Azorín admires the "spontaneous, jovial, plastic, intimate" tone of Gonzalo de Berceo.

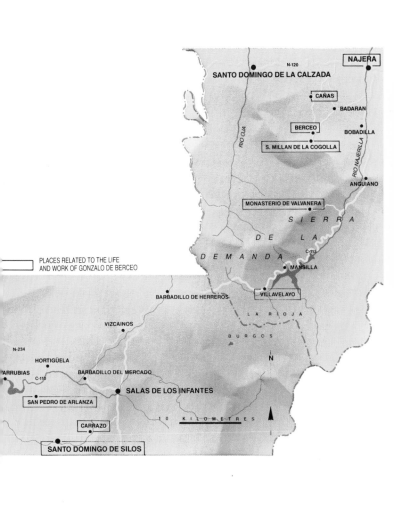

PLACES RELATED TO THE LIFE
AND WORK OF GONZALO DE BERCEO

NAJERA

N-120

SANTO DOMINGO DE LA CALZADA

CAÑAS

BADARAN

BERCEO

BOBADILLA

S. MILLAN DE LA COGOLLA

RIO OJA

RIO NAJERILLA

ANGUIANO

MONASTERIO DE VALVANERA

S I E R R A

D E   L A

D E M A N D A

C-113

MANSILLA

VILLAVELAYO

BARBADILLO DE HERREROS

L A   R I O J A

VIZCAINOS

B U R G O S

N-234

N

HORTIGÜELA

ARRUBIAS

C-110

BARBADILLO DEL MERCADO

SALAS DE LOS INFANTES

SAN PEDRO DE ARLANZA

1 0   K I L O M E T R E S

CARRAZO

SANTO DOMINGO DE SILOS

THE PLACES
OF GONZALO DE BERCEO

The traveller may arrive at Berceo and at San Millán de la Cogolla, municipalities only a little more than a kilometre apart, by various narrow but well asphalted highways: that which comes from Santo Domingo de la Calzada, the two that start from Nájera —one to the west and one to the south— to join at Badarán, and that which enters from Bobadilla, a village on the banks of the río Najerilla. By whatever way we arrive at this part of La Rioja, we shall find a fertile land of trees and meadows, reminiscent of the landscape of the Cantabrian coast. But, as everyone is free to reminisce about what he wants, Vicente Espinel saw in La Rioja a certain resemblance to Andalucía, as he wrote in his *Marcos de Obregón.*

Now in San Millán de la Cogolla, if the traveller begins by visiting the monastery of Suso —or of Arriba, in modern Castilian— he will enjoy the beech, oak and ilex woods, interspersed with a few *escarrios* (a variety of maple) which cover the neighboring hills. From 1964 until a few years ago, the monastery was cared for by a singular personality: Tarsicio Lejárraga. Facing the entrance door, next to a cherry tree, the guardian of Suso would speak of the foundation, in the sixth century, of the cave monastery of San Millán. Within the building he would comment, in verses of his own making, on these Visigothic capitals, those Mozarabic vaults, to finish by reciting some fragment of the life of San Millán, composed by his countryman Gonzalo de Berceo. Teodoro Lejárraga, successor to his father in the custody of Suso, though not heir of his poetic endowments, also gives well-studied explanations of the architecture of the monastery.

Gonzalo de Berceo, the first poet in Castilian whose name is known to us —the *Cantar del Mío Cid,* written a century before, is by an unknown author— was a rural priest ascribed to the monastery of San Millán de Suso, where he liked to compose stanzas in honour of the Gloriosa and of the saints of his devotion. This brother in sensibility to his contemporary St. Francis of Assisi —with whom he shared a conception of life far removed from the great intellectual formulations of other saints of the period, auch as St. Bonaventure, St. Albert Magnus and St. Thomas Aquinas— applied himself to write in plain vernacular language, comprehensible to his neighbours; describing not only "the miracles of Our Lady" (which occur in Toledo, Cologne, Rome, Pavia, Constantinopla, etc.) and the Martyrdom of St. Lawrence (suffered at Rome), but also the lives of local saints: San Millán (473-574), Santo Domingo de Silos (1000-1073) and Santa Oria (1042-1070?).

Gonzalo de Berceo mentions in his *Historia del señor San Millán* that this saint, born also at Berceo, pastured sheep until, by influence of the hermit San Felices, he retired to the caves in the place where the monastery of Suso now stands, because "with temporal life he was much disgusted". But, as his fame of anchorite attracted many visitors from the surroundings, he preferred to

San Millán de la Cogolla. Monastery of Suso.

(...) vevir con las serpientes,
maguer son enojosas, aven amargos dientes,
que derredor las cuevas ver tan grandes gentes [1].

Thus, to flee from the bustle of life, he entered the woods of the Montes Distercios and, in penitence and contemplation, spent forty years out there, a sort of record of wilderness solitude which Gonzalo de Berceo describes as a "feat". After being ordained priest by the bishop of Tarazona and a period as parish priest in Berceo, San Millán, now in his seventies, returned to his favourite occupation, solitude, and went to live in the caves of Suso. As he did not die until the age of a hundred and one, he had time to form a community of anchorites around him. Gonzalo de Berceo relates some prodigies worked in his lifetime by San Millán, to finish by proclaiming the miracle he worked several centuries after his death. This of all his miracles had, no doubt, the greatest historical transcendence: the host of Count Fernán González won the battle of Simancas in 939 against a host of Moors, thanks to the decisive intervention of San Millán and of St. James Apostle, both of whom, mounted on "two horses whiter than crystal", descended "through the air, at great speed", striking panic into the Moorish host.

Domingo Manso de Zúñiga, better known as Santo Domingo de Silos, "native of Cañas", as says Gonzalo de Berceo in his *Vida del glorioso confesor Santo Domingo de Silos.* The boy of Cañas became prior of San Millán de Suso, but was obliged to leave the monastery when he resisted the wishes of King García de Navarra, who proposed to reclaim the treasures that his ancestors had donated to the community of Suso. He was for a time confined in Tres

---

[1] "(...) live with the serpents, though they are disgusting and have sharp bitter teeth, than see so many people around the caves."

Celdas (three cells), a place near Tobía named for the three cells dug out of the rock by the monks Citonato, Geroncio and Sofronio; before leaving for Burgos, where King Fernando I of Castile named him Abbot of the decayed monastery of San Sebastián de Silos, in the land of Carrazo. He directed the Silos community with such honour and prudence that, at this death, the monastery became known as Santo Domingo de Silos.

In the "portaleyo" or portico of the humble monastery of Suso, Gonzalo de Berceo must have composed some of his works and, with more certainty, the *Vida de Santa Oria, virgen,* as he affirms it thus:

> *Gonzalo li dixeron al versificador,*
> *que en su portaleyo fizo esta labor*[2].

Santa Oria, who as a child had moved with her parents from Villavelayo to San Millán de Suso, lived in a bricked-up cell near the monastery, perhaps in the site which the guard at Suso calls the den of Santa Oria. Her remains and those of her mother were buried in the monastery of Suso, and are now at that of Yuso.

This monastery, that of Yuso —meaning, in old dialect, the lower monastery— is set amid San Millán de la Cogolla, a village inhabited by some 300 persons, kind and discreet, and a good supply of yawning dogs who greet the stranger with a Franciscan gaze. The monastery of Yuso, founded in the 11th century, and reconstructed and remodelled in successive ages until in the 16th century it acquired the physiognomy we now see, was a cultural and religious centre in the Middle Ages. In those days the name of San Millán de la Cogolla attracted numerous pilgrims who venerated the saint as the co-patron of Spain along

---

[2] "They called the verse-maker Gonzalo, / who in the portico performed this labour."

with St. James; but nowadays the visitors are mostly those on weekend outings, impenitent voyagers and the occasional student of our language.

Since 1973, when the 15th centenary of San Millán's birth was celebrated, and the Real Academia de la Lengua dedicated at Yuso a plaque to the Glosas Emilianenses, Spanish-speakers have again begun to take interest in this place; an interest accentuated in 1978 with an official celebration of the thousandth anniversary of the Castilian language. Approximately ten centuries have gone by since a monk of this monastery, a student of grammar it would seem, wrote some glosses in the margin of a sermon in Latin of St. Caesarius of Arles. These notes are no more than forty-three words arranged in sentences cast in early Castilian or, to be more precise, in Romance language very close to the Navarro-Aragonese dialect. To the same glossist we owe some notes in Basque, very natural in an area of Castilian, Aragonese and Basque influence. Proof of this is the fact that Gonzalo de Berceo in his works employs various words of Euskera.

Dámaso Alonso called the Emilian or San Millán glosses "the first cry of the Spanish language". A cry not only religious in nature, as Alonso Zamora Vicente has pointed out. It is true that our language is born in hesitant conversation with God, while the first testimony of French (the Strasbourg Cath of 842) is a political text, and the first writings in Italian ("L'indovello Veronese" of the early 9th century, and «Placitos de Montecasino» of about 960) turn, respectively, on a riddle and a juridical question. But the Glosses of the Emilian monk have a look about them of the hidden notes that students have always used to cheat with in examinations. So that, as Alonso Zamora Vicente concludes, the Glosses of San Millán may in their convent have the seeds of our mysticism; but in their intention lie the seeds of our picaresque tradition.

This town, San Millán de la Cogolla, to which arrive many visitors interested in the history of the Spanish language, and which was a "place coveted by the tired traveller" in the time of Gonzalo de Berceo, does not at present boast any inn or pension where the traveller may rest his bones. Nor is it possible to spend the night in the nearby town of Berceo, and the visitor must seek lodging at Santo Domingo de la Calzada or at Nájera, until at some future date the Government of La Rioja inaugurates the hostelry they are preparing in the courtyard of the monastery of Yuso.

He who decides on Nájera and takes the road that passes through Cañas, birthplace of Santo Domingo de Silos, will find there an interesting church adjoining a Cistercian monastery of the 13th century: Santa María de Cañas.

The traveller who wishes to follow the route of places mentioned by Gonzalo de Berceo, may lodge at the monastery of Valvanera, 35 kilometres by highway from San Millán de la Cogolla. For walkers there is another possibility: go up from San Millán de la Cogolla some 10 kilometres toward the Sierra de San Lorenzo, then take a shortcut on a path for some 6 kilometres through the woods to the monastery of Nuestra Señora de Valvanera, patroness of La Rioja and Cameros. This Benedictine monastery, reconstructed in recent years, conserves a Marian image of the 12th century, in a church built in the late Gothic taste on the end of the 15th. Apart from the carving of the Virgin, a masterpiece of Spanish Romanesque sculpture, the most notable thing about this monastery is its singular location: a prehistoric wilderness where, among the beeches, oaks, ilex and heather, one might not be too surprised at the appearance of a unicorn or griffin.

Gonzalo de Berceo mentions Valvanera in his *Vida de Santa Oria, virgen:*

Monastery of Valvanera.

A otro su disçípulo, Muño era llamado,
que de Valvanera fue abat consagrado[3].

Also, according to the well-founded conjecture of Father Alejandro Pérez Alonso, Gonzalo de Berceo must also have been the author of a versified history of Valvanera, composed in his "vulgar and maternal" language, of which all that has come down to us is a Latin version written two centuries later by the abbot Domingo de Castroviejo.

Going upstream along the Najerilla, a stream bordered by thick vegetation and rich in trout, a road, flanked by chestnut trees on its first stretch, leads to the reservoir of Mansilla and from there shortly to Villavelayo, birthplace of Santa Oria or Aurea. So says Gonzalo de Berceo in his *Vida de Santa Oria, virgen:*

Esa virgen preçiosa de quien fablar solemos,
fue de Villa Vellayo, segunt lo que leemos[4].

If from Barbadillo de Herreros we follow the course of brook of Pedroso, a few kilometres beyond where it empties into the río Arlanza, we find the ruins of the monastery of San Pedro de Arlanza, famous ruins which, a few years ago, were under the threat of being drowned by the waters of a reservoir. To preserve them, the Junta de Castilla y León has made an agreement to set up in the old refectory a museum on the history of the monastery. In the first half of the 10th century, Count Fernán González restored the monastery, of Visigothic foundation, and donated lands and goods to ensure its future prosperity. Thanks to Gonzalo de Berceo we know that Santo Domingo as abbot

---

[3] "Another disciple, Muño by name, / was at Valvanera consecrated abbot."

[4] "This precious virgin of whom we speak so much, / was of Villa Velayo, as we read."

of Silos cooperated in the transfer from Ávila to the abbey of San Pedro de Arlanza, of the relics of the Avilan martyrs Vicente, Cristeta and Sabina. The poet specifies the place where the Benedictine abbey stands:

> *En río de Arlanza, en una reconada,*
> *yació un monesterio, una casa honrada,*
> *San Pedro de Arlanza es por nombre clamada*[5].

Our literary pilgrimage through the territory of Gonzalo de Berceo may well end at the monastery of Santo Domingo de Silos, an establishment which, as we have said, the Riojan saint repaired and amplified when it was still dedicated to St. Sebastian. The monastery museum contains, among other valuable codices, a copy of the *Vida de Santo Domingo de Silos* by Gonzalo de Berceo, by the hand of some contemporary of the author. However, the *Glosas silenses* have come to rest in the library of the British Museum. These are glosses made in a Latin text of penitential content. A monk of Silos, about the end of the 10th century or beginning of the 11th, some decades later than the Glosses of San Millán de la Cogolla, noted a few words in the Romance language he spoke in the street. In the cloister of Silos, a capital work of Castilian Romanesque, there still stands the cypress that Gerardo Diego in a well-made sonnet called "upright fountain of shade and dreams".

---

[5] "On the río Arlanza, in a vale, / lies a monastery, and honoured house, / San Pedro de Arlanza by name."

COMUNIDAD VALENCIANA

THE VALENCIA
OF VICENTE BLASCO IBÁÑEZ

by

JOAN FUSTER

VICENTE BLASCO IBÁÑEZ
(Valencia, 1867-Menton, 1928)

For years, many years, Vicente Blasco Ibáñez was the Spanish writer most read throughout the world: in any case, the most famous of his contemporaries. Translations and cinema gave his work a wide diffusion, and built him a solid, and well remunerated, international prestige. He had a chequered youth of involvement in politics: prison, exile, almost continuous electoral success, combative journalism, duels on the field of honour, effervescent oratory, give that period of his life the classic profile of a revolutionary agitator. And his pen never abandoned these early enthusiasms. Anticlerical, republican and antimilitarist, into his narrations there filter the vehemence and the syllogisms of an ideology perhaps elementary and ingenuous, but historically effective. Literary adventure took him in 1909 to Argentina: there he soon undertook a surprising enterprise of agricultural settlement which was to prove financially ruinous. He had published pamphlets like La araña negra *(1892), a ferocious attack on the Company of Jesus. Soon after, with* Arroz y tartana, *he initiated the "Valencian cycle", the best of his work:* La barraca *(1898),* Flor de mayo *(1895),* Entre naranjos *(1900),* Cañas y barro *(1902). Later he proceeded to other places, other enterprises. Blasco did not like to cover the same ground twice. His most fortunate moment, perhaps, was in 1916 with the publication of* Los cuatro jinetes del Apocalipsis, *which immediately became a factor of propaganda in favour of the Allies in the First World War. Meanwhile, from near or far, he kept up a flow of productions published in the Castilian language. With fortune and celebrity, a tireless writer (near the end of his life, half blind, he resorted to dictation), he spent his last years on the Cote d'Azur, pursuing his obsession of hounding the Dictatorship and the Monarchy.*

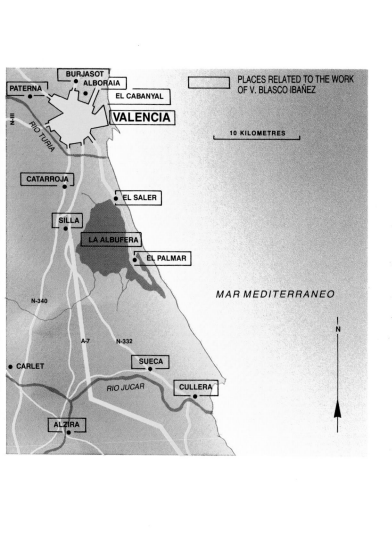

PLACES RELATED TO THE WORK
OF V. BLASCO IBAÑEZ

10 KILOMETRES

BURJASOT
PATERNA
ALBORAIA
EL CABANYAL
VALENCIA
N-III
RIO TURIA
CATARROJA
EL SALER
SILLA
LA ALBUFERA
EL PALMAR
MAR MEDITERRANEO
N-340
N
A-7   N-332
CARLET
SUECA
RIO JUCAR
CULLERA
ALZIRA

THE VALENCIA
OF VICENTE BLASCO IBÁÑEZ

Since *Arroz y tartana* (1894) or *Cañas y barro* (1902) almost a century has now gone by, and the places and people
that formed the material for the Valencian novels of Vicente Blasco Ibáñez could hardly have helped but change.
Perhaps not as much as we might expect in many aspects,
but certainly enough for us to find that, basing our vision
on those books, there remain only bits of the image we are
seeking. This is no doubt a good sign. The dynamic of time
found here a space predisposed to its demands, and has
fulfilled its function with more or less energy. The city, for
example, on spreading, and extending its necessities of
communication and traffic, has devoured half the *huerta,*
or irrigated plain, that of *La barraca* (1898) and the rest,
and also the towns of the outskirts have grown with their
own smaller industrial thrust. All these factors combine to
blur the perfumed, agrarian image of the place that Blasco
Ibáñez captured so well in his pages. Or in a contrary sense,
the area of the Ribera Alta de Xúquer has multiplied its
orange groves, and lower down also, wherever it is possible,
exportable and profitable fruit occupies the sides of the

low hills of the region. And Cabanyal of *Flor de mayo* (1895) is no longer a village of fishermen and smugglers. Of Albufera and its Devesa we could say much: about its deterioration...

Alboraia

La barraca is set in the environs of Alboraia, but its events —a rough rural, episode, of rents, rancours and fanaticism— might have had some other scene, further north or further south. Now there remain only a few *barracas*. This was the typical dwelling of the poor huerta people: straw roof, adobe walls, a shady grapevine over the entrance, a well. Now these are substituted by houses of more conventional structure, with new customs and new conveniences. The passions of the people have also varied. An exploration of the huerta must be made on foot, following the work paths, next to the canals and between the fields. The adolescent Blasco Ibáñez wandered this terrain with his five senses open to its charm, to its silent dramas, to its rites of festival and harvest. In those days the huerta was more "huerta", and the jocund vegetable growth made appetizing and cheerful company for the walker. As always when the landscape is the work of man, without geological grandiosity or thrilling spectacles of jungle or desert, the contemplation of this terrain is comforting in its cordiality and regularity. For the stranger, perhaps, the violence of the light may be somewhat aggresive. And the sweet monotony of the perfect furrows and the variety of the greens. Now, from time to time, the view is interrupted by the grey bulk of removable greenhouses: plastic coverings placed by the farmers to accelerate their *primeurs* of early fruit. Some of the remaining barracas have uralite roofs.

Valencia

They say that an Alexandrine verse of Victor Hugo defined Valencia as the city of three hundred belltowers. There may have been even more than three hundred, between parishes, convents and shrines. Recent buildings have surprassed the height of the pious towers, and the silhouette of the city has lost its former grace. The novel of Valencia is *Arroz y tartana:* that of the people and the middle class of the second half of the nineteenth century. Nobody has tried anything like it since. The present-day tourist, who approaches and passes on in search of beaches and paellas, would recognize neither the sites nor the society portrayed by Blasco Ibáñez. He had been brought up in the old alleys of small shops and artisans, with the friendship of liberals who fought in the "National Militia". When in *Arroz y tartana* —which incorporates the festive calendar of the city— a *falla* burns, the charanga band hired by the neighbours launches into the Marseillaise, as in real-life scenes when Blasco Ibáñez animated the local political life. A slight residue remains of that old Valencian lifestyle, but so attenuated it is hardly noticeable. And the venerable monuments remain: the city gates of Serranos and Quart, the Cathedral with its Miquelet, the merchant's hall —a fine civil Gothic work of the Mediterranean— a few churches saved from the flames of revolution, the palace of Dos Aguas, the museums... Valencia expanded. Blasco Ibáñez had stimulated it in an inflamed speech: *La revolución de Valencia.* His Valencia disappeared, almost. I don't believe he could be unhappy with this fact.

El Cabanyal

The city is a few kilometres from the sea. The so-called "maritime villages" —the port itself— never had an important incidence in the urban life, in spite of the mercantile

Valencia. Miquelet tower, Cathedral.

nature of the bourgeoisie and the international trade that the fruit and garden industry involved. The Cabanyal of Blasco Ibáñez —that of *Flor de mayo*— still got up to fish in the morning, and suffered frequent horrors in the storms. "And still they say that fish is dear" exclaimed the "witch of the sea" at the end of the story. "And still they say that fish is dear" was the title of a moving painting by Joaquín Sorolla, a great friend of Blasco Ibáñez. The sea of Sorolla —the Valencian sea of Sorolla— became, later in his work, a brilliant backdrop populated by ladies with elegant parasols and veils, of a Viscontian whiteness, with naked children playing in the shallows. The tragedy of the fisherman's risky life receded into the background. Something similar has happened in the economy of this coast. The Valencian littoral has become almost a continuous strip of restaurants, beach bars and discothèques, among other jocose activities, which rub shoulders with the work of loading and unloading merchandise. The inhabitants organize Holy Week festivals with lots of drums and trumpets. Blasco Ibáñez mocked these spectacles, though the people who organized them were his own voters and, presumably, readers. But this detail is of no interest.

La Albufera

To continue on our Blasco route, we must go down the highway that runs between Albufera and the Mediterranean. When Blasco Ibáñez wrote *Cañas y barro,* this highway did not exist: there was only a painful road, little trafficked. La Albufera was a vast lake, a short distance from the city and extending to Sueca and Cullera, with an island in the middle, El Palmar. The tongue of land that separates La Albufera from the sea is a pasture: the Devesa. There, in the Middle Ages, bulls pastured and snakes slid. As in La Albufera, great flocks of migratory birds nested or stopped

La Albufera.

here; the cataloguing of them would be a difficult though pleasant task. Hunting and especially fishing —eels, sea bass— were the attraction of the lagoon, reserved as patrimony of the kings. In *Cañas y barro,* Blasco Ibáñez portrays a dispute between fishermen —allies of the hunters— and the farmers. The farmer of this countryside never understood what so much still water was good for if, by some means, he could convert it to a rice field. During centuries, it seems, and by a slow and fatiguing process, gradually La Albufera was the victim of agricultural encroachment. The system consisted of filling in the lake: dumping in earth brought from another place, to reduce the area of water. The modest prosperity of Sollana, Sueca and Cullera is largely based on this operation. In El Palmar the son of a fisherman wishes to become a farmer; this is the plot. And the same wind has continued blowing. El Palmar is no longer an island as in *Cañas y barro,* but a peninsula, and La Albufera has shrunk yet further. Industrial effluents from the other side of the lake, and the insecticides now used by the farmers, not to mention the tourist industry, have made of La Albufera a dead lake, compared to what it was. An "ecological disaster", to use the trendy expression. The migratory birds, such of them as are left, avoid it. The fish are dead, of course. The Devesa has been cut up, privatized into lots for suburban summer villas. Perhaps these things have to be.

But La Albufera still makes a nice postcard. In one stretch, the highway borders the lake, and there is a spacious viewpoint by the water. A few boats come and go amid the gentle waves, toward the limpid centre —the "lluent"— or toward the canals that have formed between the "matas" or islands of mud and rushes. The spectacle has a variable grace, depending on the season and the time of day. Perhaps the best is an autumn afternoon, with the clean colours and placid climate. One last fish jumps and breaks the surface. In El Palmar we can have a fine dish of eel (imported), or rice to a traditional recipe. Nearby, in the Devesa, there is a Parador and a golf course, luxury hotels, and dozens of urbanisations. Further on, the plain extends as far as the Xúquer, ochre during some months, flooded in others, the plains green in spring and golden in autumn. All is rice. The authorities, not long ago, proclaimed they were going to step in and control the situation with the laudable intention of "preserving nature", and try to put some kind of brake on the agricultural and speculative aggresion against the lake. Perhaps they will save what is left of La Albufera, the "humid patch" of the region, and its peculiar fauna. There will be, no doubt, a lot of push and pull, and some *modus vivendi* be arrived at. The inhabitants of the place, since their ancestors first attacked it with their shovels, maintain that Man was not made for fish or birds, but the other way round. Anyway, so it says in *Génesis.*

Sueca, Cullera, Alzira

Following the route, we arrive at Sueca. Here Blasco Ibáñez had a strong following, though when in 1893 he contested a parliamentary seat here, he lost to his Consevative opponent. One day, while he was presiding an anticlerical demonstration in the street, an impertinent holy person succeed by surprise in hanging on him a scapulary of the Sacred Heart. From Sueca we may go down to Cullera, the only stretch of the coast, in these latitudes, with a bit of mountain, a lighthouse and ruins of a medieval castle. Blasco, in his novels, shifted his attention to Alzira. To go from Sueca to Alzira we cross the Xúquer (the Júcar), a generous and sometimes cruel river. In the Valencian Country, the three major rivers —the Turia, the Xúquer and the Segura— hand over their flow to the farmer and make his fields profitable. The fundamental wealth of these lands depends on the friendly water of its rivers, deriving into innumerable canals, troughs, furrows and runnels. But these same rivers can go wild when the weather becomes impertinent, and their floods can be devastating. On not a few occasions, the Valencians have had occasion to think of their rivers in a parody of the Biblical proverb: "The river giveth, the river taketh away; blessed be the name of the river." Dams moderate the floods now; but dams have bee known to collapse, wiping out whole towns, with trees, animals and persons floating dead on the water, on their way to the sea. Blasco Ibáñez chose Alzira as the scene for a description of one of these floods. This is in *Entre naranjos*. Human precautions were not then what they are today; and today they leave much to be desired. Mitigation of the disaster could only come by supernatural hand. In Alzira, San Bernardo and his sisters María and Gracia, martyrs in Christian faith —all children of a Moorish king, converted to Christianity— were the mediators before the divinity. Nowadays, with the agnosticism that is about, the exalted processions of *Entre naranjos* are seen no more, for better or for worse.

In Alzira we may contemplate one of the loveliest and most satisfactory "landscapes" in the geography of Blasco Ibáñez, and which Blasco had no time to see. The expansion of the orange orchards has occurred since the novelist's time. The visitor, whom one imagines as being curious and supplied with some funds, may install himself in the low hills that surround Alzira, and look. What he sees will be a deliberate wood, a calculated accumulation of branches, spreading all along the Ribera Alta: by the edge of the Xúquer and the land directly or indirectly irrigated by it. The people of Alzira are prosperous; there are rich folks in this place. The population has taken up the industrial challenge, and the bosses here are no longer those of *Entre naranjos*. We cannot even find out whether there is some

Wagnerian singer, like the one Blasco Ibáñez features in his book: a Valkyrie of banner-like and victorious cry. Blasco loved Wagner as much he did Victor Hugo, and it would be difficult to say which of them exercised the greater formative influence on him. Ther style of Blasco Ibáñez —setting aside his bilingual syntax and his brutal adjectives— is, in the novelistic scene of his time in Spain, a rhetorical emulsion of a strange vitality. Among his younger countrymen of recognized fame in Castilian, Azorín (1873-1967) and Gabriel Miró (1879-1930), language and literature part ways: they are not eloquent. Or they don't sing.

Catarroja: and back to Valencia

From Alzira we return to Valencia. We do so by the interior; that is, leaving the "humid patch" of La Albufera on our left. The highways, toll roads or not, are easy. What is to be seen and is seen, hardly existed when Blasco Ibáñez wrote. We pass through Catarroja. Catarroja has a "port" on La Albufera: it had some fishermen with rights on the lake, and a musical band for the fiestas of El Palmar, and industrious farmers. Catarroja is now an appendix to Valencia, with factories, warehouses and services. This bit of the huerta —for it *is* huerta— has become part of the conurbation. A bit further on, without noticing the difference amid the strip development, and we are in Valencia. It is no longer the Valencia of Blasco. It is, and it isn't. Blasco Ibáñez left a heritage: a sort of street-life verve, linked to his personal charisma. It soon faded away. Two furious pamphlets, *Una nación secuestrada. Alfonso XIII, desenmascarado* (1924) and *Lo que será la República española* (1925) where to be his testament. In 1933, his remains were brought back from Menton to Valencia, where they occupy a niche, abandoned and sad, in the civil cemetery. *Sic transit...*

PAÍS VASCO

PÍO BAROJA:
HIS LAND AND HIS PEOPLE

by

JULIO CARO BAROJA

PÍO BAROJA
(San Sebastián, 1872-Madrid, 1956)

Among the Spanish writers who, in a more or less conventional manner, have been included in the Generation of '98, Pío Baroja is, no doubt, the "novelist" by antonomasia. Although he did not fail to cultivate other genres (essay, theatre, autobiography), his most intense attentions, during more than half a century, were devoted to the novel.

He studied Medicine at Madrid and Valencia, and took his doctorate, significantly, with a thesis on "Pain". He practised Medicine in Cestona, and there began to write and acquired a consciousness of being Basque, by his own admission. His first published work, Vidas sombrías *(1900) is composed of short narrations. The novels that follow, which are grouped in trilogies, are set either in the Basque country or in the city of Madrid. Apart from novels with contemporary background, he wrote many others that occur in the nineteenth century. The first of these is* Zalacaín el aventurero *(1909). Later, with* El aprendiz de conspirador *(1913), he began a series under the general title of* Memorias de un hombre de acción, *whose protagonist is a relative of his own mother: Eugenio de Aviraneta.*

From 1921 Baroja spent much of the year with his mother

at "Itzea", a house he had bought and restored in Vera de Bidasoa. Here he brought together a very curious library and a collection of prints related to he life of nineteenth-century personalities, and to episodes in the history of that century. At the age of nearly 84 he died in Madrid, surrounded by official incomprehension and the admiration of Spanish and foreign writers. Hemingway declared on many occasions that Baroja was one of his masters.

Like all great novelists, Baroja was an exceptional witness of his period, a profound observer, not without a lyrical, profoundly Romantic vein. Antonio Machado, who much admired him, wrote in an expressive poem that Baroja had picked "the last leaf of the Romantic rose".

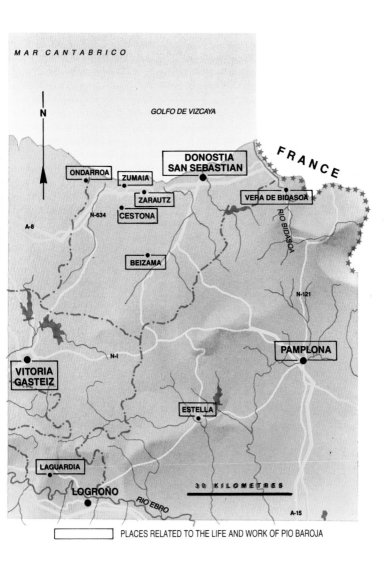

MAR CANTABRICO

GOLFO DE VIZCAYA

FRANCE

N

DONOSTIA
SAN SEBASTIAN

ONDARROA

ZUMAIA

ZARAUTZ

VERA DE BIDASOA

CESTONA

N-634

A-8

RIO BIDASOA

BEIZAMA

N-121

PAMPLONA

N-I

VITORIA
GASTEIZ

ESTELLA

LAGUARDIA

30 KILOMETRES

LOGROÑO

RIO EBRO

A-15

PLACES RELATED TO THE LIFE AND WORK OF PIO BAROJA

PÍO BAROJA:
HIS LAND AND HIS PEOPLE

I.   *The observer and his scope*

The vision one may have of a country if he is born in it, is usually distinct from that of a stranger. Some believe that both are complementary. Others, that the foreigners in general see better; which personally I doubt. He who sees best is the native, but the native endowed with great intelligence and certain particular faculties. I believe that these occur above all in the great novelists. Think of what Gogol, Tolstoy, Turgenev or Dostoyevsky have given us to know about Russia; of what Dickens has reflected of the merry or sombre England of his time. And here, what has been observed in us by Cervantes and Galdós. In this series we may put the vision of Spain in general and of the País Vasco in particular, offered by Pío Baroja in his triple condition of Basque much tied to his country, resident of Madrid and assiduous traveller. These visions may only reach a select group of attentive readers. Because the majority of people (perhaps today more than ever) prefer to see any sort of framework of a political type, with more of vain rhetoric than real content.

In Baroja's case there are particular circumstances, which we must know in order to judge his vision of the País Vasco and people. In the first place, his birth in San Sebastián, on the Day of the Innocents of 1872, in a bourgeois family of liberal traditions. Baroja had seven Basque surnames and one Italian. His great-grandfather Querubín Nessi had been born at Como and came up the north of Spain early in the nineteenth century, at the time of the struggles between French and Asturians. In the second place, his progenitors, for four or more generations, had practised liberal professions. Among them were printers and editors, pharmacists, merchant mariners, lithographers, goldsmiths. People of provincial cities, but city people; with a predominance of liberal ideology. This in a land, like the País Vasco in the nineteenth century, where Carlism was great force, must be viewed as of prime importance. Finally his father Serafín Baroja y Zornoza (1840-1912), mining engineer, Basque poet and a smiling, benevolent man, was markedly anticlerical, though his wife was a pious and fairly rigorous woman.

The vision of the world that can begin with that of a child born in such circumstances (and above all, if the child is a bit turbulent and imaginative) must of force be somewhat peculiar. But to understand it we must take yet another factor into account. From soon after his birth until the age of twenty, the family had to change their residence many times, to Madrid, Pamplona, Valencia, owing to the father's transfers. After finishing his medical studies and practising medicine as municipal doctor of Cestona in Guipúzcoa, Baroja not only returns to spend some time in the country, but also discovered his Basque roots, as he himself declared. It is during this period also that he begins to write, and compose the sketches for some of the stories he was to publish in his first book *Vidas sombrías* (1900), among which several have a Basque setting.

From then until his death in 1936, his relation with the country grew, and in 1912 he settled at Vera de Bidasoa, at the northern end of Navarra, with the French frontier on one side and Guipúzcoa on the other. During his long sojourns there, he wrote much of his work, and got to know the country much better.

So it may be said that Baroja was able to give a very complex and ample vision of the country itself and the people throughout many years: from the second half of the 19th century to the first half of the twentieth. Such a vision reflects, no doubt, a filial fondness; but is none the less critical for that. Among the characters of his novels there are plenty of Basques who act in a more or less heroic, more or less poetic mode. There is no lack, however, of personalities of a less sympathetic or even sinister type; portrayed directly, it may be more directly than the others.

II. *Four Basque settings, with proposal for a route*

As we know, Baroja had a custom of gathering his novels into trilogies to which he gave a common name, though each novel was independent. Thus one of these trilogies, soon established, is called *Tierra vasca* and comprises *La casa de Aizgorri* (1900), *El mayorazgo de Labraz* (1903) and *Zalacaín el aventurero* (1909). In another, slightly later novel, *Las inquietudes de Shanti Andía* (1911), grouped with others under the general title of *El mar,* there is a fourth vision of the life of the men of the country in relation to their surroundings. Because *La casa de Aizgorri,* dated at Marañón on 17 July 1900 and written in dialogue form, gives a sombre vision of an industrial milieu, the unattractive aspect of industry, and this at a time when the Basque industrial-

Vera de Bidasoa. "Itzea", the Barojas' house.

ists were most proud of what they were doing. The novel's personalities are, in part, decadent or degenerate, in part idealist, as is the protagonist. The ambit in which the action takes place (later illustrated by Ricardo Baroja) is that of a Guipuzcoan Village. The author, during his practice of medicine at Cestona, between 1894 and 1895, had observed much about the first worker's agitation, and the effects of alcoholism in the country.

El mayorazgo de Labraz has a different character. In 1900 and in the company of Ramiro de Maeztu, Baroja had toured Álava and La Rioja, lands that had deeply impressed him. There he was to conceive this second novel, which he began by writing in dialogue form and then recast in another manner. Labraz is a compound, built of what had been seen in various towns; and among the personalities there are some taken from other surroundings. The novel, much along Romantic lines, portrays the southern part of the region, which was less known to the novelist, though the surname Baroja, or rather, Martínez de Baroja, proceeds from there. One of the villages of Peñacerrada is called Baroja.

The contrast between the setting of *Labraz* and that of *La casa de Aizgorri* is absolute. Labraz is a town static and anchored in the past. It lives on its traditional prejudices. The South of Álava still has towns full of strength and character, like Laguardia, described by Baroja in *El aprendiz de conspirador* (1913). Seeking then, to give in these pages a route to be followed through Basque territory to the thread of Barojan texts, it seems preferable to begin by entering the Basque country by way of the area described in *El aprendiz de conspirador,* the second novel of the trilogy *El mayorazgo de Labraz,* that is, by the south. From the Alavese Rioja we go up to the north, to a central Guipúzcoa: that of *La casa de Aizgorri,* and from there descend to the sea, as in *Las inquietudes de Shanti Andía,* at a classic port,

between San Sebastián and Motrico, or even some port to
the west of Vizcaya, of which possibly the novelist was also
thinking.

A different ambience, with its central personality, is
described in *Zalacaín el aventurero,* a novel also illustrated
by Ricardo Baroja, and which has enjoyed more popularity than the earlier ones. The hero's native town, Urbía,
is a compound, but in great part corresponds to what Cestona still was at the time when Baroja was municipal doctor
there. Te action takes place during the second Carlist War,
and the writer puts to use many of his father's memories.
Among the secondary personalities there are portraits of
persons, too, that Baroja knew in Cestona, such as "Pi-
chía". Te repertory of Basque songs that might be made
between those mentioned in the novel and those actually
transcribed, is interesting for various reasons. First of all,
there are some whose the music has never been transcribed;
others, with lyrics of historical circumstance, like *Gu guera,*
announcing the second Carlist War; other, of great lyri-
cism. Baroja was always very sensitive to popular song, and
thought it one of those elements that most characterize an
epoch and a people. The action of *Zalacaín* takes place
within canons that are, up to a certain point, "classic", as
at least one shrewd critic has observed. The hero, like
ancient ones, dies young. Apart from this, it gives an idea of
the war quite contrary to that which may be found in other
novels and writings of the epoch, in which, for example,
the priest Santa Cruz, a well-known Guipúzcoan Carlist
leader, is glorified and uplifted. It is also very hostile to
the Navarrese Carlism of cities like Estella. Furthermore
the novel's action largely develops in the area of the French
frontier, and the hero is buried in the French Basque town
of Zaro. So that in the proposed route we may later take a
turn toward the east, through Navarra Atlántica, proverbial
land of contraband, to enter the land of Labourd and Baja

Navarra, and then further south to the land of Estella, a city which also appears in *Zalacaín.*

The fourth novel to which we have referred, *Las inquietudes de Shanti Andía,* has a less conflictive character, as far as the country is concerned. It is grouped with another two in the trilogy *El mar.* The maternal family of the writer's mother, the Goñi Alzate family, could boast various merchant mariners from the days of sailing ships. The frigate "La bella vascongada", drawn and framed in a salon of a great aunt of the novelist, doña Cesárea, is, more or less, that of the House of Aguirre, in the fourth chapter of the first part of the novel. In "Itzea" we find today, in what is called the "green room", all that the novelist could see, a hundred and some years ago, in San Sebastián. These family memories joined in him with his childish explorations of the port and with the persons and types that later came to his attention there, such as an old ship captain, don Francisco Iriberri, who told terrible anecdotes of the days of the slave trade. *Shanti Andía* is one of the few Spanish novels of the sea. It has a great documentary value and, from the folkloric point of view, it features customs and songs of the San Sebastián of other days, not recorded elsewhere. This novel was also illustrated by Ricardo Baroja and Ramón de Zubiaurre.

There are others in the series *El mar,* which are *Los pilotos de altura* (1929) and *La estrella del capitán Chimista* (1931) with a Basque background. And not only this. Baroja in composing them had access to a sort of memoirs of diaries of a certain Vizcayan mariner of the mid-nineteenth century, named Abarva. This, a work handwritten in excellent calligraphy, but crude in verbal style, Baroja returned to those who had lent in him, and it has since disappeared. In sum, the four Barojan novels of the early part of the century, which happen in the País Vasco, give an idea of life in very different parts of it, from an original and pro-

Coast of Guipúzcoa. From Igueldo to Machichaco.

found vision, which was later to futher expand or define itself.

III. *Widening the vision*

There is no lack, above all, in the first two novels, of an element that might be defined as symbolist, typical of the period in which they were written, but which later faded out of the Barojan manner. But we must take it into account, because it also fits the fundamental ideology of the writer in that period, which made him see features of Basque society invisible to other observers. Thus in *Labraz,* the proud and attractive air of the village is combined with ossification, inertia and corruption of customs, covered by a certain Phariseeism of forms. Is *La casa de Aizgorri,* other vices are described. In both cases, what is written corresponds to direct observation, in a critical moment of the life of Spain, and to a desire of liberation or of overcoming problems.

In *Zalacaín* we may observe the same desire, expressed in historically clearer from. The hero dies at the age of 24, in 1876. During the war he has lived a free and independent life in a country of mainly Carlist ideology. Zalacaín, essentially, is anti-Carlist, as Baroja was. But apart from this ideological ingredient, there is a wealth of descriptions superior to that of the two previous novels. We may remember, in *Zalacaín,* that of the town of Urbía, and those of many places in Guipúzcoa and the north of Navarra, where the smugglers and guerillas circulate. And later, the description of Estella. It is not only in these novels of Baroja's first period where we may find descriptions of the country, or lyrical pages inspired by it. Apart from some stories of *Vidas sombrías, mixtificaciones de Silvestre Paradox* (1901), a vision that corresponds to the novelist's childhood memories; he lived in the capital of Navarra from 1881 to 1886, and his sister Carmen was born there.

We must not think, of course, that in such writers we can find information catalogued as in a guide of technical text. We are dealing with rapid impressions, which reflect background and, above all, circumstance. Much later, in his old age, the novelist received a commission to write a sort of guidebook, published at Barcelona in 1953 with the title of *El País Vasco,* and reprinted after his death, with abundant illustration. But, from 1912 on, he wrote many interesting pages in different circumstances. The long series began of *Memorias de un hombre de acción,* whose protagonist in Eugenio de Aviraneta, and in which there are several novels with episodes set in the Basque country.

Suddenly, in the first of these, *El aprendiz de conspirador,* dated from his house at Vera, in October 1912, there is a curious description of the South of Álava and a reconstruction of life in Laguardia in 1837, beginning with a description of the city and its surroundings. In this series there are also several novels, or parts of them, that take place in Basque-French territory or, more concretely, in a city that always exercised a great attraction on our novelist: Bayonne or Bayona. Already in *Los caminos del mundo* (1914), the city appears, later to be the scene of other action.

There are four later novels of major interest from our point of view: *El amor, el dandismo y la intriga* (1922), and above all, those that really constitute another trilogy, to wit: *Las figuras de cera* (1924), *La nave de los locos* (1925) and *Las máscaras sangrientas* (1927). A Basque-French historian said that the image of life in Bayonne during the first Carlist War, drawn by Baroja in the first of these novels, was perfect.

It may also be said that the central story of *Las máscaras sangrientas* is among Baroja's most dramatic ones. In writting in he had before him an event that had occurred recently: a mysterious crime had taken place in a certain town of Guipúzcoa called Beizama, which was the occasion of a controversy strongly involving the whole country, with certain political nuances, relative to the perpetrators of the murder of two women of ill fame, mother and daughter, who were found dead in their farmhouse.

IV. *Reality and idealisation: the value of folklore*

The novelist, unlike the historian, has full liberty to perform transpositions of reality. But Baroja, in works that are not novels and which contain impressions and even confidences, also reflected his preoccupation with the Basque country and people. Thus in the *Nuevo tablado de Arlequín* (1917) there are various articles on the country, especially notable being one on what was then still called "Bizkaitarrismo", i.e. Basque nationalism.

In *Juventud, egolatría* (1917) and *Las horas solitarias* (1918) there are personal memories and lyrical or melancholic impressions of life in the village or its outskirts; some pointed observations on the spirit of certain cities (which have since changed much), and several portraits of persons. There is also another work of November 1918, which came out in 1919 in the guise of a mook lecture, bearing the title of *Monumentum Catastrophicum* which today may still seem of current relevance to many. Here again we see how Baroja never let himself be blinded by his fondness for his country. Whenever his image of the country is exempt from political considerations, Baroja gives free rein to his poetic instinct and creative imagination. This is especially manifest in *La leyenda de Jaun de Alzate,* published in 1922 when the novelist, at the age of fifty, already considered himself a fairly old man. It is difficult to hink of an imaginative work in which the folklore of a country has been so much utilized, and in manner less "traditionalist", in the political sense the word then had. Baroja always manifested a frank hostility to the Basque traditionalists. In *La leyenda de Jaun de Alzate* he uses all sorts of traditions, but these are of pre-Christian origin or, simply, un-Christian. The novelist thus gave his answer to the thesis of the official traditionalists. In essence, *Jaun de Alzate* is a poetic work.

Lastly, in 1932 he published another trilogy including *La famiolia de Errotacho, El cabo de las tormentas* and *Los visionarios,* in which the early part is based on recent events that had taken place near his house in Vera. These were actions of the anarcho-syndicalists, in whom Baroja had always had an interest. In 1936 there appeared *El cura de Monleón,* a novel which paints an image of a young Basque priest dominated by doubt. The story of this novel was based, in large part, on the confidences of an ex-seminarist of Vitoria. As may well be imagined, the novel did not find favour in many circles in the country. In 1943 and in uncomfortable circumstances, he published *El caballero de Erlaiz,* a nostalgic look at Basque life in the final period of the Enlightenment.

Leaving the novels and personal books to one side, there is a considerable quantity of small essays and articles in which Baroja developed Basque themes, describing types, customs, landscapes. We need only review the indices of compilations such as *Intermedios* (1931) or *Vitrina pintoresca* (1935) to notice this.

V.   *An image of compounds*

In sum, the image of the País Vasco and people is, for Baroja, as an observer throughhout many years, a composed and dynamic image. Other persons, especially politicians and men on faith, or men of the system in general, prefer, for their own interests, static and total images, without contradictions or nuances: the Typical Basque is like this, and not like that; and the country, too. Nor can these people conceive thow a thing that is part of one, and which one loves, can have negative and even disgusting aspects. However experience indicates the opposite: the obseesion for unity and perfection spoils the picture. The first maker of compounds is Nature herself.

For a long time, the men of a land as small as Guipúzcoa have perceived in it three parts: the uplands ("Goierri"), the lowlands ("Beterri") and the coast ("Kostalde"). Each land has too a different society. In other days a woodland ("Baserri") was also spoken of, in contrast to the unwooded land and its respective inhabitants. The city or town was clearly differentiated from the country. The criterion of *composition* may be seen in other orders. From the worker or bourgeois of the factory towns, to the woodcutter or shepherd of the hills there was an immense distance, and the common language was ramified into dialects and subdialects wherever it was spoken with spontaneous fluency. Of the distinct regions of the País Vasco proper we need say no more: but if we include Navarra, which is a most ancient ethnic and political entity, but by no means a physiographic one, that is another question. Even the ancient geographers, in the territory of the Vascones, which included present-day Navarra and parts of Aragón and La Rioja, divided it in a southern region, suitable for agriculture, and a northern, wooded one: the *ager* and the *saltus.* This distinction may be further subdivided, for there are notable differences also in the north part, between the Atlantic and the high Pyrenean lands.

Finally, let us insist on the composite nature of the image obtained by a reading of Baroja's works: obviously, it is that of a novelist, not of an "ideologist", not even in the positive sense that word may have. The novelist does not judge, he describes. He lives in surroundings where many other people exist. Taken together, these surroundings please him and the persons excite his interest. The novelist may describe misery, sadness, horror, even in the country he most loves, as did Dostoyevsky. The ambience where these actions take place is quite another question. Here the novelist has his predilections: everywhere he finds something that especially attracts his attention, whether it repels or pleases him. Baroja knew the whole country well. Perhaps certain parts of Vizcaya were those he least favoured; obviously, he had his preferences. Above all he preferred the area of Bidasoa, where he settled, his reputation of "bad man of Itzea" changing to that of a lovable neighbour. He denounced things that to him seemed ugly, mental mannerisms and abuses. But ultimately, he was moved by love when he wrote about his land and the people to which he belonged.

BIOGRAPHICAL NOTES
ON THE CONTRIBUTING
AUTHORS

Carmen Bravo-Villasante

A writer born in Madrid, Carmen Bravo-Villasante is the holder of, among other things, a Doctorate in Philosophy and Letters and the National Prize for Literature. She is the author of numerous biographies, most notable among them being: *Vida de Bettina Brentano* (1957), *Vida de Juan Valera* (1959), *Vida y obra de Emilia Pardo Bazán* (1962), *Galdós* (1970), *Vida de un poeta: Heinrich von Kleist* (1971), *Una vida romántica: la Avellaneda* (1967), *El alucinante mundo de E. T. A. Hoffmann* (1973), and *Puschkin* (1985). She has translated Hölderlin, Goethe, Rilke, E. T. A. Hoffmann, J. M. Barrie and other writers. Carmen Bravo-Villasante obtained the prestigious Premio Nacional Fray Luis de León for her translation *Los elixires del diablo* of E. T. A. Hoffmann.

She is also known as the author of a history and anthology of Children's Literature in Spain, Iberoamerica and the World, and of a *Diccionario de autores de la literatura infantil mundial* (1985); also of various other books on the subject of children's literature. Her essays include: *Biografía y Literatura* (1969), *Pepita Jiménez, mujer actual* and *La mujer vestida de hombre en el teatro español del Siglo de Oro* (1977). She is a member of the Hispanic Society of America.

Rubén Caba

Born in Madrid in November 1935, at whose Universidad Central he obtained degrees in Law and Philosophy. For nine years he directed a public opinion research firm in Madrid; in 1972 he dropped this activity, considering it incompatible with his literary work.

His first literary text was a cinema script on the *Libro de buen amor,* appearing in 1970, and his first book a political opinion survey: *389 escritores españoles opinan* (1971). Though he has published some collections of poems —*Ímpetu, pasión y fuga* (1972) and *Carta en cuaderna vía* (1982), which received the first prize at the IV "Arcipreste de Hita" Poetry Concourse—, he generally prefers to work in the field of narrative: *Por la ruta serrana del Arcipreste* (1976), a travel book; *Islario* (1980), a novel; *Hispán e Iberia* (1981), a story; and *La puerta de marfil* (1988), a novel.

He has contributed to many publications: *El País, Diario 16, Informaciones, Los Cuadernos del Norte, Viajar,* and *El Independiente,* and has given courses on the *Libro de buen amor* and *Don Quijote.*

Julio Caro Baroja

Julio Caro Baroja was born in Madrid on 13 November 1914, and grew up in an artistic and intellectual ambit where, as a child, he met great figures of the Spain of the early twentieth century: Azorín, Ortega, Valle-Inclán, Azaña, Unamuno. His father, Rafael Caro Raggio, was a publisher and printer with artistic leanings. And his mother, Carmen Baroja y Nessi, was the sister of Ricardo and Pío Baroja. He studied Philosophy and Letters at Madrid, and privately studied Prehistory and Archaeology with Obermaier. Outside the University, he had many dealings with the Basque anthropologists and prehistorians Telesforo de Aranzadi and José Miguel de Barandiarán.

After occupying for eleven years the post of Director of the Museo del Pueblo Español, he spent some time in the Sahara territory, then under Spanish mandate. From this experience came his *Estudios saharianos* (1955). He devoted later study to the history of ethnic minorities such as Moriscos and Jews, and to ethnographic themes of a descriptive nature, especially upon Navarre. In 1962, with an already copious oeuvre, he entered the Real Academia de la Historia.

Since 1986 he has also been a member of the Real Academia Española. He has obtained the "Premio Príncipe de Asturias" (1984) and the "Premio Nacional de las Letras Españolas" (1985).

Of his extensive bibliography we may mention *Las brujas y su mundo* (1961), translated into various languages; the trilogy composed of *El carnaval* (1965), *La estación de amor* (1979) and *El estío festivo* (1984); *Las formas complejas de la vida religiosa* (1978); *La aurora del pensamiento antropológico* (1983); and *Los fundamentos del pensamiento antropológico moderno* (1985). As a memorialist he has published, among other works, *Los Baroja* (1972) and *Semblanzas ideales* (1972). Julio Caro Baroja is also known for his drawings and paintings.

Juan Cruz Ruiz

Journalist and writer. Born in Puerto de la Cruz, Tenerife, in 1948. He has been a writer for *El Día* in Tenerife and for *El País* of Madrid, of which he has been London correspondent, director of Culture, and Editor of opinion articles. He is presently the chief writer for the Culture section.

As writer he has published the novels *Crónica de la*

nada hecha pedazos (Benito Pérez Armas prize, 1972), *Naranja* (1975), *Retrato de humo* (1982), *El sueño de Oslo* (Azorín prize, 1987), *Cuchillo de arena* (1989), and *En la azotea* (1989).

Juan Cueto Alas

Born at Oviedo on 1942. Degrees in Law (Oviedo), Political Science (Algiers) and Journalism (Madrid). Professor of Philosophy at the University of Oviedo until 1975. Editor of the collections *Júcar Universidad, Espasa Mañana, Etiqueta rota* and *Sindéresis.* Editor of the *Enciclopedia temática de Asturias* now being published. Columnist and critic of *El País* from its foundation. Founder and director of the cultural review *Los Cuadernos del Norte,* with ten years of publication. Director of the private television network *Canal Plus.*

He has published, among others, the following books: *Guía espiritual de Miguel de Molinos* (1974), *Guía secreta de Asturias* (1976), *Los heterodoxos asturianos* (1977), *Fragmentos* (1977), *Mitologías de la modernidad* (1982), *Exterior noche* (1983), *La sociedad de consumo de masas* (1983), and going to press soon: *Pasiones catódicas* and *Las letras del espíritu.*

He has contributed to numerous publications both national and foreign: *Triunfo, Revista de Occidente, Papeles de Son Armadans, Liberation, La Quinzaine Littéraire,* etc.

He has won, among others, the journalism prizes *César González Ruano* and *Cuco Cerecedo.*

Luis Mateo Díez

Luis Mateo Díez was born at Villablino, León, in 1942, and has resided in Madrid for over twenty years. He was a founder and director of the magazine *Claraboya,* published at León in the 1960s. His first book of short stories appeared in 1973, titled *Memoria de hierbas.*

He has since published: *Apócrifo del clavel y la espina* (1977, with revised and definitive edition in 1988), *Relato de Babia* (1981), *Las estaciones provinciales* (1982), *La fuente de la edad* (1986), *Brasas de agosto* (1989) and *Las horas completas* (1990). In 1987 he obtained the Premio de la Crítica and the Premio Nacional de Literatura for his novel *La fuente de la edad.*

José Esteban

Has divided his literary vocation between criticism, novels and publishing. A fruit of his triple activity has been the incorporation into Spanish culture of forgotten authors such as Ciges Aparicio, Alicio Garcitoral, Joaquín Arderíus and many more, by way of prologues, editions, and studies of their works.

He is also the author of an edition of the aphoristic work of Bergamín, of another on Valle-Inclán (Valle-Inclán as seen by...) and, in collaboration with Gonzalo Santonja, *Los novelistas sociales españoles, 1928-1936.*

El himno de Riego (1984) and *La España peregrina* (1988) constitute his novelistic production up to the present.

As a Galdosian, he is the author of *Guadalajara en la obra de Galdós* (1985) and *La cocina en Galdós* (1991) as well as of many lectures and studies related to the work of the Canarian novelist.

A Castilian from Sigüenza, Guadalajara, he has resided in Madrid since 1956.

Joan Fuster

Joan Fuster (Sueca, 1922) has published almost a hundred books of essays and cultural history. He studied at the University of Valencia, where he has also been Professor of Catalan Philology. Part of his work is centred on litrerary and sociopolitical themes connected with the Valencian Country, among these being the figure of Vicente Blasco Ibáñez. He resides in his native city, near the areas that were the setting for the first novels of Blasco. Of his bibliography we may mention: *El descrèdit de la realitat* (1959), *Nosaltres els valencians* (1962), *El País Valenciano* (1962), *Diccionari per ociosos* (1964), *Consells, proverbis i insolencies* (1968), *Literatura catalana contemporánea* (1972), *Contra Unamuno y los demás* (1975) and *Llibres i problemes del Renaixement* (1989).

Among other distinctions, he has obtained the Premi d'Honor des Lletres Catalanes (1975) and the Premi de les Lletres del País Valenciá (1981). He is a doctor Honoris Causa by the University of Barcelona and the Universidad Autónoma de Barcelona.

José Antonio Gabriel y Galán

Born at Plasencia, Cáceres, on 24 October 1940.

Degrees in Law and Journalism at University of Madrid. Studies at the Sorbonne in Paris. Journalistic work in many media, and numerous contributions to literary and journalistic publicacions, especially in *Fotogramas* (theatre critic), Agencia Efe, *Cuadernos para el Diálogo, El País, Diario 16.* Presently editor and director of the literary review *El Urogallo.*

Founding member and General Secretary of the Spanish PEN club, he has written for the theatre: a version of

La velada en Benicarló by Manuel Azaña (teatro Bellas Artes, Madrid, 1980-81); texts of *Las furias* (Mérida, Madrid, 1986). Also for the radio: *Tiempo del 68* (Radio Nacional, Jan.-Apr. 1985) and for the TV: adaptation of *El obispo leproso* by Gabriel Miró. He has translated *Anábasis* by Saint-John Perse (1983).

Novels: *Punto de referencia* (1972, finalist for Biblioteca Breve prize); *La memoria cautiva* (1981, March scholarship); *A salto de mata* (1981); *El bobo ilustrado* (1986, finalist for Premio Nacional de Literatura).

Poetry: *Descartes mentía* (1977); *Un país como éste no es el mío* (1978); *Razón del sueño* (1986); and a collection of all these: *Poesía, 1970-1985* (1988).

In 1990 he received the first Premio Eduardo Carranza de Literatura for his novel *Muchos años después.*

Salvador García Jiménez

García Jiménez was born on 20 December 1944 at Cehegín, Murcia. Professor of Language and Literature; Doctor in Letters for his thesis *La influencia de Franz Kafka en la narrativa española,* he has published the following books.

Poetry: *Tono menor para un desconcierto* (Premio Aldebarán of Seville, 1974); *Épica de náufrago* (Accésit to Premio Adonais, Madrid, 1980); and *Gris encendido* (Premio Polo de Medina, Murcia, 1980), obtaining also in the last-mentioned year the Vicente Aleixandre Prize in Madrid.

Narrative: *Puntarrón, Tres estrellas en la barba, Coro de alucinados, Por las horas oscuras, Odio sobre cenizas* and *Agobios de un vendedor de biblias,* which obtained the following prizes: Nacional Universitario de Salamanca, 1969; Ciudad de Palma, 1974; Ciudad de Murcia, 1974; Ateneo de Valladolid, 1974; Armengot de Castellón, 1977, and Gabriel Sijé, 1984. His short stories have won him these prizes:

Gabriel Miró (Alicante, 1980); Antonio Machado (Madrid, 1980); La Felguera (Asturias, 1985) and Hucha de Plata (Madrid, 1987). In recent years he has published *La paloma y el desencanto* (1981), an anthology of his stories, and the novels *Angelicomio* (1981), *Myrtia* (1985), *La peregrinación* (grant from the Ministry of Culture; Premio la Manga for novels, 1985), and *Caelum Caeli* (Premio de Narrativa Ciudad de Alcalá de Henares, 1988).

Ian Gibson

Ian Gibson was born in 1939 in Dublin, where he studied French and Spanis at Trinity College. After teaching Spanish Literature in Belfast and later at the University of London, he abandoned academic work in 1975 to devote his time exclusively to writing. At this time he had just published, to great international acclaim, his first book, on the murder of Federico García Lorca. Till 1978 he lived in France, when he moved with his family to Spain to begin his major biography of the Granadine poet, the first volume of which was published in 1985 and the second in 1987, with the title of *Federico García Lorca.* Ian Gibson is the author of ten books; among the most recent we may note *La noche que mataron a Calvo Sotelo,* 1982; and *En Granada, su Granada... Guía a la Granada de Federico García Lorca.* 1989. He lives in Madrid, a city he loves and hopes never to leave. He has recently worked on a television series for the BBC on today's Spain.

Ildefonso-Manuel Gil

Was born in Paniza, Campo de Cariñena, Zaragoza, in 22 January 1912. Bachelor in Law at the Universidad Central, Doctor in Philosophy and Letters at the Univ. of Zaragoza. After the Spanish Civil War, spent over twenty years teaching Spanish literature in U.S. universities. Now Professor Emeritus of the City University of New York. Since 1985, he has resided in Zaragoza.

Since the appearance of his first book *Borradores,* in 1931, with poems written between 14 and 18 years of age, he published 25 books of poetry, the most recent being *Las colinas* (1989). Others include *Poemas de dolor antiguo* (1945), *El tiempo recobrado* (1950), *Luz sonreída, Goya, amarga luz* (1972), and the anthologies *Poesía* (1953), *Hombre en su tierra* (1980) and *Vuelta al amor en 54 poemas* (1986).

As narrator he obtained in 1950 the Premio Internacional de Primera Novela, with *La moneda en el suelo,* since translated to French and Portuguese. Two other novels, *Juan Pedro, el dallador* (1953) and *Pueblonuevo* (1960); and several volume of stories, notably *Amor y muerte y otras historias* (1971) and *La muerte hizo su agosto* (1980), complete his published fictional work.

He has been honoured with the Gold Medal of the City of Zaragoza; several streets and plazas in Zaragoza and its region are named after him. He is Numerario of the Academia Norteamericana de Lengua Española, Correspondiente de la Real Academia Española and of the Instituto de Coimbra; member of the Spanish Society of New York. He presently directs the Institución Fernando el Católico, Fundación de la Diputación de Zaragoza.

José María Gironella

Born at Darnius, Gerona, in 1917, held various jobs in his youth: chemist's apprentice, bellboy, bookseller; until his revelation as a novelist with *Un hombre* (1946). But the first found fame and a wide public with *Los cipreses creen en*

Dios (1953), first novel in a trilogy about the Spanish Civil War, completed with *Un millón de muertos* (1961) and *Ha estallado la paz* (1966). A tireless traveller, he has been on all the continents, and has written a number of articles and books on travel: *El Japón y su duende* (1965), *Personas, ideas, mares* (1965), *En Asia se muere bajo las estrellas* (1968), *El escándalo de Tierra Santa* (1978) and *El escándalo del Islam* (1982).

His works have been translated into French, German, English, Italian, Finnish, Hebrew and Japanese; not to mention Catalán, his mother tongue.

He has received various prizes: the Nadal, 1946, for *Un hombre;* the Nacional de Literatura, 1955, for *Los cipreses creen en Dios;* the Thomas Moore, of Chicago, 1955, for the same novel; the Planeta, 1971, for *Condenados a vivir;* and the Ateneo de Sevilla, 1987, for *La duda inquietante.*

José Hierro

Was born at Madrid in 1922. Poet and art critic. Author of various books of verse, notably *Alegría* (1947, Adonais prize), *Quinta del 42* (1953), *Cuanto sé de mí* (1958, prizes Crítica and March), *Libro de las alucinaciones* (1964, Crítica prize). He has obtained the National Literature prize for his *Antología poética* (1954), and the Príncipe de Asturias prize (1981), for the ensemble of his poetic work; and recently, the Premio de las Letras Españolas (1990).

He has written numerous monographs on contemporary artists: *Pancho Cossío, Farreras, Francisco Mateos, Redondela* and others. Doctoral theses in Europe and America on his poetic work. In the opinion of the poet and critic Aurora de Albornoz, Hierro is a "bridge poet between the first group of postwar poets and the following generation; a bridge too between the poets of the 27 and the poetry of the present day; and in his *Libro de las alucinaciones* many observers glimpse an anticipation of trends that have imposed themselves years later".

José Jiménez Lozano

Jiménez Lozano was born at Langa, Ávila, in 1930.

Among his essays: *Los cementerios civiles y la heterodoxia española* (1978); *Sobre judíos, moriscos y conversos* (1982); *San Juan de la Cruz. Poesía* (1983); *Guía espiritual de Castilla* (1984); *Los tres cuadernos rojos* (1986); *Ávila* (1988); *Los ojos del icono* (1988).

Among his novels and narrations: *Historia de un otoño* (1971); *El sambenito* (1972); *La salamandra* (1973); *El santo de mayo* (1976); *Duelo en la casa grande* (1982); *Parábolas y circunloquios de Rabí Isac Ben Yehuda (1325-1402)* (1985); *El grano de maíz rojo* (1988); and *Sara de Ur* (1989).

In 1988 he received the Premio Castilla y León de las Letras for all his work; and in 1989, the Premio Nacional de la Crítica for his book of short stories *El grano de maíz rojo.*

José María Merino

José María Merino was born at La Coruña in 1941, and spent his childhood and adolescence in León. He studied Law at Madrid, where he now resides.

He first wrote poetry. His works in this genre have been recently published under the title *Cumpleaños lejos de casa* (1988).

He has published the novels *Novela de Andrés Choz* (1976), *El caldero de oro* (1981) and *La orilla oscura* (1985); and the book of stories *Cuentos del reino secreto* (1982) and *El viajero perdido* (1990).

He is also author of a trilogy of adventure novels that take place in the days of the Conquest of America: *El oro de los sueños* (1986), *La tierra del tiempo perdido* (1987) and *Las lágrimas del sol* (1989).

He won the "Novelas y Cuentos" prize in 1976 for *Novela de Andrés Chos,* and received the "Premio de la Crítica" in 1985 for *La orilla oscura.*

Baltasar Porcel

Baltasar Porcel was born in Mallorca in 1937 and divides his time between his native island and Barcelona. A tireless traveller and writer, he has published novels, stories, theatre, essays, biographies and numerous articles in periodicals.

His first novels *Solnegro* (1961), *La luna y el velero* (1963), *Difuntos bajo los almendros en flor* (1969) describe, between myth and reality, the rural world of Mallorca. This cycle cuminates in *Caballos hacia la noche* (1975). Subsequent narrative works, though not unrelated to the family cycle of Andratx, introduce more cosmopolitan themes: *Las manzanas de oro* (1980), *Los días inmortales* (1984) and *Primaveras y otoños* (1986). In any case, Porcel's work reflects an eminently Mediterranean world, poetic and mythical but none the less vital and real.

His creative work has earned him various prizes: the "Sant Jordi", the "Josep Plà", the "Ciudad de Palma", the "Crítica Española" and the "Internazionale Mediterraneo" of Italy. In the journalistic field, Porcel has created a very personal style in newspaper opinion articles and interviews, and has received the journalism prizes "Ramón Godó" and "Mariano de Cavia".

His Complete Works are presently in process of publication, an unusual thing for an author of his age. Also Porcel, has revived the nineteenth-century tradition of the novel published by instalments: his latest work, *El divorcio de Berta Barca,* first saw the light in the summer of 1989, in the pages of the daily *La Vanguardia.*

Julio Manuel de la Rosa

Born at Sevilla in August 1935. Teaches Contemporary Spanish Literature in the Journalism Department of the CENP, in Sevilla.

In 1971 his novel *Fin de semana en Etruria* obtained the Sésamo Prize. He also publishes much work in news papers and in specialist magazines. Prize of the Ateneo de Sevilla for Short Stories in 1975. He is the author of the following novels: *La explosión* (1966), *Croquis a mano alzada* (1974), *La sangre y el eco* (1979), *Las campanas de Antoñita Cincodedos* (1987).

He has published essays: *Cesare Parese* (1973), *Apuntes sobre novelistas sevillanos* (1981) and *Luis Cernuda y Sevilla. Albanio en el Edén* (1982), with a prologue by Juan Goytisolo.

He has written three books of short stories: *No estamos solos* (1962), *De campana a campana* (1964), and *Nuestros hermanos* (1975).

Miguel Sánchez-Ostiz

Born at Pamplona in 1950. Lawyer; frequent contributor to the periodical press.

Author of the novels *Los papeles del ilusionista* (1982), *El pasaje de la luna* (1984), *Tánger Bar* (1987), *La quinta del americano* (1987) and *La gran ilusión* (1989); of the books of poems *Pórtico de la fuga* (1979), *Travesía de la noche* (1983),

De un paseante solitario (1985) and *Reinos imaginarios* (1986); as well as the volumes of essays *La negra provincia de Flaubert* (1986), *Mundinovi* (1987) and *Literatura, amigo Thompson* (1989).

In 1989 he obtained the Premio Herralde de Novela for *La gran ilusión.*

Gonzalo Santonja

Gonzalo Santonja, born at Béjar, Salamanca, has a Doctorate in Hispanic Philology from the Universidad Complutense and a diploma in Documentation, and has received various distinctions for his writing and research work.

Besides being a contributor to various publications such as *Informaciones, El País, Liberación, Cuadernos Hispanoamericanos, República de las Letras, Diario 16, El Mundo,* he is the author of, among other books, several studies of a socio-literary character, such as *Del lápiz rojo al lápiz libre* (1986), *Figuras y tendencias de la novela social española* (1987) written in collaboration with José Esteban, and *La república de los libros* (1989); of several anthologies and critical editions: *La novela proletaria* (1979), *Cristal del tiempo* by José Bergamín (1984) or the *Libro de las maravillas del mundo* by *Incierta memoria* (1988) not easy to pigeonhole in a specific genre. In 1986 he was named Honorary Fellow in Writing by the University of Iowa (EE.UU.).

In 1989 obtained the City of Segovia Essay prize for his work *La república de los libros.*

Andrés Sorel

Born at Segovia during the Civil War, of Castilian father and Andalusian mother.

Exiled for political reasons in París, 1971-74, he there directed the weekly *Información Española.*

Founder of *Diario Liberación* which he presided throughout its existence, directing the cultural section.

Since December 1984, Secretary General of the Asociación Colegial de Escritores de España.

Directs the literary review *República de las Letras.*

He has written critical studies and biographies of José Martí, "Che" Guevara, León Felipe, Luis Cernuda, José María Arguedas, etc.

Contributor to newspapers and reviews in Spain, Germany, the U.S., Sweden, Mexico, etc.

He has given lectures at universities in Spain, the U.S., Germany, Cuba, Switzerland, Finland, etc.

He has published a book of short stories: *Crónicas de amor y muerte en varias ciudades del mundo* (1973), various novels: *Free on board Carolina (Como la enfermedad, como la muerte)* (1974), *Discurso de la política y el sexo* (1978), *El perro castellano* (1978), *Crónica de un regreso* (1982), *Concierto en Sevilla* (1982), and the following essays: *Guerrilla española del siglo* XX (1970), *Cuarto mundo: emigración española en Europa* (1974), *Introducción a Cuba* (1974), *Guía popular de Antonio Machado* (1975), *Castilla como agonía* (1975), *Miguel Hernández: escritor y poeta de la revolución* (1977), *Yo, García Lorca* (1977), *Miseria de nuestra cultura* (1980), *Castilla como agonía. Castilla como esperanza* (1975), *Liberación. Desolación de la utopía* (1987), *Dolores Ibarruri. Memoria humana* (1989).

Jesús Torbado

Born in León, in 1943. After a childhood spent in a village of Tierra de Campos and adolescence in a school of friars, he studied philosophy and journalism at Madrid, and at an early age began working for the Madrilenian press: also travelling, first hitchhiking over Europe, later visiting many other parts of the world. He also began his career as a writer. In 1965, at the age of 22, he obtained the Alfaguara prize for novels with his book *Las corrupciones.* This book has been followed by some twenty others. The most notable include *En el día de hoy* (Planeta prize, 1976), *Los topos* (1977), *Moira estuvo aquí* (1971), *La ballena* (1982) and the travel books *La Europa de los jóvenes* (1969), *Tierra mal bautizada* (1968) and *Camino de plata* (1989). His latest work (1990) is the novel *Yo, Pablo de Tarso.*

He has been a frequent contributor to newspapers and magazines as a writer of articles and chronicler of travel. Also he has written for television and is the author of several cinema scripts. He has taught journalism in Brazil and given lectures in many cities. Some of his works have been translated into seven languages. He has received numerous awards for stories and articles, such as the *Hucha de Oro* and the *Antonio Machado* for short stories, and the *Mariano de Cavia* in journalism. When he is not journeying over the face of Spain, or in lands further removed —he is often in Asia— he lives in a town near Madrid.

Manuel Vázquez Montalbán

Writer and journalist, born at Barcelona in 1939. Poet included by Castellet in the anthology of Los Nueve Nosísimos, forming a link between the poets of experience (Gil de Biedma, Barral, González) and those of the "novísima" sensibility. An experimental novelist *(Cuestiones marxistas),* chronicler of society (the Carvalho cycle), and of historical or individual conduct (*El pianista,* 1985; *Los alegres mucha-*

chos de Atzavara, 1986; *Cuarteto,* 1988). Essayist on collective memory (*Crónica sentimental de España,* 1971) or on the means of creation of social consciousness (*Palabra libre en la ciudad libre,* 1979; *Manifiesto subnormal,* 1970). He has in common with Plà a liking for travel, for the Catalan country that Plà lived in and described, and a controlled love of gastronomy.

In 1979 he obtained the Premio Planeta for his novel *Los mares del Sur.*

SOURCES OF ILLUSTRATIONS

SOURCES OF ILLUSTRATIONS

Maps:

Javier Belloso, 22, 23, 41, 49, 67, 87, 109, 129, 147, 167, 189, 209, 229, 247, 267, 287, 307, 331, 347, 365, 385, 403, 423, 447, 465, 483, 501.

Photos:

AGROMAYOR, Luis, 39, 151, 213, 254, 341.
AISA, 43, 451.
ARNÁIZ, 116.
BERLÍN, Blanca, 411.
BROSSA, Mario, 136, 429.
C.P. EE.UU., 132.
CASTAÑO, Juan Luis, 372.
CIGANOVIC, 74, 271.
GARRIDO, A., 158, 488.
GONZÁLEZ GRANDE, J. L., 93, 294, 510.
GOYA, 506.
GROS, F., 436.
LARRION PIMOULIER, 453, 456.
LAX, 314.
LÓPEZ OSÉS, A., 474.
LÓPEZ-ALONSO, Ramón G., 100, 172, 174, 196, 201, 240, 259, 469.
MASSATS, 53, 55, 408.
ONTAÑÓN, Francisco, 113, 218, 234, 297, 339, 355.
ORONOZ, 311, 389, 394.
PASCUAL, Juan José, 71.
PÉREZ SIQUIER, C., 490.
PUENTE BRIALES, A., 281, 369.